D0222175

American Difference

Second Edition

USED BOOK

DEC 1 2 2019

SOLD TO AZTEC SHOP, LTD

We dedicate this book to our families. Thanks for lending us to each other over the years, Hannah and Liam Staudinger, and Raymond, Magdalene, and Katherine Wolf.

USED BOOK

Sara Miller McCune founded SAGE Publishing in 1965 to support the dissemination of usable knowledge and educate a global community. SAGE publishes more than 1000 journals and over 800 new books each year, spanning a wide range of subject areas. Our growing selection of library products includes archives, data, case studies and video. SAGE remains majority owned by our founder and after her lifetime will become owned by a charitable trust that secures the company's continued independence.

Los Angeles | London | New Delhi | Singapore | Washington DC | Melbourne

American Difference

A Guide to American Politics in Comparative Perspective

SECOND EDITION

Lori M. Poloni-Staudinger
Northern Arizona University

Michael R. Wolf
Indiana University–Purdue University Fort Wayne

FOR INFORMATION:

CQ Press
An Imprint of SAGE Publications, Inc.
2455 Teller Road
Thousand Oaks, California 91320
E-mail: order@sagepub.com

SAGE Publications Ltd.
1 Oliver's Yard
55 City Road
London, EC1Y 1SP
United Kingdom

SAGE Publications India Pvt. Ltd.
B 1/I 1 Mohan Cooperative Industrial Area
Mathura Road, New Delhi 110 044
India

SAGE Publications Asia-Pacific Pte. Ltd.
18 Cross Street #10-10/11/12
China Square Central
Singapore 048423

Copyright © 2020 by CQ Press, an Imprint of SAGE Publications, Inc. CQ Press is a registered trademark of Congressional Quarterly Inc

All rights reserved. Except as permitted by U.S. copyright law, no part of this work may be reproduced or distributed in any form or by any means, or stored in a database or retrieval system, without permission in writing from the publisher.

All third party trademarks referenced or depicted herein are included solely for the purpose of illustration and are the property of their respective owners. Reference to these trademarks in no way indicates any relationship with, or endorsement by, the trademark owner.

Printed in the United States of America

Library of Congress Cataloging-in-Publication Data

Names: Poloni-Staudinger, Lori, author. | Wolf, Michael R., author.

Title: American difference : a guide to American politics in comparative perspective / Lori M. Poloni-Staudinger, Northern Arizona University, Michael R. Wolf, Purdue University Fort Wayne.

Description: Second Edition. | Los Angeles : CQ Press, an imprint of SAGE Publications, Inc., [2019] | Includes bibliographical references and index.

Identifiers: LCCN 2018043003 | ISBN 9781544325330 (Paperback : acid-free paper)

Subjects: LCSH: United States—Politics and government. | Democracy—United States. | Comparative government.

Classification: LCC JK31 .P58 2019 | DDC 320.973—dc23

LC record available at https://lccn.loc.gov/2018043003

This book is printed on acid-free paper.

Acquisitions Editor: Monica Eckman
Editorial Assistant: Sam Rosenberg
Content Development Editor: Lauren Schultz
Production Editor: Myleen Medina
Copy Editor: Michelle Ponce
Typesetter: Hurix Digital
Proofreader: Rae-Ann Goodwin
Indexer: Joan Shapiro
Cover and Interior Designer: Alexa Turner
Marketing Manager: Erica DeLuca

SUSTAINABLE FORESTRY INITIATIVE

Certified Chain of Custody
At Least 10% Certified Forest Content
www.sfiprogram.org
SFI-01028

19 20 21 22 23 10 9 8 7 6 5 4 3 2 1

BRIEF CONTENTS

DETAILED CONTENTS

TABLES, FIGURES, AND PHOTOGRAPHS

TABLES

FIGURES

PHOTOGRAPHS

PREFACE TO THE SECOND EDITION

As professors who teach courses on comparative politics and American politics, we wrote the first edition of this book out of a passion to explain both the similarities and differences American politics has with other democracies. This motivation has not abated in the four years since the first edition. We know colleagues who teach and study comparative politics or international relations become frustrated with how the study of American politics can at times seem like it lacks comparative context. This book is for you. We also know colleagues who teach and study American politics who scratch their heads at how other democracies run elections, govern themselves, or come up with the types of policies produced. This book is for you, too. It is a genuine attempt to place American politics in a broader comparative context in a brief format. On a normative note, we are concerned with evidence that suggests younger citizens do not value democracy as much as their parents. This book is for them as well, intended as a way to explicate both the beautiful and ugly aspects of democracy and to understand how these aspects situate in comparative context. Democracy has not looked pretty in recent years to be sure, but democracy beats its alternatives every time, even if it has been bruised by selfish political leaders and a dose of citizen neglect. Democracies do not provoke war with each other. They trade with each other, share each other's company, and enrich each other's economic and cultural livelihoods. Democracy is vital for the free world and for American society. American democracy is exceptional, and it needs every generation knowing why it is and engaged in sustaining it.

Numerous classic books and articles have discussed how American politics differs from other democracies. They provide the theoretical and historical explanations for why American politics are exceptional. In fact, the book draws heavily from findings already catalogued by such authors as Tocqueville, Hartz, or Lipset. Nevertheless, with so much contemporary political use of the term *American exceptionalism*, we take a step back to explain the term's scholarly origins and the term's practical application for American politics today. American political institutions, citizen values, and public policies today are as much a consequence of American values and institutions historically as they are of the actions of current politicians, status of current political conditions, or a result of citizens' beliefs today. This is a key theme to the book: America's political development has made contemporary American politics quite exceptional.

What the book does do differently from other works is to concentrate also on the similarities American politics shares with the political dynamics of other democracies. This includes broadly shared values, attitudes, institutions, and policies. Therefore, the historical origins and subsequent consequences of American exceptionalism for contemporary politics are better understood when juxtaposed against the numerous similar ways American democracy compares to other democracies. Comparative politics scholars and students know that the United States often does not fit easily in comparative studies. Frankly, the United States is often studied as its own case alone or is not included in cross-national comparative studies, so it is no wonder that the theme of United States as "different" is so pervasive. True, the United States is exceptional, and these differences are important to note. The United States is not entirely unique, however. That portion of comparison has needed more attention in comparative politics. We hope students and instructors find that we have balanced the similarities and differences well.

There are many areas that we do not address as much as we could with a longer volume or additional themes. Students of American history and other nations' histories may wonder why we did not include more about formative historical points or figures. Also, we address the complicated simultaneous interactive effects of founding political beliefs and institutional design on contemporary political beliefs and institutions, but our path-dependent argument does not tackle the exact chain of events of this sequence. Other classics in this area cover this in more depth, but we simply do not have the space to sufficiently cover this exhaustively and provide detailed analysis of contemporary American politics from a comparative perspective in a brief book. We also do not address how American foreign policy differs from other democracies. Questions over why a superpower acts like it does on the world stage are extremely interesting and important, but such an addition would require additional chapters and a shift from the very focused themes of the book. The book's length and focus mean that we necessarily leave many interesting aspects to other scholars and books. The second edition expands and updates each chapter, and we add several new chapters. First, we add a chapter on civil rights and liberties (Chapter 5) and a chapter on constitutional arrangements (Chapter 6). We also expand the chapter on institutions (Chapter 7) and attempt to explain to the reader and adopters why in a comparative context discussion of legislative and executive branches together makes the most sense. In this second edition, we divided discussion on elections into two chapters—one on institutions (Chapter 10) and one on behavior (Chapter 11). The book is designed to be a stand-alone text for a broad set of classes in comparative politics or American politics or as a companion text to American politics or comparative politics textbooks. It was fun to work with each other while creating this book, and we hope readers learn from and enjoy it as much as we learned from and enjoyed working with each other.

ACKNOWLEDGMENTS

We want to recognize several people who were very helpful in the writing and editing of this book, both the first and second editions. Carmen Burlingame and Dr. Candice Ortbals, and her 2014 Honors American Politics students at Pepperdine University provided helpful editing and suggestions on the first edition of the book. Christopher Harrison, Myann Bradley, and Julianne Updike were conscientious research assistants on the second edition making Lori's job much easier and providing both authorship and editorial help in some of the breakout boxes. The authors are also indebted to Robert Rohrschneider for his scholarly guidance and encouragement over the years and to Russell Dalton for his invaluable and detailed comments on the first edition. J. Cherie Strachan is a walking literature review and champion of civic education for American college students. Georgia Wralstad Ulmschneider's fingerprints are on many pages of this manuscript due to her mastery of comparative judicial systems and civil liberties. James Toole and Craig Ortsey also lent suggestions on key sources and insights. Barbara Blauvelt ensured (as always) that the trains ran on time in Fort Wayne during the book's original writing. During the second edition, Teri Luce provided backup in Fort Wayne, and Heaven Johnson held faculty at bay to give Lori time to write in Flagstaff. Thank you all for your invaluable service to our departments. We also appreciate the suggestions made by the various anonymous reviewers on edition one and particularly for this second edition, and we thank them for their time. Finally, we want to thank Charisse Kiino, Monica Eckman, Erica DeLuca, Sam Rosenburg, Michelle Ponce, Myleen Medina, and the entire editorial and production staff at CQ Press. It has been wonderful to work with you.

ABOUT THE AUTHORS

Dr. Lori M. Poloni-Staudinger (PhD, Indiana University, 2005) is a professor in the Department of Politics and International Affairs at Northern Arizona University and associate dean for research, faculty affairs, and graduate programs in the College of Social and Behavioral Sciences at Northern Arizona University. She was statewide coordinator for Arizona Deliberates, an organization focused on increasing public deliberation in Arizona, and a Kettering Foundation Fellow. Her research and publications focus on social movements, political contention and extra-institutional participation, and political institutions, mainly in Western Europe. Her recent work examines questions around women and political violence. She was a Distinguished Fulbright Fellow at the Diplomatic Academy in Vienna, Austria, and has served as a consultant for the Organization for Security and Co-operation in Europe. She also taught at University of the Basque Country in San Sebastian, Spain.

Dr. Michael R. Wolf (PhD, Indiana University, 2002) is a professor and department chair in the Department of Political Science at Purdue University Fort Wayne. His research focuses on comparative and American public opinion and political behavior. He has recently published on the nature and effects of political discussion in democracies and the dynamics of political compromise and political incivility. He is a research fellow with the Mike Downs Center for Indiana Politics and former Lugar Senior Fellow, 2017 Arts and Sciences Distinguished Lecturer, and partner with the Kettering Foundation.

CHAPTER ONE

AMERICAN POLITICS FROM A COMPARATIVE PERSPECTIVE

Y̶ou have probably all heard the phrase "of the people and for the people" when hearing about democratic government, but what does that mean? Why in the United States does "of the people and for the people" equal three branches of government and a U.S. president who generally stays in office for a full term no matter his popularity, but in the United Kingdom it can mean early elections and leaders yanked off the stage when public opinion sways against them? Does democratic government mean the individual with the most votes wins like we see in the United States, or does it signify power sharing and compromise like we see in Italy or Germany? Do other democracies have an electoral college? When Americans hear the word *democracy* they likely think of the president, separation of powers, a winner-take-all election system, and checks and balances. When other countries' citizens hear the word *democracy*, they probably think of parliaments, proportional representation, and coalition formation. Why would the word *democracy* bring one set of ideas to mind for Americans and yet conjure up an entirely different set of ideas for people living in other democracies? Exploring American politics from a comparative perspective helps to explain why Americans view the meaning and practice of politics differently from other democratic citizens around the world. In 1936, Harold Lasswell famously said that politics is about "who gets what, when and how."[1] We know, however, that not every government looks the same, and even governments that we group together as democracies do not look the same. Why are they different? If politics really is about "who gets what, when and how," examining democracies from a comparative perspective helps us better understand *why* who gets what, when, and how it is similar or different in the United States as compared to other democracies.

WHAT DOES IT MEAN TO EXAMINE AMERICAN POLITICS FROM A COMPARATIVE PERSPECTIVE?

American students can often see their friends change over the years in class pictures—from pigtails in elementary school, to awkward middle school years, to the contemplative senior portrait. For those who do not move, students go to school together for over a decade because the United States typically has a common curriculum from kindergarten through twelfth grade. This means, that for the most part, American kids receive a universal education, with everyone pretty much having the same sort of curriculum in one school building. While there may be tracks within schools, and some kids take AP classes while others don't, you generally see your friends in gym and at lunch and take other classes like sex ed or health all together. Everyone who goes to high school in Bad Axe, Michigan, for example, goes to a universal high school. In other countries, education works differently. In Germany or Austria, kids enter different educational tracks after fifth grade. Teachers, in consultation with parents, recommend kids enter either a college preparatory, technical, or mid-level and lower-level vocational educational track.[2] It is hard to imagine a fifth-grade teacher having as much influence in the United States as to where a parent would send a kid for middle school. Why?

The answer lies in part with the American belief in **individualism**, or the idea of favoring individual freedom of action over collective or state control, as well as the well-developed social welfare system in other countries. In the United States, parents would likely be suspicious of a public official having so much control over determining a child's educational future. Most Americans would also favor allowing the individual child the opportunity to work hard and succeed rather than predetermining the child's educational attainment. Further, Germans, Austrians, and citizens in other democracies believe more in looking out for the entire society more than individuals, meaning that skilled and unskilled laborers are relatively well paid, with job security, paid vacation, universal health care, and promises of state-funded retirement. So a plumber and a surgeon share common work benefits, making any pressure to attend college less strong in some social democracies than it is in the United States. What is the result? The more collective views of Germans and individualist views of Americans lead to dissimilar acceptance of authority over the individual, which leads to enormous differences on policies such as education, social services, and labor. In short, citizens *expect* and *accept* very different things from their governments.

Gun control provides a poignant example of how these differential expectations play out in real policy debates. In March 1996, a gunman armed with four handguns entered Dunblane Primary School in Dunblane, Scotland. He killed sixteen children and one adult before taking his own life. Less than a year later, the British Parliament decisively passed a law banning private ownership of nearly all guns, which is still in effect today and maintains high levels of public support. In December 2012, a gunman entered Sandy Hook Elementary School in Newtown, Connecticut, killing twenty children and six adults, before taking his own life. In the months that followed, the country remained divided about the best course of action regarding gun control. Congress did not pass any comprehensive legislation; government action came solely in the form of executive orders, not through legislative action; and no substantive changes were made regarding gun ownership in the United States. In fact, there have been almost 300 school shootings since Sandy Hook! Why do we see the stark difference between responses to similar shootings in the United Kingdom and United States? The answers lie in part with differences in political culture and democratic governmental structure in the United States compared with the culture and democratic structures in the United Kingdom. The emphasis on individual liberties and the difficulty of changing public policy meant that the American response led to more debate over principles than action, whereas the more collectivist views in the United Kingdom and ease of changing policy led to dramatic policy change.

Comparative politics is a subfield of political science just like American politics is a subfield of political science. Yet, while American politics is focused on understanding the political culture, behavior, and institutions in the United States, comparative politics is focused on analyzing and comparing political culture, behavior, and institutions across political systems. Thus, **Americanists**, or political scientists who specialize in American politics, examine how politics works under American democracy. **Comparativists,** or political scientists who specialize in comparative politics, may look at the way in which different democracies behave in different situations, understanding that there are many democracies around the world and that they do not all look the same. To explore American politics from a comparative perspective, then, means asking how politics in the United States is similar to and different from politics in other advanced industrial democracies. For example, why do we see differences in such areas as education, social services, gun control, and fiscal policies, yet we see similarities in terms of competitive party systems, values of freedom, and high levels of economic growth? The United States shares many foundational democratic characteristics with other advanced industrial democracies. We discuss these similarities in Chapter 2. However, the United States also differs from other democracies in terms of political culture, institutions, and political parties and elections, themes explored throughout the book.

IS AMERICAN DEMOCRACY THE BEST TYPE OF DEMOCRACY?

The position of the Americans is therefore quite exceptional, and it may be believed that no democratic people will ever be placed in a similar one. . . . Let us cease, then, to view all democratic nations under the example of the American people.[3]

American exceptionalism is sometimes used to express the idea that the United States is unique among and superior to other countries. By extension, proponents of American exceptionalism argue that American-styled democracy is the "best" form of government. Alexis de Tocqueville (quoted above) held to the idea that not only is the United States different, but its difference has allowed it to develop the *best* way to organize a government. You may have heard of the idea that the United States is a "City on a Hill." This language, emanating from the New

Testament, has been used throughout history to refer to the uniqueness, and some believed exceptional nature, of the United States. John Winthrop in 1690 told the Massachusetts Bay colonists that their community would be a "city upon a hill" and watched by the world. This religious-like approach to America's uniqueness gave rise to the belief that the United States is a special and blessed country and a Shining City upon a Hill, like that discussed in the Bible. In subsequent years, politicians like John F. Kennedy and Ronald Reagan returned to the City on the Hill metaphor to bring to mind America's uniqueness and superiority as a beacon of hope for the world.

In other usage, however, American exceptionalism simply means that the United States is different, not better than other countries. Other countries, too, believe that they are an example for the world to follow. In Chapter 3, we explore these varied meanings of American exceptionalism, favoring the idea of looking at how American democracy stacks up against other advanced industrial democracies on objective measures rather than suggesting that American democracy is a better type of democracy. Thus, these authors, while each proud Americans, do not ascribe to the idea that the United States would be the "best" democracy to be emulated the world over. Instead, exceptionalism is an analytical angle with great leverage to explain strengths and quirks in American politics that might otherwise be dismissed as normal or maybe not even be noticed. As we travel through this book, we hope that students read with an eye to understanding why the United States is unique and the best type of democracy for *the American system* but not objectively superior in context than other forms of democracy around the world.

In fact, many scholars of American politics have criticized the narrowness of American political beliefs compared to other democracies. While Tocqueville admired American democracy as noted above, he also said,

> I know of no country in which, speaking generally, there is less independence of mind and true freedom of discussion than in America. . . . In America the majority has enclosed thought within a formidable fence. A writer is free inside that area, but woe to the man who goes beyond it.[4]

The uniformity of thought and embrace of individualism leaves Americans feeling threatened by other political beliefs, even if they are modest and democratic. Louis Hartz argued that Americans' "irrational" devotion to "Americanism" and limited government leads Americans to overreact to other ideologies. This explains why the hysteria that some Americans held socialist thoughts led to the red scare in the 1950s, where some Americans' civil liberties and civil rights were bulldozed out of fear that communism would spread.[5] Due to this uniformity of thought, Americans do not recognize other ideological beliefs, and modest social welfare spending gets called "socialism" even while it is small relative to any other democracy. Other scholars say that this adherence to limited government and skepticism toward government progressivism leaves the American system unable and unwilling to deal with pressing issues until there is a crisis—like the Civil War or the Great Depression—when the government has no other choice but to act.[6]

Despite these critiques, American democracy may in fact be the best type of democracy for the United States given the uniqueness of its notions of social contract and political culture; other democracies based upon other notions of social contract and culture have found ways of organizing better suited to their own circumstances. For the sake of analysis, this theme of exceptionalism meaning the *difference* of American government rather than *superiority* of American government will be a theme for inquiry that we carry throughout the book. It is also important to recognize, however, that the United States shares much in common with other advanced industrial democracies. In fact, the United States may not be as dissimilar from other democracies as de Tocqueville or Winthrop thought. Broad commonalities shared as democracies will be explored in Chapter 2. Throughout the book, then, we point out both the similarities and differences between the United States and other democracies as we explore American politics from a comparative perspective.

WHY IS IT IMPORTANT TO EXAMINE AMERICAN POLITICS FROM A COMPARATIVE PERSPECTIVE?

Public policy is not made from a common viewpoint across democracies. In other words, the policy priorities that a country has are influenced by the political culture and institutions (i.e., parties, elections, electoral law, voting behavior) unique to each country. Often we become trapped in our own conceptions of what is appropriate for public policy challenges, institutions, and appropriate political behavior. Examining American politics from a comparative perspective will allow us to "unpack" some of these preconceptions and better understand American politics by studying how other democracies face challenges and do politics. For example, when a person puts on green-colored glasses, they see their environment as green but cannot detect the color of anything that is green. When another person looks at the same environment through purple colored glasses, the same happens with the color purple. In a sense, Americans are socialized into their political worldview as if the United States had put on a pair of green glasses. The political world is tinted from their established viewpoint. Let's say Italy's glasses are purple, and they see the same environment but in purple. While it is natural to have such a worldview and tint based on their particular experiences, Americans cannot distinguish what is green, and Italians cannot discriminate what is purple. These become almost blind spots because of their tinted view. Viewing the environment through another set of glasses can help Americans see the blind spots they would not see otherwise.

Why are American politics different? Differences in political history and political culture have led to differences in institutional preferences, manifested in differences in voting behavior. In short, culture and institutions have intermingled to have long-standing influence on the policy preferences and voting behavior of publics in advanced industrial democracies. American democracy is *one* form of democracy, and when examined comparatively, one learns how American democracy is a unique form of government because culture and institutions have blended in a different way in the United States than they have in other countries. When readers examine each component of American political life comparatively, they will better understand how American democracy is a distinctive form of government and how other democracies function successfully, albeit differently, and readers will more fully understand American politics.

Before we focus on the differences between democratic government practiced in the United States as compared to other countries, we must first understand what these countries have in common. The United States is not the world's only democracy. So what is it that makes a democracy a democracy? Are there common characteristics that all advanced democracies share? Returning to a lens metaphor, when the United States puts on the glasses and looks at a tree, it sees a green tree. When Italy puts on the glasses and looks at the same tree, it still sees the same physical tree; the tree just happens to be purple when viewed through Italian lenses. The same is true with democracy. There are certain core concepts that remain unvarying across all democracies. When the United States looks at these concepts, it sees democracy. When Italy, Australia, Canada, or any other democracy looks at these concepts, they also see democracy. The countries just may look at the world slightly differently, in essence seeing democracy tinted in different ways. We learn in Chapter 2 that the United States has more in common with other democracies than we may think, sharing unique binding characteristics as democracies.

WHAT TO EXPECT IN THE FOLLOWING CHAPTERS

In the following chapters we will explore American politics from a comparative perspective. Each chapter will address a new topic, with definitions of key concepts, and then explore how those concepts work comparatively. Breakout boxes and special feature sections will allow in-depth exploration of these concepts in unique ways.

- Chapter 2 will begin by focusing on definitions of democracy and focus on those characteristics the United States shares with other advanced industrial democracies, that is, the broad similarities between the United States and other democracies.

- Chapter 3 will explore the idea of American exceptionalism and focus on the ways in which the United States is different from other democracies by exploring the concepts of liberal democracy and social democracy.

- Chapter 4 deals with political culture, first by defining political culture and discussing how culture is measured, then exploring different types of political culture and comparing American political culture to political culture in other democracies. This chapter will also examine ideology and the relationships between political culture, social capital, and civic culture.

- Chapter 5 examines the relative protection of civil rights and civil liberties in the United States compared to other democracies. Fitting the American political culture, the American Constitution and Bill of Rights protect civil liberties more vigilantly than do other democracies' constitutions. In turn, the United States has less explicit protections for civil rights due to its political culture, era of constitutionalism, and expression (or lack of expression) of rights and liberties directly in the Constitution and Bill of Rights.

- Chapter 6 explores constitutions further. We begin by defining federal democracy as found in the United States as compared to unitary democracy as found in countries like the United Kingdom and France. We then look at other constitutional differences and similarities such as longevity and majoritarianism versus consociationalism.

- In Chapter 7, we also explore national governing institutions, looking at conceptions of parliamentarianism versus presidentialism, two very different, yet successful ways of organizing the executive and legislative branches of democratic systems. We also examine how judicial systems function in the United States as compared to other democracies.

- Chapter 8 looks at interest groups. The chapter begins with a discussion of interest group arrangements found in the United States compared to interest group arrangements found in many other advanced industrial democracies. Interest groups are examined from a life-cycle approach, and both the positive and negative aspects of interest groups as well as the modes of action undertaken by groups are discussed.

- Chapter 9 continues the discussion of interest articulation by addressing political parties. In particular, we discuss how the American two-party system is unique from other multiparty or single-party democratic systems. In order to understand the uniqueness of the American party system, this chapter addresses party formation and how American party formation differed from party formation in other democracies as well as discusses electoral change and value change.

- Chapter 10 examines elections and electoral institutions. The chapter begins by discussing the different types of electoral systems and electoral law in advanced industrial democracies. We explore the ramifications this has on stability of government and representativeness of government.

- Electoral behaviour is discussed in Chapter 11. The chapter delves into political behavior and attitudes of American voters as compared to voters in other democracies. In this chapter, we discuss different approaches to attitude formation as well as the changing attitudes and voting behavior found in the United States and other advanced democracies.

- Chapter 12 revisits the questions posed in the introduction to this chapter: What does it mean to study American politics from a comparative perspective? *How* and *why* is American democracy different, and what similarities are shared with other advanced industrial democracies? In short, what have we learned from the other chapters in this book?

HOW TO USE THIS BOOK

Each chapter is comprised of several components. First, the chapters are sub-divided into sections. The section heads alert readers to the important topic covered in the paragraphs that follow. Second, within each section, key terms are bolded. Generally, a definition of the term will follow the term itself. A list of these terms appears at the end of each chapter for study reference. There are also boxes located in each chapter. The boxes should not be seen as supplementary or optional reading; they are integral to understanding the concepts introduced in the chapter. Readers should refer to boxes for explanation, illustration, and deeper understanding of concepts. Some chapters also present graphs, maps, and/or data. These should also be examined closely by readers as they help to explain the concepts introduced in the text. The conclusion of each chapter provides a summary of the material; however, they should not be read instead of the chapters. The summary conclusions should be used to help solidify knowledge gained by reading the full chapters. The "points to remember" provide highlights from each chapter, but again should not be used as a substitute for reading the chapter but as a way to self-test knowledge. The review questions at the end of each chapter can also be used as a way to self-test and think more analytically about topics. Finally, we provide a short list of additional readings at the end of each chapter if you would like to explore further any of the topics covered in this book.

KEY TERMS

American exceptionalism 3	Americanists 3	Individualism 2
	Comparativists 3	

REVIEW QUESTIONS

1. What are the distinctions between using American exceptionalism as an admiration of the promise of American democracy used by figures, scholars, and politicians throughout history and the use of American exceptionalism as a mechanism to study the differences in American democracy from other democracies?

2. When President Trump uses "Make American Great Again," how does this fit with the historically positive view of American exceptionalism and the promise of American democracy and way of life?

3. Louis Hartz discussed the common liberalism of political thought among Americans and warned that it leads Americans to overreact to political thought that is outside the American political norm. Explain how this might explain today's polarized American politics. At the extremes, for instance, could this help explain the fear of immigration and multiculturalism that has led to some embracing strong right-wing nationalism in response? Does it explain how the fear of populist authoritarianism has led to radical resistance by some of the militant left?

NOTES

1. Harold Lasswell, *Politics: Who Gets What, When and How* (New York, NY: Whittlesey House, 1936).

2. While there is some parental choice, school tracking in Austria and Germany is fairly common and has been cause for political concern in recent years. The ÖKD, a political party in Germany, for example, incorporated in their platform the idea of universal education, similar to the United States, as a political reform. When the author's own children were in school in Austria, for example, there were debates about which school they would attend should they stay in country as their language skills were not strong enough for the highest track school while their academics were.

3. Alexis de Tocqueville, *Democracy in America* (New York, NY: Penguin Classics, 2003), 363.

4. Alexis de Tocqueville, *Democracy in America* (New York, NY: Harper Perennial, 1988), 254-255.

5. Louis Hartz, *The Liberal Tradition in America* (New York, NY: Harcourt, Brace and World, 1955), 9-14.

6. Walter Dean Burnham, *Critical Elections and the Mainsprings of American Politics* (New York, NY: W. W. Norton & Company, 1971).

CHAPTER TWO

SIMILARITIES BETWEEN THE UNITED STATES AND OTHER DEMOCRACIES

Even though President Donald Trump is viewed to be closer to President Vladimir Putin of Russia than previous U.S. Presidents have ever been with any Russian or Soviet leader, Western allies and the United States closed ranks against Russia around two key events in the spring of 2018. First, in March 2018, in an event that played out like a James Bond movie, former Russian intelligence officer Sergei Skripal and his daughter, Yulia Skripal, were poisoned with a nerve agent while in Salisbury, U.K. In response to this, more than 20 Western allies expelled over 100 Russian diplomats accused of being spies. In the United States alone, there were 60 expulsions. This show of Western solidarity to expel Russian diplomats was the largest seen since the Cold War. The strength of shared values among the Western allies was summed up in British Prime Minister Theresa May's statement to Parliament: "I have found great solidarity from our friends and partners in the EU, North America, NATO and beyond over the past three weeks as we have confronted the aftermath of the Salisbury incident. . . . And together we have sent a message that we will not tolerate Russia's continued attempts to flout international law and undermine our values."

Second, in April 2018, Syrian leader Bashar al-Assad launched a chemical attack against his own people in what has been a long line of war crimes committed by the Syrian regime. Analysis showed the use of a nerve agent and chlorine gas, with up to 500 people poisoned and dozens killed due to the chemical weapons in the attack. The international community (including Donald Trump who previously retaliated with missile strikes after a chemical attack in Syria in 2017) was quick to condemn the attack. Russia and Syria have denied involvement. (Russia has been previously suspected of supplying chemical agents to Syria and aiding the Assad regime in attacks against rebel strongholds). The call for a response was taken to the United Nations Security Council. There, as in the case above, we saw "the West" against Russia, with the United States, France, and the U.K. linking arms to vote against Russian proposals, and Russia voting against the proposal from the Western countries. Such action has clearly drawn a line in the sand, with the United States, U.K., and France striking Syria simultaneously as punishment for the chemical attacks—even though they did not affect their countries directly—and Russia doing everything it could to support Syria's military. Thus, it appears that the international community, particularly our democratic cousins, are willing to come together when chemical attacks are at play, weapons so ghastly that the democratic world has agreed that they have no place in combat situations or international affairs 100 years after their use in Europe during World War I and around 75 years after their use against Jews by the Third Reich.

Why are we seeing this shared purpose among Western countries in direct opposition to Russia? The answer lies in part with the sentiments expressed by Theresa May above—the similar purpose and characteristics the United States and all democracies share. Before these similarities are highlighted, it is important to ask, *what is a democracy*? Not surprisingly, democracy is a multifaceted concept. Scholars have provided different theories about and measures to indicate just what a democracy is as well as how democratic a country is. Others have challenged a Western-centric understanding of democracy and question the type of democracy promoted in the United States and other Western countries. We will explore many of these theories and concepts to see how similarly the United States stacks up to other democracies.

Most Americans have a sense of their country being remarkably democratic. Following numerous typical measures of democracy, that sensibility is warranted. In particular, American government provides numerous democratic structures, encourages sectors of society to express themselves in the political process, offers broad political participatory opportunities, provides vast democratic freedoms to its citizens, and has a socioeconomic structure that backs up democratic citizenship. Across these many disparate measures of democratic life, many other democracies score similarly to the United States. Thus, this chapter demonstrates how American democracy fits within a broader grouping of governing type that scholars refer to as **advanced industrial democracies**. This type of democracy is not without critique. Obviously, the fruits of democracy are not spread evenly, and some have become dissatisfied with democracy. The end of the chapter looks at frustrations with contemporary democracy more closely.

DEFINITION OF DEMOCRACY

The word *democracy* comes from the Greek word *dēmokratía*, meaning "rule of the people." In its earliest usage it described the type of political system in place in some Greek city-states, like Athens, in the fifth through fourth century BCE, where people were allowed and expected to participate in their governing. (Of course, in ancient Greece, this right of participation did not extend to women, slaves, or foreigners.) Democratic government, or rule by the people, can be contrasted with **authoritarian** government, where governing power rests with the state instead of the people, even if people can hold their own religious or social beliefs. In authoritarian governments, citizens do not participate in their own governing. A **totalitarian** government is an extreme type of authoritarian system where the government maintains absolute, or total power, over all aspects of life—political, economic, and social. Democracy can also be contrasted with systems like **monarchy** (rule by one individual, often a king or queen), **oligarchy** (rule by small group of rich or powerful elite), and **theocracy** (rule by religious elite). While this is not an exhaustive list of governing types, these are broad types of governments against which we can contrast democracy. Since this book primarily compares the United States to other democracies, the remainder of this chapter will focus discussion in that area.

Democracy today is generally used to refer to **representative democracy**, or a system of government where citizens select leaders to make decisions on their behalf. For example, in the United States, citizens elect members of Congress who then make laws on their behalf. Similarly, in the United Kingdom, British citizens elect Members of Parliament (MPs), to legislate on their behalf. Because the framers of the U.S. Constitution saw danger in the majority forcing their will and infringing on the rights of the minority, they advocated for representative government. In *Federalist 10*, James Madison argues, "A pure democracy can admit no cure for the mischiefs of faction. A common passion or interest will be felt by a majority, and there is nothing to check the inducements to sacrifice the weaker party. Hence it is, that democracies have ever been found incompatible with personal security or the rights of property; and have, in general, been as short in their lives as they have been violent in their deaths."[1] When Madison states "democracy," he is referring to direct democracy and here advocating for representative democracy. This representative, or **republican**, form of government has survived and defined democracy for centuries, though there are critics, highlighted in the following section, who say that representative democracy does not provide sufficient power to the public or allow equal distribution of wealth in contemporary advanced industrial democracies. Representative democracy can be contrasted with **direct democracy**, where citizens vote directly on a policy issue, and other forms of democracy that will be highlighted in Table 2.2.

The similarities among advanced industrial democracies may be more easily pointed out by their common indicators than by any single definition. Nailing down specific conditions that make a country an advanced industrial democracy remains difficult, so political observers often point to one of the following qualifying indicators. We do not propose that any one of the following definitional components (or lack thereof) of advanced industrial democracy trumps another, but in advanced industrial democracies we tend to see a combination of (1) procedural democracy, (2) high political contestation and high political participation, (3) expansive individual and public freedoms, and (4) high levels of socioeconomic development.

PROCEDURAL DEMOCRACY

When most American political scientists refer to democracies, they are referring to the **Schumpeterian** definition of democracy, named after Austrian-Hungarian-American economist and political scientist Joseph Schumpeter (1883–1950). In 1942 Schumpeter developed a **procedural definition** of democracy stating that

"[T]he democratic method is that institutional arrangement for arriving at political decisions in which individuals acquire the power to decide by means of a competitive struggle for the people's vote."[2]

This definition is considered procedural because it focuses on the *process* of voting. The focus on voting as a yardstick for democracy has also been called **electoralism**.

In other words, for Schumpeter, representative democracies are those where politicians campaign for people's votes, achieve power, and make public decisions. This procedural definition contrasts with the **classical definition** of democracy in two ways. The classical definition was based on the eighteenth century idea that the will of the people and the common good are reflected through decisions made by representatives elected by the citizenry. First, Schumpeter argued that individuals differ in their conception of what constitutes the **common good** (i.e., something that is beneficial for all). Second, individual knowledge of political matters is limited, so that individual interest may not actually lead to the long-term common good of the society.[3]

Obviously, using voting as the yardstick for democracy is not without problems. Many societies have had individuals vote for a leader (Saddam Hussein's Iraq or Putin's Russia, for example) that would in no way qualify being called democracies. Thus, voting alone is not a sufficient indicator for democracy. Procedural definitions of democracy, then, are minimalist definitions of democracy, focusing on elections and voting as the yardstick by which political systems are measured as democracies.

PUBLIC CONTESTATION (COMPETITION) AND INCLUSION (PARTICIPATION)

American political scientist Robert Dahl (1915–2014) expanded upon the idea of Schumpeterian democracy by arguing that a key characteristic of a democracy is the responsiveness of the government to the preferences of citizens who are considered political equals in the political system. Dahl understood that no country could reach the ideal of being completely responsive to its citizens. For a democracy to work best, citizens need to be able to formulate and signify preferences and have these preferences weighted equally in the conduct of the government. In order for this to happen, certain institutional guarantees are necessary (see Table 2.1).[4] The forms these institutions take, however, are different due to the political cultures and historical developments of individual countries, as we discuss in the following chapters.

Two key components are necessary for vibrant democracy—or what Dahl called **polyarchy** or "rule by many": **inclusiveness** (or participation by large numbers of citizens) and **public contestation** (what he deemed liberalization, or the competition among social groups for a policy position). Thus, polyarchies

Table 2.1 Requirements for Democracy according to Robert Dahl

In order for people to have the opportunity to:	The following institutional guarantees are required:
Formulate Preferences	–Freedom to form and join organizations
	–Freedom of expression
	–Right to vote
	–Right of politicians to compete for support
	–Alternative sources of information must be available
Signify Preferences	–Freedom to form and join organizations
	–Freedom of expression
	–Right to vote
	–Eligibility for public office
	–Right of politicians to compete for support
	–Alternative sources of information must be available
	–Free and fair elections
Have Preferences Weighted Equally in the Conduct of Government	–Freedom to form and join organizations
	–Freedom of expression
	–Eligibility for public office
	–Right of politicians to compete for support and for votes
	–Alternative sources of information must be available
	–Free and fair elections
	–Institutions for making government policies must be dependent on votes and other expressions of preference

Source: From Robert Dahl, *Polyarchy: Participation and Opposition* (New Haven, CT: Yale University Press, 1972).

include large numbers of citizens (inclusiveness) in policymaking and are marked by an atmosphere that allows competition between the ideas of these citizens. It is through contestation, or competition, among the ideas of groups or individuals that governments arrive at a policy decision. In other words, in polyarchies, groups of citizens are competing against each other in the marketplace of ideas to arrive at policy outcomes. While ninety-two countries meet criteria of inclusiveness and contestation, we will mainly concern ourselves in this book with advanced industrial democracies, or those countries that are democracies and also have high levels of freedom and economic development (conditions we will highlight below). These include the countries that make up the European Union, Switzerland, Norway, Canada, Australia, New Zealand, Israel, Japan, South Korea, the United States, and potentially others.

A spatial representation plotting advanced industrial democracies based upon inclusiveness and contestation as of 2000 can be found in Figure 2.1. All advanced industrial democracies are located in the upper right-hand corner with high levels of inclusiveness and contestation, but variation among them exists. The Nordic countries have the highest levels of *both* contestation *and* inclusiveness. The United States, on the other hand, has as high as contestation scores as Norway and Sweden but scores somewhat lower on inclusion. While Germany has inclusion levels like Norway and Sweden, it has lower scores than the United States on contestation. Australia, France, and the United Kingdom all have lower contestation *and* inclusion scores than the United States. This illustrates an important point: *variation exists among advanced industrial democracies concerning contestation and inclusion, but they generally clump together on the higher range of both, even if not uniformly between the two components.*

Moving the definition of democracy beyond procedural requirements and expanding his definition beyond just contestation and inclusiveness, Dahl focused on democracy as a system of fundamental rights that includes the following six ideal traits democracies try to maximize:[5]

- Effective participation: All citizens must be afforded a chance to make their views known before a collective decision is taken.

- Equality in voting: Every citizen has an equal opportunity to vote, and each vote is counted as equal.

- Gaining enlightened understanding: Each citizen has opportunities for learning about relevant alternative policies and their consequences.

- Final control of the agenda: Citizens decide how its members choose which items get placed on the agenda.

- Inclusion: Every citizen is entitled to participate.

- Fundamental rights: Each of these features is a fundamental right that is part of the ideal order.

A further point put forward by Dahl is important here as well. Most advanced industrial democracies developed public contestation, or debate over ideas, prior to having high levels of inclusion. So in most countries, sectors of society competed in politics at the elite level prior to **mass enfranchisement**, or when voting rights were extended to the entire citizenry. Here the United States stands as somewhat different. The right to vote was given out broadly in the United States to citizens of all social classes, though not originally to all races or women; whereas other countries held back the right to vote for lower classes longer. This will be a key distinction explaining how the United States is different in subsequent chapters.

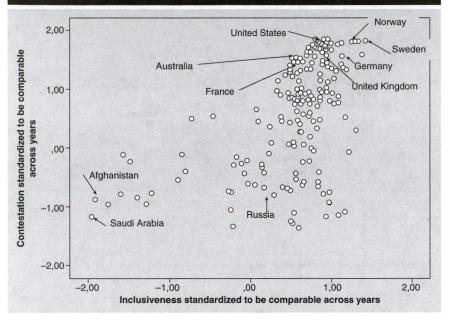

Figure 2.1 Dahl's Polyarchy: Levels of Contestation and Inclusion, 2000

Source: Data from Macro Guide: Polyarchy and Contestation Scales, http://www.nsd.uib.no/macrodataguide/set.html?id=33&sub=1.

FREEDOMS

So far, the similarities between the United States and other advanced industrial democracies have focused on institutions providing democracy procedurally and high levels of contestation and public inclusion. For any observer of American politics, one key component of American democracy not yet discussed is freedom. Americans can quote Patrick Henry's "Give me liberty or give me death," have state mottos like "Live Free or Die," and fly the famous flag with a coiled snake and the phrase "Don't Tread on Me!" Perhaps nothing else is as centrally voiced by Americans for its importance to their conception of being American as is their embrace of their freedom. Interestingly, despite the great connection between the American ethos and identity and freedom, the United States shares objectively measured indicators of freedom with other advanced industrial democracies.

The Freedom House Organization, an independent, nonpartisan watchdog organization, measures the level of freedom in a country, focusing particularly on political rights and civil liberties.[6] The complex measures for each country's

Figure 2.2   Level of Freedom Worldwide, 2018

Countries highlighted in black are designated free or partially free in Freedom House's 2018 Survey.

Source: Freedom House, http://www.freedomhouse.org.

political rights and civil liberties score determine if a country is free, partially free, or not free (see Figure 2.2). Democracies are those seen as "free" based upon the Freedom House scores. Although, most democracies have a score of 1.0 (lower scores equal more freedom), the United States' political rights score dropped to 2 (partly free) in 2018, giving it an overall score of 1.5. While this is still in the "free" category, it is higher than other democracies. While there are some exceptions, there is quite a bit of overlap between the Freedom House variables, Dahl's public contestation and participation, and Schumpeterian procedural democracy. Democracy, not surprisingly, fits hand in glove with citizens' freedoms.

SOCIOECONOMIC DEVELOPMENT

One of the most controversial correlates of democracy is socioeconomic development. It is controversial because no one wants to suggest that a society needs wealth or specific social development features in order to be democratic. Luckily, socioeconomic development is neither required for nor determinative of democracy. Thus, the authors are not claiming that high levels of socioeconomic development are necessary for democracies; yet, this is a theme dominant in international politics. Regardless of personal belief, higher levels of socioeconomic development have historically run parallel with democracy and have been a recurring component of the study of democracy for different reasons.

First, many such studies grew out of post–World War II scholarship trying to explain how to strengthen burgeoning democracies. This scholarly pursuit was particularly timely given the failure of German and Italian democracy prior to World War II and the Cold War fear that without strong democracy some countries might pursue Soviet-style communist government. Though critics argued that the Western-backed policies that attempted to bring about the social structural changes championed by this scholarship ended up weakening these countries' governments and stunting democracy, these scholars did find that a combination of economic development, social structural conditions, and democratic institutions all existed together in advanced industrial democracies.

Second, socioeconomic advancement likely related with other important features of democracy such as an educated and participatory public. In a particularly noteworthy study, American political sociologist Seymour Martin Lipset tested the Greek philosopher Aristotle's arguments that societies with a large middle class will tend toward healthy democracy.[7] Lipset found that in addition to effective governing institutions, democracy did correlate with a greater presence of a middle class. In particular, he found that societies with greater economic development and industrialization, education levels, and citizen wealth sustained democracy best.[8] These were not meant to be determinative but suggested that social and economic conditions often bolstered and stabilized democratic processes. Therefore, there is no magic menu of criteria for democracy, and societies often change, yet higher rates of educational achievement, economic development, and institutions that promote middle-class participation in the marketplace of ideas tend to correlate with democracy—both in the United States and among other advanced industrial democracies.

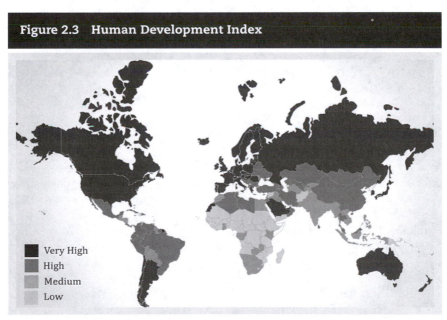

Figure 2.3 Human Development Index

Very High
High
Medium
Low

Source: Map based upon data from the United Nations Development Programme, 2017, http://www.hdr.undp.org.

Economists use different measures to assess the economic development of a country. One measure is **gross domestic product (GDP)** per capita, or the market value of all goods and services produced in a country per person. Another measure commonly used is **human development index (HDI)**, which measures life expectancy, literacy rates, education levels, and standard of living. Advanced industrial democracies have high levels of HDI and GDP per capita (see Figures 2.3 and 2.4).

From these maps, it is clear that quite a bit of overlap exists between the socioeconomic statistics, procedural democracy, Freedom House scores, and representative democracies with high public contestation and participation. Nevertheless, some caveats are in order. First, socioeconomic status does not determine democracy. Some wealthy countries do not score highly on freedom or democratic scores (see Saudi Arabia, Iran, or China), whereas other less wealthy countries score well (see India and South Africa). Second, democracies and socioeconomic dynamics change. Indeed, some scholars have moved away from relying on economic indicators for democracy, arguing that wealth measurements alone mask inequities in these societies and have highlighted a new set of criteria. These advanced industrial democracies are in fact now "postindustrial" societies, containing a large portion of citizens frustrated with the idea that more democracy does not necessarily equate with higher quality of life.[9] In other words, socioeconomic factors do not correlate with some perfect democracy. Nor is there a "perfect" democratic endpoint the United States or other democracies have achieved.

Figure 2.4　GDP per Capita

Advanced industrial democracies display the highest GDP/capita.

Thousands
- > 47.91
- 30.79 - 47.91
- 18.48 - 30.79
- < 18.48

Source: GDP per capita in 2017 US$. Data from the World Bank, http://www.worldbank.org.

Like other advanced industrial democracies, Americans often complain that they wish they had more say in their government (see Box 2.1). In fact, common critiques have blossomed about all advanced democracies not being democratic enough in large part because critics are unsatisfied with the representative nature of modern democracies. Critics have suggested other types of democracy from contemporary representative democracy, such as those highlighted in Table 2.2, would better articulate citizens' wishes in the governing of their country. These critiques have blossomed in part because some segments of the populations think that elected representatives are more responsive to special interests (a topic we cover in Chapter 9), or wealthy segments of the population, rather than the popular will of the people. In part, this happens because in republican government, citizens turn over decision-making power to representatives to act on their behalf. Thus, elected officials need to make judgment calls, and these calls can be out of step with citizens' preferences. These critiques have led many citizens to pine for, if not to call for, more direct forms of democratic participation.

BOX 2.1

Frustration With Representative Democracy

Sometimes democracy is messy and its benefits not equally distributed across members of society. When this happens, we will often see individuals acting in concert to push their demands on their governments. There are countless examples of such social movements (see Chapter 8). This box will highlight three recent examples of dissatisfaction with representative democracy: Brexit, The Women's March, and the Tea Party. **Brexit** refers to the British exit from the European Union (EU). On June 23, 2016, voters throughout the United Kingdom (England, Scotland, Wales, and Northern Ireland) went to the polls to vote on whether to stay in the EU or to leave. By a narrow margin of 51.9 percent of those who voted, Britons voted to leave. They are scheduled to exit the EU at 11p.m. on March 29, 2019. Most economists agree that exiting the European Union will decrease real per-capita income over the medium and long term.[14] Why then did the British vote to leave? To understand this, we have to look at where there was support for Brexit. Scotland, Northern Ireland, and the city of London voted overwhelmingly to remain in the EU; however, in England and Wales, areas that were relatively less educated, had lower incomes, and higher unemployment were more likely to vote to leave.[15] Incidentally, these were also areas outside of city centers. In other words, those in rural areas were move likely to want to Brexit. In fact, it seems as if the Brexit vote was more a manifestation of dissatisfaction with the unequal distribution of wealth in the U.K., driven in part by differences in education and location, the same mechanisms we see driving the vote for right wing candidates in Europe (like Marine le Pen, see Chapter 9)[16] and the Tea Party movement in the

(Continued)

(Continued)

United States (discussed next). In 2018, support for Brexit has dropped across the U.K., with Northern Ireland grumbling about joining the Republic of Ireland and Scotland once again considering a referendum on exit from the U.K. Even within England and Wales, support has fallen, and a majority of Britons now favor a new vote. The government in the U.K., however, has not called for such a vote, and as of late 2018, British exit from the EU is planned to occur.

Similar to those who support Brexit, Americans who identify with the Tea Party tend to live outside major populations centers. That said, they tend to be slightly more educated than the average U.S. electorate. They also tend to be White and older. The **Tea Party** is a conservative movement within the Republican Party in the United States that began in the immediate aftermath of the election of Barak Obama. While some in the Tea Party have racist leanings, the majority of Tea Party supporters call for lowering of the national debt and reduction in taxes.[17] While they often self-identify as Independents, most members of the Tea Party have a strong record of voting Republican. Tea Party voters are also angry with Washington, DC. A majority were upset with how Washington was working. Only 1 percent in 2012 approved of the work of Congress, and most wanted a smaller role for the federal government. Flying flags that said, "Don't Tread on Me," Tea Party adherents believed the United States was on the wrong track and that a fundamental change in the way the country was governed was needed. Tea Party unease with the U.S. government contributed in part to the election of Donald Trump, as he played directly into these frustrations as the proclaimed antiestablishment candidate of the Republican primary and eventual winner of the 2016 presidential race.

While Donald Trump's presidency can be traced back to Tea Party frustration with democracy, The Women's March and subsequent "resistance" movements grew out of dissatisfaction with the election of Donald Trump in 2016. As explained in Chapter 7, Trump won the presidency with almost 3 million fewer votes than Clinton, yet won the electoral college vote and thus the presidency. This left many people dissatisfied with the Trump presidency, particularly women and people of color. The Women's March grew into a worldwide protest event on January 21, 2017, the day after Donald Trump's inauguration. The march in DC, known as the Women's March on Washington, is the largest single protest event ever recorded in the United States; between 3,267,134 and 5,246,670 people participated in Washington, DC, with 7 million participating worldwide (see Chapter 8 for more on the Women's March).[18] By comparison, Trump's inauguration the day before drew between 3 to 6 million. The march subsequently grew into a social movement that continued to agitate for its key demands—women's rights, reproductive rights, immigration reform, healthcare reform, racial equity, worker's rights, LGBTQIA rights, and environmental protection. Annual marches also take place to commemorate the first march and are attended by those who remain dissatisfied with the outcome of the 2016 presidential election and who feel as if their concerns are not being addressed in Washington.

Table 2.2 Alternative Forms of Democracy From Representative Democracy

Type	Definition
Deliberative Democracy	In contrast to a procedural focus on voting found in representative democracy, **deliberative democracy** (also called discursive democracy) focuses on citizen deliberation and public consensus building in the democratic process. Through public deliberation, laws achieve **legitimacy** through consensus building and majority rule in public meetings, forums, and conventions. Deliberative democracy has its roots in Greek philosophy and has seen modern-day application in environmental policy making and election reform with examples seen in the United States' Green Party, Canadian election reform, and sustainability conversations in Australia.
Direct Democracy	Direct democracy is a form of government where citizens vote on issues directly rather than vote for representatives who then vote on the issues. Deliberative democracy can sometimes take the form of direct democracy. Also having its roots in ancient Greek governance, direct democracy today is manifest in referendum, initiative, and recall. **Referenda** are votes on whether or not a law should stand and be binding. **Initiatives** are usually put on ballots by citizens and circumvent the representative process by going directly to the public for a vote on legislation. **Recalls** give the public the authority to remove an elected representative from his or her position. We see modern-day examples of direct democracy in the United States (mainly at the state and local levels in western states) and Switzerland. The framers of the U.S. Constitution were opposed to direct democracy because they thought it could result in **tyranny of the majority**, when the majority tramples over the rights of the minority.
Radical Democracy	Radical democracy has mainly been used when talking about **social movements**, large informal or formal groups of individuals organized around an issue or cause, and argues that social movements need to challenge neoliberal assumptions of democracy, in particular the connections between capitalism and democracy. In this view, democracy is achieved through difference, challenge, and dissent. Radical democracy is associated with many left-wing movements in several countries, including the Socialist Party in the United States and Abahlali base-Mjondolo, the shack dwellers movement in South Africa. The Occupy Movement in the United States, discussed in Box 2.1, is also an example of radical democracy combined with direct democracy.

Most Americans likely wouldn't call for practicing democracy in any other way than they already practice it, but that doesn't mean our version of democracy should be adopted to improve life for all countries universally, nor do the conditions of being an American necessarily make us happier than the citizens of other countries. The World Happiness Report ranks countries based on results pooled from six indicators applied in the Gallup World Poll survey. Scores run from 0 (lowest) to 8 (highest). The current report includes data from 2015 to 2017, with Finland topping the world in terms of respondent happiness. Using the six indicators of income, healthy life expectancy, social support, freedom, trust, and generosity, has become a comprehensive process for comparing the satisfaction of citizens and residents across nations. Reported data can be used to track changes in individual countries over time, regional variations at the international level, and national differences of neighboring populations within regions.[10] The United States ranks 21st on the World Happiness Index, well below many other advanced industrial democracies but still above others, like France and the U.K. (see Figure 2.5).

As stated above, democracy is not without its critics, and living in a democracy does not necessarily make one happier. The critique of representative democracy as commonly practiced in advanced industrial democracies is not a uniquely American critique. This critique is found in democracies all over the world. Further, it demonstrates, as Dahl stated, that democracy is not a static condition or an endpoint. Rather, democratic citizens continue to place demands on governments and push to satisfy democratic demands. There has been recent attention given to the decrease in support for democratic institutions across advanced industrial democracies (see Table 2.3 for country level data), and this decrease in support for democracy is stronger among younger generations than older. For example, only

Figure 2.5 World Happiness Index

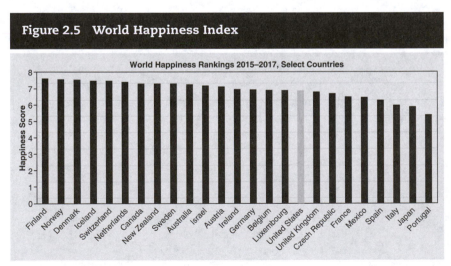

Source: J. Helliwell, R. Layard, and J. Sachs, *World Happiness Report 2018* (New York, NY: Sustainable Development Solutions Network, 2018).

Table 2.3 Aggregate Support for Democratic Principles, Select Countries

	People can practice their religion freely %	Women have the same rights as men %	Honest elections are held regularly w/ choice of at least two parties %	People can say what they want w/o censorship %	The media can report news w/o censorship %	People can use the Internet w/o censorship %
United States	84	91	79	71	67	69
Canada	62	94	81	61	65	60
France	52	83	66	67	46	50
Germany	71	92	76	86	73	69
Italy	75	82	73	62	64	61
Spain	58	88	79	76	75	69
U.K.	68	92	76	57	58	53
South Korea	49	64	62	56	52	50
Japan	24	60	60	57	45	40
Australia	54	92	75	52	57	53

Data from Pew Research Center http://www.pewglobal.org/2015/11/18/1-support-for-democratic-principles. Numbers are aggregate percentages of respondents who agree and are not broken by age.

30 percent of American millennials say that it is important to live in a democracy compared to 75 percent of people born before 1930. In fact, in a 2010 poll, fully 24 percent of younger Americans said that democracy was a *bad* form of government.[11] This is not a phenomenon unique to the United States. Foa and Mounk have found a similar cohort pattern across all longstanding democracies, including the United Kingdom, the Netherlands, Sweden, Australia, and New Zealand, "with the proportion of younger citizens who believe it is essential to live in a democracy falling to a minority."[12] This statistic mirrors a concomitant decrease in trust (see Chapter 4) among younger generations as well.

In short, younger generations are skeptical of all sorts of democratic institutions, including political parties, institutions, and minority rights. They are also open to authoritarian interpretations of democracy, with at least 20 percent of individuals in most advanced industrial democracies saying that "having a strong leader who doesn't have to bother with parliamentary elections" is a good thing. The percentage of people who agree with this statement has increased in every democracy over time, and as of 2017, was at 30 percent in the United States.[13] The decrease in trust and decrease in those who think democracy is important should trouble readers of this book. Is this a sign of democratic decay? It has led some scholars to warn of democratic **deconsolidation,** or the sliding back from liberal democracy to nondemocratic forms of government.

Recent manifestations of dissatisfaction with democracy include Brexit in the United Kingdom, the Tea Party movement in the United States, and the Women's March, which started in the United States and spread throughout the world. Thus, on dissatisfaction as well, the United States is similar to its advanced industrial counterparts.

CONCLUSION

When looking at democratic procedure, contestation and inclusion, freedoms, and level of socioeconomic development, the United States is very similar to other advanced industrial democracies. That is, the United States is not unique in its democratic society; it is more like other societies and their governing systems than it is dissimilar. This chapter found that procedurally, the United States is like other democracies. The United States practices a representative form of democratic government, where citizens are enfranchised to vote for representatives. Further, the United States, like other advanced democracies, displays high levels of contestation and inclusion, thus making it a near polyarchy. In addition, the United States has similar levels of objectively measured freedom when compared to other advanced industrial democracies. In fact, advanced democracies display the highest levels of freedom. Finally, advanced industrial democracies, including the United States, have high levels of economic development. Even in terms of dissatisfaction with Western-styled democracy, the United States stacks up similarly to other countries, and democracies are not always the "happiest" based on objective measures.

Therefore, it can be erroneous to set the United States aside as its own unique democratic case. American exceptionalism, or difference, highlighted in subsequent chapters, should not suggest that the United States is a unique form of democracy. Rather, it is a typical advanced industrial democracy across broad measures, sharing core features with other advanced industrial democracies but one with distinct—perhaps even remarkably so—political beliefs and institutions.

POINTS TO REMEMBER

- The word *democracy* comes from the Greek word *dēmokratía*, meaning "rule of the people," distinct from other forms of government like authoritarianism, totalitarianism, monarchy, oligarchy, and theocracy.

- Representative democracy, practiced in the United States and other advanced democracies, is a form of government where citizens elect representatives to make decisions on their behalf.

- Procedural democracy, also referred to as Schumpeterian democracy, differs from classical definitions of democracy and focuses on elections as the yardstick for determining if a country is or is not a democracy.

- Polyarchy, coined by Robert Dahl, refers to those countries (like the United States and other advanced industrial democracies) that have high levels of both contestation and inclusion.

- The Freedom House scores measure levels of freedom in countries worldwide. The United States, like other democracies, scores "very high" in terms of level of freedom, yet its political rights score has dropped in 2018.

- Socioeconomic development can be measured with indices like GDP per capita and HDI. Advanced industrial democracies have high levels of socioeconomic development.

- Some argue that representative democracy is not sufficient and does not guard against inequalities and instead call for other forms of democracy including direct democracy, deliberative democracy, and radical democracy.

- Distrust of democracy has increased over time while belief in the importance of democracy has decreased across all advanced industrial democracies. This decrease is most pronounced in younger generations.

KEY TERMS

REVIEW QUESTIONS

1. What does the word *democracy* mean? What is its origin?

2. What do we mean when we refer to representative democracy? Procedural democracy? Electoralism?

3. What is a polyarchy? How does this relate to levels of inclusion and contestation in a country?

4. According to Dahl, which six traits do all democracies possess?

5. What is mass enfranchisement?

6. What indicators are used to assess democracy? How do democracies score on these indicators?

7. In what ways are all advanced industrial democracies similar?

8. What are some critiques about representative democracy? Why do these critiques exist?

9. What is tyranny of the majority?

10. What are referendum, initiatives, and recall?

11. Are you concerned about democratic decay? Do you think it is important to live in a democracy? Why, or why not?

SUGGESTED READINGS

Baker, Kendall L., Russell J. Dalton, and Kai Hildebrandt. *Germany Transformed*. Cambridge, MA: Harvard University Press, 1981.

Dahl, Robert. *Polyarchy: Participation and Opposition*. New Haven, CT: Yale University Press, 1972.

Dalton, Russell J., Scott C. Flanagan, and Paul Allen Beck, Eds. *Electoral Change in Advanced Industrial Democracies: Realignment of Dealignment?* Princeton, NJ: Princeton University Press, 1984.

Dryzek, John. (1990). *Discursive Democracy: Politics, Policy, and Political Science*. Oxford, UK: Oxford University Press, 1990.

Inglehart, Ronald. "The Silent Revolution in Europe: Intergenerational Change in Post-Industrial Societies." *American Political Science Review* 4 (1971): 4, 991–1017.

Inglehart, Ronald, and Christian Welzel. "How Development Leads to Democracy: What We Know about Modernization." *Foreign Affairs March/April* (2009).

http://www.foreignaffairs.com/articles/64821/ronald-inglehart-and-christian-welzel/how-development-leads-to-democracy.

Lipset, Seymour Martin. *Political Man: The Social Bases of Politics*. New York, NY: Anchor Books, 1959.

Lipset, Seymour Martin. "Some Social Requisites of Democracy: Economic Development and Political Legitimacy." *American Political Science Review* 53, no. 1 (1959): 66–105.

Madison, James. *Federalist No. 10: "The Same Subject Continued: The Union as a Safeguard against Domestic Faction and Insurrection." New York Daily Advertiser*, November 22, 1787.

Schumpeter, Joseph A. *Capitalism, Socialism, and Democracy*. New York, NY: Harper, 1942.

NOTES

1. James Madison, *Federalist No. 10:* "The Same Subject Continued: The Union as a Safeguard against Domestic Faction and Insurrection," *New York Daily Advertiser*, November 22, 1787.

2. Joseph A. Schumpeter, *Capitalism, Socialism, and Democracy* (New York, NY: Harper, 1942).

3. Schumpeter, *Capitalism, Socialism, and Democracy*.

4. Robert Dahl, *Polyarchy: Participation and Opposition* (New Haven, CT: Yale University Press, 1972).

5. Dahl, *Polyarchy*.

6. According to the Freedom House definitions of these in its "Freedom in the World 2017" report, political rights are based on electoral process, political pluralism—like Dahl's contestation above, and participation, while civil liberties include freedom of expression and belief, associational and organizational rights, rule of law, and personal autonomy and individual rights.

7. Seymour Martin Lipset, *Political Man: The Social Bases of Politics* (New York, NY: Anchor Books, 1959).

8. Lipset, *Political Man*. Also see Seymour Martin Lipset, "Some Social Requisites of Democracy: Economic Development and Political Legitimacy," *American Political Science Review* 53, no. 1 (1959): 66–105; Kendall L. Baker, Russell J. Dalton, and Kai Hildebrandt, *Germany Transformed: Political Culture and the New Politics* (Cambridge, MA: Harvard University Press, 1981).

9. Ronald Inglehart, *Culture Shift in Advanced Industrial Society* (New Jersey: Princeton University Press, 1990).

10. John F. Helliwell, Richard Layard, and Jeffrey Sachs, *World Happiness Report 2018* (New York, NY: Sustainable Development Solutions Network, 2018).

11. Roberto Stefan Foa and Yascha Mounk, "The Signs of Deconsolidation," *Journal of Democracy* 28, 1 (January 2017): 5–15.

12. Foa and Mounk, "The Signs of Deconsolidation," p. 6.

13. Foa and Mounk, "The Signs of Deconsolidation."

14. Thomas Sampson, "Brexit: The Economics of International Disintegration," *Journal of Economic Perspectives* 31, no. 4 (2017): 163–184. doi:10.1257/jep.31.4.163.

15. Sascha O. Becker, Thiemo Fetzer, and Dennis Novy, "Who Voted for Brexit? A Comprehensive District-Level Analysis," *Economic Policy* 32, no. 92 (2017): 601–650. doi.org/10.1093/epolic/eix012.

16. Becker, Fetzer, and Novy, "Who Voted for Brexit?"

17. Angie Maxwell and T. Wayne Parent, "A 'Subterranean Agenda'? Racial Attitudes, Presidential Evaluations, and Tea Party Membership," *Race and Social Problems* 5, no. 3 (2013): 226–237.

18. Matt Broomfield, "Women's March Against Donald Trump Is the Largest Day of Protests in U.S. History, Say Political Scientists," *Independent*, archived from the original on January 25, 2017.

CHAPTER THREE

AMERICAN EXCEPTIONALISM

At the winter Olympics in South Korea in 2018, you could see people wrapped and decorated with the flags of the different countries competing. Many Americans were among them, wrapped in the stars and stripes of the American flag. When the Olympics ended, most fans put away their flags and patriotic wear until the next Olympics or worldwide sporting event. This is not as much the case for American fans. When you travel around the United States, it is not uncommon to see the American flag flying everywhere—from your local McDonald's to churches, to car dealerships to people's own front lawns. In other countries, this is less of the case. In other countries, you are less likely to see a flag flying from any building other than government buildings. While in the United States it is almost a requisite that you fly a flag several times a year, in Germany, for example, in part because of their dodgy past with nationalism, people would look at you strangely if you had a flagpole raised in your yard. In fact, when Germany won the Soccer World Cup in 1990, some Germans commented how proud they were of their team but had reservations about the level of flag waving. The ubiquitous patriotic displays in the United States fit with Americans' historical sense of being special or exceptional. But, what does it mean to say that the United States is exceptional?

In Chapter 2 we discussed the many similarities between the United States and other advanced industrial democracies. The United States is similar to other democracies when we examine democratic practice, competition (contestation), participation, freedom, socioeconomics, and even frustrations. This raises the question, if democracies are so similar, why do scholars discuss American exceptionalism? Part of the answer stems from the very different focus of scholarship between scholars who study American politics—referred to as **Americanists**—and those who compare aspects of governance among different countries, referred to as **comparativists**. Most Americanists focus in great depth on specific areas of American political institutions, parties, interest groups, or political behavior, and for good reason, most American politics textbooks draw from the detailed work of Americanists. Thus, when some scholars look at the United States relative to other advanced industrial democracies, it can lead them to view the United States as unusual, unique, or even special. In fact, early observers of American democracy, like Alexis de Tocqueville (see Box 3.1), noted the unique aspects of

American democracy. In the past, some people have referred to this idea of the United States as special, or superior, as American exceptionalism; however, this is an incorrect understanding of the term. Viewing the United States as special distorts a comparative look at American democracy. The scholarly definition of **American exceptionalism** focuses not on the degree to which the United States is superior to other countries but instead on how the United States is *different* from other advanced industrial democracies. This is because the true meaning of exceptionalism is not superiority or special but unique. When we consider the root of exceptionalism is *exception*, we can better understand American exceptionalism as the idea that the United States is an exception, or sometimes different than, other democracies.

The key component of the answer as to why the United States is different lies in the significant difference in the founding conditions in the United States compared to other countries. Those conditions and subsequent political life have predisposed Americans to view what makes government **legitimate**, or popularly accepted, differently from citizens of other advanced industrial democracies. When a government has legitimacy, it is seen as having the right to rule. In other words, when citizens view a government as legitimate, they accept that government's authority. De Tocqueville and others saw citizen deliberative experiences, such as town hall meetings, as an opportunity to build not only ties among citizens but also the legitimacy of the governmental system.

BOX 3.1

Alexis de Tocqueville

Alexis de Tocqueville (July, 29, 1805–April 16, 1859) was a French thinker and historian who most famously wrote the two-volume *Democracy in America* based on his observations from travels in the United States. He is credited with providing an early basis of work for sociology and political science, particularly in the United States. De Tocqueville wrote of his travels through America during the time of President Andrew Jackson, when the fabric of American life was under dramatic transformation. He wanted to elucidate the difference between the fading aristocratic order in France and the "new" democratic order emerging in the United States.

De Tocqueville, ever the supporter of liberty, remarked on the American penchant for liberty and

▶ **Photo 3.1** Alexis de Tocqueville, *Democracy in America* (1899), accessed via Wikimedia Commons.

equality. He also is known for his affection for American-styled citizen involvement, where he spoke highly of the New England town hall–styled democracy and **associational life**, where people form and rely upon social networks, as a way for Americans to come together and forge an American consciousness and solve problems. He saw deliberation, consensus building, and decision making among citizens as a way to forge a stronger and better democracy. We see his legacy today in town halls and citizen participation across the United States.

DIFFERING VIEWS OF GOVERNING LEGITIMACY

Humans do not weigh all experiences equally. Rather, some memories and experiences in our life forever shift views of how the world works and propel us toward certain careers or even ways of life. Such formative events tend to strike people in their adolescence, high school, or college years and likely imprint particular worldviews from that point forward. You have likely experienced friends who had very different experiences than you in these times, and despite your previously close relationship, you just have not remained as close because one or both of you "changed"—you both may not understand "what happened" to the other to make them the way they are today. Countries may have similar decisive "adolescent" experiences that crystallize particular views of how governance should operate. In other words, other nations scratch their head and wonder why American politics is odd.

One formative event in the "adolescence" of a country is the nature of the democratic revolutionary moment of a people, or the historical conditions and popular wisdom at the time a nation democratized. Why would Americans choose to view their government as legitimate when other democracies, sharing democratic values and love of freedom, choose their own patterns of **legitimate government?** Social contract theorists were political philosophers who answered this sort of question (see Box 3.2). Beginning in the **Enlightenment Era** (late seventeenth through eighteenth centuries)—in Western philosophical, intellectual, and scientific life where reason was advocated as the primary source of legitimacy and sway, and traditional beliefs and authority were questioned—these theorists argued that government legitimacy came from citizens entering a **social contract**, or the implicit agreement among citizens to grant government legitimacy in exchange for certain protections from the state. As political philosopher Thomas Hobbes (1588–1679) then argued, people proactively decide to leave the anarchy and danger that would exist among people in an ungoverned world—what these theorists termed the **state of nature**. Thus, legitimacy of government came from people deciding to be governed rather than legitimacy coming from the **Divine Right of Kings**, the idea that a monarch gains legitimacy from God, which defined why royalty held government legitimacy prior to this philosophical challenge. While all democracies ultimately share the view that government gains its legitimacy from the people, the nature of what government should ultimately be doing to fulfill its end of the contract differs by the conditions a country faced as it democratized. In the case of the United States, its democratic revolutionary moment borrowed directly from social contract theorist John Locke, who said that only governments that were limited would be legitimate.

BOX 3.2

Enlightenment Thinkers[1]

▶ **Photo 3.2** John Locke, Library of Congress, www .loc.gov.

John Locke was an English philosopher and physician who lived from August 9, 1632 to October 28, 1704. An important philosopher of the Enlightenment Era, his thoughts on liberalism greatly influenced American thinking at the formation of the country and today. His thoughts are reflected in liberal democracies. Locke coined the idea that governments ought not to infringe on the life, liberty, or property of citizens if they are to be legitimate.

▶ **Photo 3.3** Maurice Quentin de La Tour, "Portrait of Jean-Jacques Rousseau (1712–1778)," accessed via Wikimedia Commons.

We see his ideas enshrined in the United States' Constitution, making the United States very much "locked into Locke."

French philosopher Jean-Jacques Rousseau (1712–1778) focused thoughts on the common good, arguing for placing the common good above individual rights and private property. His thoughts are reflected in social democracies' emphasis on social welfare and state responsibility to citizens.

According to Locke's view of the social contract, government arises out of an agreement among people and a willingness to be governed and collectively follow given rules. Additionally, government provides an ordered society. Locke also believed that people have particular "natural rights"—from the state of nature—and a legitimate government should never take these rights away. These natural rights, according to Locke, are life, liberty, and property. When Thomas

Jefferson eloquently penned America's reason for splitting from England, he borrowed directly from Locke and his notion of legitimacy by inserting a slightly changed form of Locke's natural rights in the Declaration of Independence— *life, liberty, and the pursuit of happiness*—to explain why the English king had violated the social contract and was no longer legitimately the leader of the American people.

For Americans, Jefferson's borrowing of Locke's phrase captured their belief that unalienable rights were not given to citizens by the government but by their Creator and could not be taken away from them by government. In fact, Americans did not just use Locke for the Declaration of Independence but have continually returned to the protection of individual life, liberty, and pursuit of happiness (or property) as necessary conditions for government to be considered legitimate. When the United States' first constitution—the Articles of Confederation—could not protect the individual unalienable rights of American citizens due to **tyranny of the majority**, or the idea that the majority can pursue choices that are not favorable to the minority whose rights are not protected, the framers of the Constitution met to reinvent American institutions to make them less open to democratic pressure in order to protect individual liberties. In particular, under the Articles of the Confederation, citizens' property rights were threatened from riots and rebellions against lenders foreclosing on debtors' land, so the authors of the Constitution rebalanced the trade-offs of democratic rule relative to individual protection of liberty with the latter winning out.

Anti-Federalist critics felt the Constitution would not limit government power enough relative to citizen rights. Indeed, *Anti-Federalist 1* predicted some of the frustrations Americans express with the size and scope of today's federal government. Ultimately, as a concession to Anti-Federalist concerns, the Bill of Rights—the first ten amendments to the Constitution—specifically highlighted key citizen rights the government could not take away (see Chapter 5 for more on this). Not surprisingly, the Fifth Amendment lists the many conditions under which the government cannot hold or prosecute citizens. This includes the limitations that people cannot "be deprived of life, liberty or property, without due process of law; nor shall private property be taken for public use, without just compensation."

Unfortunately prior to the Civil War, the Supreme Court cited the very concept of life, liberty, and property as the reason why former slave Dred Scott was not free despite being in a free state. Because Scott was not a citizen he did not have rights, and because the government could not legitimately take away a citizen's property, which Scott was considered to be in slavery, Scott's freedom was revoked because of his former slaveowner's property rights. Later, after the Civil War, Americans explicitly articulated that states could not take away their citizens' rights of "Life, Liberty, and Property" without a due process of law in the Fourteenth Amendment. This is not a debate that was put to bed in the 1800s. In 2018, the Supreme Court ruled in a 5 to 4 ruling on *Trump v. Hawaii* that the United States could ban travelers from certain countries (known as the Trump travel ban or Executive Order 13769 and Presidential Proclamation 9465). Again, because they were not citizens, travelers to the United States did not have the right to life, liberty, and the pursuit of happiness, and the majority opinion ruled that President Trump had made a sufficient national security argument to disfavor some countries citizens' travel to the United States.

With life, liberty, and property—or the pursuit of happiness—always at its centerpiece, Americans have viewed government's legitimate role as extremely limited in their lives (liberty) and in the marketplace (property). Scholars of American exceptionalism note the particularly deeply ingrained "Lockean liberalism" of American political life as something which marks the United States as unique.

Locke was not the only social contract theorist, and other societies viewed the notions of legitimacy put forward by other social contract theorists as superior. French thinker Jean-Jacques Rousseau thought that legitimate government produced the **common good**—or so-called by Rousseau, collective will (common interest)—and while recognizing that humans are naturally free, was more willing to place collective will above individual rights as the central pursuit of a legitimate government.[2] (See Box 3.2) For example, he argued that while some people were endowed with natural abilities in science or industry, the advances those people made should benefit all of society, both financially and in terms of quality of life. Thus, he was more likely to support limitations on private property ownership and profit. As we will see shortly, this view of the collective will fit better with the views of other democracies' citizens in their democratic revolutions. So a key difference between the United States and other democracies stems from a philosophical view of legitimate government and the balance between individual citizen liberties and collective will.

The unique nature of this view of legitimacy is not simply an old-world vs. new-world distinction. When Canada formed its first government not directly governed by the United Kingdom, it authorized that the Canadian government should "make laws for the peace, order, and good government of Canada"—a sharp distinction from notions of government being limited so as not to threaten life, liberty, and the pursuit of happiness seen in the United States' founding. Further, notions of the collective will being paramount to individual liberties were codified into the constitutions of these democracies as will be highlighted in later sections. In sum, relative to other democracies, the notion of American governmental legitimacy rests on liberty and independence.

FUNCTIONAL EXPLANATIONS FOR AMERICAN EXCEPTIONALISM

A distinct chicken-and-egg dilemma exists when trying to explain just how much Locke's view of protection of liberties drove Americans' subsequent beliefs in and attraction to limited government or whether Americans' love of liberty just made Locke's arguments more attractive. Most likely both help to explain the distinctiveness of Americans' political beliefs. Certainly the historical conditions Americans experienced helped to formulate American political beliefs and these beliefs subsequently have stayed in the collective American conscience over time. That is, the American experience led the United States down one political path while other democracies chose another path. According to such path-dependent explanations, we cannot explain contemporary distinctions among these democracies without explaining the divergent directions these countries chose hundreds of years ago. **Path-dependent explanations** are those where outcomes of the present are determined by decisions made or circumstances presented in the past. Two fundamental and interconnected explanations put forward by scholars of American exceptionalism help to explain the difference in the United States.

1. **The self-selection of who came to America.** It took a particularly risk-taking individual to decide to leave everything behind to travel to live in a new world sight unseen. As American political scientist Louis Hartz (1919–1986) noted, this voyage to the new world highlights a spirit of individual independence.[3] Scholars broadly highlight the self-selection of colonial Americans as a key influence on the subsequent focus on United States individualism. Obviously this explanation is not universal. Hundreds of thousands of slaves were brought in chains as property and not due to a free-will itch that needed to be scratched. Further, the old world did not completely empty out its risk takers in America. Nevertheless, a substantial portion of the American public ended up predisposed to view the rewards of life coming from individual risk taking rather than collective outcomes. This continues today in the national narrative that "if you work hard you can succeed" and the idea of "picking oneself up by one's bootstraps," even though studies show that one's adult social class is largely determined by the social class into which one was born.

2. **The lack of feudalism and socialist movement.** America's lack of **feudalism**, a system for structuring society around relationships derived from the holding of land in exchange for service or labor, bolstered this individualism because it freed individuals from psychologically connecting one's future to the collective viewpoint of a particular class.[4] Feudalism, which existed during the Middle Ages in Europe, meant that peasants, or lower-class people, worked the land for an overlord. In the old world, feudalism created significant class divisions and consciousness in all areas of economic, social, and political life and ultimately led to the **socialist movement**—a movement based upon workers' rights and social ownership of the means of production.

3. **Constitutional stability and rigidity.** The government of the United States created by the Constitutional Convention in 1787 was a bold experiment. At the point of the writing of the Constitution, no government existed anywhere in the world like the United States. What is particularly remarkable about American democracy is the staying

power of its Constitution (discussed more in Chapter 5). Over time, more democracies came on board across the world and crafted new institutions that fit the spirit of those times. Those evolved institutions were not adopted by the United States. The relative rigidity of the stable U.S. Constitution and Bill of Rights reinforced principles of the social contract and limited government while democratic principles and institutions kept evolving in other democracies.

Here, the United States is clearly the "exception"—Americans had no demands for socialism. In other countries, a new urban working class developed a class consciousness born of frustration with an often cruel industrializing society with dangerous working conditions, child labor, squalor, and no real social, economic, or political power. Indeed, English novelist Charles Dickens's view of London may be as insightful as German philosopher Karl Marx's (see Box 3.3) for why the lower classes were broadly ripe for revolt in these countries. The bitter economic, social, and political inequalities led this class to embrace the socialist movement's promise of social and economic equality, and very importantly, the political power of the right to vote. As political scientist Louis Hartz argued, "actually socialism is largely an ideological phenomenon, arising out of the principles of class and the revolutionary liberal revolt against them which the old European order inspired."[5] Changing the social, political, and economic order for the benefit of the working-class masses drove the socialist movement in Europe. The only way to improve one's political, social, and economic lot was to bind arms with one's fellow workers and class members to gain the right to vote and political power, which would in turn lead to government owning or regulating the marketplace for better economic equality, provision of decent public housing, and assurance of a more equal social order. Thus, gains were to be made through collective rather than individual struggle.

Even though the same harsh working conditions faced the American working class, the socialist movement never gained a foothold in the United States because it was not attractive to working-class Americans. First, the social order of these European societies had already been rejected by Americans when they fled feudalism. Second, most working white men already had the right to vote so the political appeal of the right to vote did not attract the American working class. Third, despite sharing similar urban working-class life conditions with Europeans, the American working class, as Hartz argued, had the availability of land, and American natural "abundance" meant that workers had economic options. The European working class could not "go west" to homestead or prospect natural resources because land ownership had already been exhausted. Therefore, improving one's life in the United States was not solved by joining together with fellow workers; it meant striking out on one's own. Thus, *Americans' economic and political welfare was an individually determined good rather than collectively achievable.*

These exceptional conditions at the American founding through the Industrial Revolution in the nineteenth century put the United States on a different democratic path from other democracies. These conditions and founding principles were reinforced by the stability and rigidity of the U.S. Constitution, which kept Americans on this path by protecting civil liberties over the common good when they conflicted at key points in history. Other democracies forged a different path, influenced by the socialist movement and constitutions that protected principles of the common good. Understanding why contemporary democracy differs between the United States and others requires as much concentration on America's distinctive democratic path as on any current institutional, policy, or rhetorical dissimilarities with other democracies. The starting point on this path led the United States toward a much more liberal democracy, while most other democracies ended up as social democracies due to differing starting points on their trails of democracy.

BOX 3.3

U.S. and Europe in the 1800s

▶ **Photo 3.4** Karl Marx by Friedrich Karl Wunder, accessed via www.marxists .org.

When Karl Marx wrote "Workers of the World, Unite!" for economic and political power, most Americans were not buying the argument because a greater extent of economic and political power was already possible in the United States without uniting. Just how different were Americans and Europeans at this time? In 1848, the working class revolted throughout European countries for economic and political power. Similar squalid conditions existed for the working class in American cities, but rather than linking together with fellow members of the working class, many American workers gave up everything to bolt westward to seek the riches of the gold rush just a year later in 1849. French writer Victor Hugo captured the mood of collective European nineteenth century class heroism and death in the novel *Les Misérables*. Meanwhile, Americans were reading about heroic figures such as an individually resourceful Natty Bumppo in James Fenimore Cooper's *Leatherstocking Tales* or Horatio Alger stories about a farm boy who becomes a senator.

SOCIAL DEMOCRACY AND LIBERAL DEMOCRACY

Liberal democracy is a political system built around a belief in representative and limited government, regular and competitive elections, the rule of law, multiple channels for political participation, limited state control over the economy, and the protection of civil rights and liberties. Americans tend to use the terms *liberal* and *liberalism* differently from others around the world, focusing on the ideological meaning of liberalism rather than more often used classical or economic meanings. In order to understand the meaning of liberal, it is important to remember that the words *liberal* and *liberty* come from the same Latin base, *liber*, meaning free. Many of you take liberal arts courses because a well-rounded education makes one a free and superior citizen, unable to be duped by myth, fooled by faulty logic of governing authority, or shackled by ignorance. An important source of academic freedom and citizen power comes from libraries—which also share the same root. In other words, liberalism focuses on the notion of individual freedom and extends ideas of freedom to the economic marketplace and political power. Therefore, liberal democracy incorporates elements of classical and economic liberalism and is not to be confused with American ideological liberalism (see Table 3.1). Liberalism ideologically in other democracies more closely fits the foundations of classical and economic liberalism.

Liberal democracy can be contrasted with social democracy. **Social democracy** also recognizes the primacy of freedoms and liberty. We saw this in the discussion of the similarities between all advanced industrial democracies in Chapter 2, but social democracy places much greater emphasis on the social welfare responsibilities of governments. Borrowing more from ideas of Rousseau than Locke, economic equality and political equality are both seen as equally important in social democracies, and economic redistribution policies are often embraced as a way to add fairness and justice to the system. Not to be confused at all with **socialism**—an economic system where the state rather than the market determines production, distribution, and pricing and where property is government

Table 3.1 Meanings of Liberalism	
American Ideological Liberalism	Approach to society based on greater government involvement in people's lives as a way of redistributing wealth, equalizing opportunity, and righting social wrongs.
Classical Liberalism	Approach to government based on limiting government power through a social contract (constitution) and respecting personal freedoms and the rights of individuals.
Economic Liberalism	Belief in private property including a hands-off (**laissez-faire**) approach to the economy and promotion of a free market driven by supply and demand.

owned—social democracy advocates greater regulation of the marketplace for the common good and greater regulation of democratic decision making to meet the general will than does liberal democracy. That said, as a governing and economic system, it is far closer to liberal democracy than socialism.

While the United States follows more of a liberal democratic model, many European democracies, especially in Nordic countries, follow a social democratic model. Both liberal and social democracies are welfare states. A **welfare state** is one where the government plays a key role in providing a "safety net" and passes policies aimed at protecting and promoting the economic and social well-being of its citizens. The United States, like all other social and liberal democracies, is a welfare state. Its welfare system is just more constrained than the welfare systems in social democracies, meaning that it prefers to leave some social welfare items, like health care or higher education, to private entities or market forces. In social democracies, we generally see a more expansive welfare state with government-run healthcare systems, subsidized education, and broader social welfare systems. In these systems, there is far greater tax responsibilities and redistribution of wealth for social welfare policies. As OECD (developed countries) data in Figure 3.1 demonstrate, the percentage of a country's total economy that is taxed in social democracies far exceeds—and sometimes nearly doubles—the same rate for the United States. In some cases nearly half of the economic production (gross domestic product) is taxed. Further, Figure 3.2 provides the other side of the coin: what are governments doing with that taxed income? The same social democracies that tax at high percentages redistribute that tax revenue through social programs.

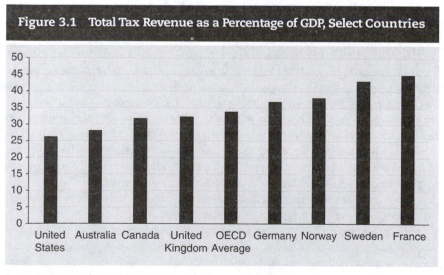

Figure 3.1   Total Tax Revenue as a Percentage of GDP, Select Countries

Source: OECD 2015, https://data.oecd.org/tax/tax-revenue.htm

Figure 3.2   Total Public Social Spending as a Percentage of GDP, Select Countries

Source: OECD (2018), Social spending (indicator). doi: 10.1787/7497563b-en (Accessed on March 19, 2018)

This raises another point. We are often comparing apples and oranges when one tries to explain government spending when the *size of countries' economies differ*. To understand this, think about financial aid. Can we compare a family budget using percentages if one family makes $30,000 per year and one makes $500,000? Does it mean the same thing for each family to spend 10 percent of their income on education? Will it equally affect each family's ability to buy groceries or maintain a basic standard of living? The same applies when comparing government spending when the size of economies differs, highlighting a further component of how remarkable the United States is on taxation and social spending. The United States is the largest economy in the world and could tax more than other countries and still meet obligations of modern states, and it could spend more on social welfare than other countries with spare room for other policy needs given its economic power. But it doesn't. In fact, it taxes and spends far less relative to other much smaller-sized economies. It does so out of public preference and because of views surrounding legitimate governing policy choices. Social democracies tax their citizenry as well and provide public services at a much higher rate than the United States, especially given the size of their economies. There are not protests in the streets of these social democracies based on government taxation and social spending levels. Indeed, it is often when the broad social welfare programs get curtailed that people hit the streets.

An important point to remember is that no democracy is completely liberal or social, and all of these advanced industrial democracies share competitive democracy, free markets, and other core democratic freedoms. These democracies can be found along a continuum from those that embrace more social democratic models—where government is seen to be legitimate when it provides for a stronger social welfare state for the collective benefit—to those that embrace more liberal democratic models—where limited government is the benchmark of legitimacy (see Figure 3.3).

How central is social welfare to governmental legitimacy in these social democracies? In social democracies, we see that social rights are enshrined in constitutions. In fact, every European constitution contains social rights (called positive rights). For example, Section 15 of the Finnish constitution states that "public authorities shall, in the manner stipulated in greater detail by Act of Parliament, secure for everyone adequate social welfare and health services and shall promote the health of the population."[6] In other words, the Finnish government is legitimate in so far as it provides for the social welfare of the country, including healthcare. The German Basic Law (constitution) also codifies social rights. Article 20 of the Basic Law explicitly states that Germany is a *social* federal state. Rights found in the federal and state constitutions in Germany include rights to housing, employment, and social security. The South African constitution goes further than any other constitution in the guarantee of social rights, and it has in fact been looked to as a model by countries drafting new constitutions.[7] The South African constitution explicitly guarantees the right to food, water, housing, health care, and social security. In addition, South Africa permits individuals to petition the Constitutional Court on the grounds their social rights have been violated. Thus, while the United States' Constitution limits government and focuses on the rights upon which the government cannot tread, or those things the government *cannot* do, constitutions in social democracies codify the social responsibilities of government and specify what government *must* do. This is an idea we revisit in Chapter 5.

Whether or not a country is more liberal or social in its approach to democracy has policy implications, particularly as related to the cost and provision of **public goods** and services (see Box 3.4 for an example), those goods and services provided by government as opposed to private enterprise. Even when these **social goods** are not constitutionally guaranteed, social democracies provide a strong safety net for citizens and more publicly funded social services than liberal democracies. Social services can range from universal health care, to retirement benefits, to state-funded day cares. Social democracies provide these services publicly more so than liberal democracies. One area of social service, parental leave, provides an interesting example. The United States is the only advanced industrial democracy

Figure 3.3 Continuum of Liberal to Social Democracy

Japan				Finland
Australia			Germany	Norway
United States	United Kingdom		France	Sweden

Liberal Demoracy- -→ Social Demoracy

BOX 3.4

The Cost of College Education

In social democracies, the cost of many social goods, a good or service that benefits the largest number of people in the largest possible way, are subsidized by the taxpayer. For example, in France, if you are sick, you can go to the doctor and be treated without any out-of-pocket expense. You do not have to have insurance because insurance is public, or provided through the government. Another social good is college education. While in the United States the cost of college education is subsidized through grants and loans that the graduate then needs to repay, in many social democracies of Europe, the cost of college education is lower in the first place because the cost is covered by the taxpayer. For example, the average cost of yearly tuition for a four-year degree in the United States in 2013 was $13,856, an 1120 percent increase since 1978. In 2017, the average cost was just over $20,000. In Germany, by comparison, it was $933 in 2013. Germany abolished tuition in 2014, and today students pay fees of about $500 per term. In the table below, we see the average cost of college education as of 2017. Note, we break out private and public for the United States, but other countries include the average of all types of institutions. Even compared with the Commonwealth countries—Canada, United Kingdom, and Australia—that have higher levels of tuition compared to mainland Europe, the U.S. costs are considerably higher. Additionally, U.S. students are graduating with significantly more debt than students in other countries. This is because even in places where tuition is similar to that of the United States, the number of students who qualify for subsidization of their tuition is higher. Thus, on average, U.S. students graduate with $37,000 in debt, while in the U.K., on average, they graduate with $30,000 in debt and in Germany $2,400 in debt.[8]

Country	Education Costs
Germany	Free
France	<$1,000
Sweden	Free
Finland	Free
Netherlands	Approx. $2,500
United Kingdom	Approx. $8,000
Australia	Approx. $5,000
Canada	Approx. $5,000
United States	$8,700 (public 4 year); $21,000 (private 4 year)

Source: Student Loan Review, The Cost of College Education around the World, https://www.studentloanreview.com/college-cost-around-the-world-infographic.

to not mandate paid parental leave (either maternity or paternity), although a parent can take up to 12 weeks of unpaid leave under the Family and Medical Leave Act (FMLA). Other advanced industrial democracies mandate paid leave (see Figures 3.4 and 3.5), including maternal leave (for mothers) and paternal

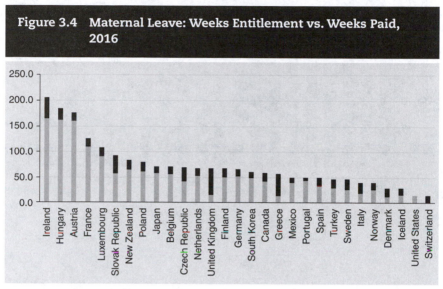

Figure 3.4   Maternal Leave: Weeks Entitlement vs. Weeks Paid, 2016

Source: OECD, OECD Family Database, http://www.oecd.org/els/family/database.htm. The light gray represents paid leave, the dark gray represents number of weeks of leave to which a mother is entitled.

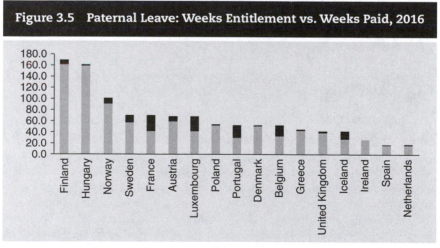

Figure 3.5   Paternal Leave: Weeks Entitlement vs. Weeks Paid, 2016

Source: OECD, OECD Family Database, http://www.oecd.org/els/family/database.htm. The light gray represents paid leave, the dark gray represents the number of weeks of leave to which a father is entitled. The United States is not on the chart because it does not guarantee paternal leave.

Figure 3.6 Paid Vacation and Holidays

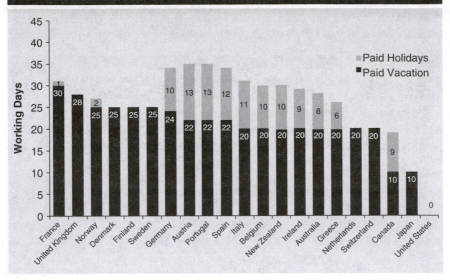

Source: OECD (2010), Society at a Glance 2010: OECD Social Indicators, OECD Publishing, http://dx.doi.org/10.1787/soc_glance-2008-en.

leave (for fathers). This means that it is *required that companies give, and workers take, parental leave.*

In social democracies, we also see states supporting paid vacation. In this regard, the United States is very different from other democracies. The United States is the only advanced industrial democracy that does not support paid vacation as mandated by federal law (see Figure 3.6), although locally variations may exist based on state law or local statutes.

CONCLUSION

This chapter focused on American exceptionalism, or the uniqueness of the United States, explaining that this difference can be understood by looking at the unique historical conditions at the time of the country's founding. Lockean ideas of legitimacy defined American democracy from its founding, and the lack of feudalism, a propensity for risk taking, and natural abundance helped lead to an American system that is different from other advanced industrial democracies. This uniqueness is manifested in the fact that the United States has a more liberal form of democracy that is much longer standing than other democracies, while other democracies are more social in their democratic orientation. In turn, this influences tax and social policies, with the United States having lower taxes, less social spending, and fewer guaranteed social rights than other advanced industrial democracies. As we will see in the following chapters, this difference combined with different political culture (discussed in Chapter 4) leads to differences in institutions and interest articulation through interest groups and political parties (discussed in Chapters 6, 7, 8, and 9) and electoral institutions and behavior (discussed in Chapters 10 and 11).

POINTS TO REMEMBER

- American exceptionalism refers to the idea that the United States is an exception, or different, from other democracies.

- A key difference between the United States and other democracies stems from a philosophical view of legitimate government and the balance it draws between individual citizen liberties and collective will.

- The founding conditions in the United States compared to other countries differed. Those conditions and subsequent political life have predisposed Americans to view what makes government legitimate, or popularly accepted, differently from citizens of other advanced industrial democracies.

- American government borrows from ideas of Locke that limited government is best and that government is legitimate when it protects life, liberty, and property (the pursuit of happiness). This differs from other ideas of social contract, based upon collective good.

- The United States is a liberal democracy. Liberal democracies combine classical and economic ideas of liberalism.

- Liberal democracy can be contrasted with social democracy. Liberal democracies focus more on limited government and protection of individual rights, and social democracies focus on the protection of social rights and expansive welfare states, or social safety nets.

- Social democracies tend to have higher levels of taxation but also higher levels of social spending and provision of social services.

KEY TERMS

American
    exceptionalism 32
Americanists 31
Associational life 33
Common good 36
Comparativists 31
Divine Right
    of Kings 33
Enlightenment Era 33

Feudalism 37
Laissez-faire 40
Legitimate 32
Legitimate
    government 33
Liberal democracy 39
Path-dependent
    explanations 37
Public goods 43

Social contract 33
Social democracy 40
Social goods 43
Socialism 40
Socialist movement 37
State of Nature 33
Tyranny of the
    majority 35
Welfare state 41

REVIEW QUESTIONS

1. What is the key distinction between what comparativists and Americanists study?

2. What do we mean when we refer to American exceptionalism?

3. Describe the historical conditions that differed at the founding of the U.S. democracy as compared to European democracies. How do these founding differences help to explain differences in American government today?

4. In what way is American democracy influenced by the thinking of social contract theorist John Locke? How does this differ from the thinking of Rousseau?

5. How does a liberal democracy differ from a social democracy? What are some policy implications of this difference?

SUGGESTED READINGS

Hartz, Louis. *The Liberal Tradition in America: An Interpretation of American Political Thought since the Revolution.* New York, NY: Harcourt Brace, 1955.

Liptak, Adam. "'We the People' Loses Appeal with People around the World." *New York Times*, February 6, 2012.

Pascal, Elizabeth. "Welfare Rights in State Constitutions." *Rutgers Law Journal* 39, no. 4 (2008).

NOTES

1. Pictures and background from philosophypages.com.

2. Ernest Barker, *Social Contract: Essays by Locke, Hume and Rousseau, Introduction* (Oxford, UK: Oxford University Press, 1960), vii–xliii.

3. Hartz, *The Liberal Tradition in America: An Interpretation of American Political Thought Since the Revolution* (New York, NY: Harcourt Brace, 1955).

4. Hartz, *The Liberal Tradition in America*.

5. Hartz, *The Liberal Tradition in America*, 6.

6. Elizabeth Pascal, "Welfare Rights in State Constitutions," *Rutgers Law Journal* 39, no. 4 (2008): 863.

7. Adam Liptak, "'We the People' Loses Appeal with People around the World," *New York Times*, February 6, 2012.

8. Martin, Emmie, "Here's How Much It Costs to Go to College in 25 Countries around the World," *CNBC* (2017). https://www.cnbc.com/2017/10/13/cost-of-college-tuition-around-the-world.html.

CHAPTER FOUR

POLITICAL BELIEFS
Political Culture and Ideology

Going grocery shopping in Spain can sometimes be a full-contact sport as senior citizens throw elbows and have no qualms pushing you out of their way as they reach for a coveted piece of cheese or juicy peach. No one in Spain thinks anything of this. In fact, Americans who continually say "excuse me" or try to keep a "personal space bubble" while passively waiting their turn at checkouts are looked at as somewhat bizarre. One can't imagine that elbow throwing and pushing would be considered "normal" behavior at the local Whole Foods. Why is one set of behaviors acceptable in one location but seen as completely unacceptable in another? It has to do with a difference in what is deemed culturally appropriate.

As Chapter 2 and Chapter 3 demonstrated, the United States shares many similarities with other advanced industrial democracies, but it also has much that marks it as unique and sets it apart. These earlier chapters provided numerous societal-level measures of these similarities and differences. But, how do American beliefs about democracy stack up to those of their advanced industrial cousins? What evidence is there that all democracies share common beliefs, or is the United States different from other advanced industrial democracies in this regard? This chapter begins by looking at political cultural similarities between the United States and other advanced industrial democracies. Then, we highlight key distinctions of American political cultural beliefs relative to other democracies. Finally, the unique nature of American political culture helps to explain how American political ideological debates tend to be narrower than those of other advanced industrial democracies, which means American political debates may be fierce, but they are contained within a tighter band of ideology than the mainstream political debates of other advanced industrial democracies.

POLITICAL CULTURE

Explaining the role of political culture has always perplexed scholars of politics. Identifying what political culture is and how one nation's culture differs from another's remains difficult because culture—much less political culture—is such an intricate and not very tangible concept. Anyone who has been to a cultural festival recognizes unique components of culture. People wear specialized clothing, listen and dance to characteristic music, and eat distinctive foods. A trip overseas—even to advanced industrial democracies—can produce a culture shock. It takes a while to acclimate to the culture, to act in a polite way, and frankly not to shake one's head at what is "normal" elsewhere. For example, one of the author's kids attending school in Spain was shocked by the more authoritative nature of Spanish teachers and pursuit of conformity and collectivity among students rather than individuality. Additionally, playground culture in Spain is much less "democratic" than culture on an American playground; teachers and adults rarely intervene in the disputes between children, leaving kids oftentimes to duke it out to get their way on the soccer field or jungle gym. Be assured, most other societies shake their heads at an American culture they admire but find curious. Spanish teachers find the United States' emphasis on individuality and American children's excessive opinions exasperating and American adults as too overinvolved in playgroup scuffles.

In other countries, people live their daily lives differently than they do in the United States—the way they behave, interact with others, act in the marketplace, and even how they eat food and argue about sports and life. Merely traveling from an airport and witnessing folkways of driving in some countries by swerving

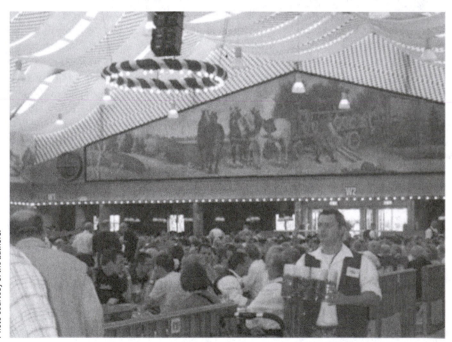

Photo courtesy of the authors.

▶ **Photo 4.1** Scenes from the German Oktoberfest, a mainstay of German culture.

through lanes, locking up brakes, and endlessly honking, brings a level of culture shock until one realizes that this is the normal thing to do in that country. This provides broad fields of study for social scientists—sociologists, anthropologists, and economists—who spend considerable time explaining how people behave differently publicly, historically, or in the marketplace. Not surprisingly, the way people interact politically differs as well, and political scientists concentrate on how shared beliefs and values of countries differ.

Most scholars blend many of the following key features into what we will use as our definition of **political culture**: the shared political norms, values, and beliefs of a citizenry about politics. The term *political culture* refers specifically to attitudes toward the political system and attitudes toward the role of citizens in the system. Since societies socialize children into a shared set of beliefs, we use political culture to link the broader social indicators emphasized in previous chapters with evidence from individual-level attitudes found in surveys and election studies.

If politics is defined as who gets what, when, and how, then countries' political cultures will differ by *how* their citizens believe such decisions should get made. What is the legitimate level of public debate? Does everyone have to be satisfied with policy outcomes, or does the majority simply always win? How much deference do you have to give to authority in these decisions? The political culture of a country decides the answers to these questions in decisions of who gets what, when, and how; captures citizens' satisfaction about their political system; and influences their attitudes about their own role in their political system.

Political culture is also central because a government's institutions had better produce decisions over who gets what in a way that fit citizens' beliefs. If not, those institutions fail. We see this in numerous ways. First, when countries transition to democracy from other forms of government, political leaders design institutions to fit the existing political culture. When a country's social beliefs and political institutions do not mesh, democracy peters out, fails, or gets overthrown. Matching political culture to institutions is not a one-way street nor is it just an issue for developing democracies. The political institutions of so-called **consolidated democracies**—democracies that are longer-lived, have survived transitions of power, and have well-developed institutions, like advanced industrial democracies—shift when the incremental revisions of political culture mean the beliefs of citizens no longer meet the institutional set-up. The United States altered its institutions historically to expand participation (former slaves, women, eighteen-year-olds) and make offices more responsive (direct election of senators, primary election for party nomination) when the gradually shifting values of society outpaced institutional ability to meet the society's expectations.

To comprehend American political culture, we must first recognize how Americans' beliefs are similar to and different from beliefs held in other advanced industrial democracies. We begin first by looking at similarities between the political beliefs in the United States and other advanced industrial democracies. These democracies share a civic political culture where people engage in politics, believe that citizens play an important role in government, and generally trust fellow citizens. As Chapter 3 demonstrated, American culture differs in part because Americans favor limited government more than citizens of other democracies. On one hand, American democratic beliefs and interpersonal social relationships will be similar to other democracies, while Americans differ from other countries on the process of how to make decisions over who gets what, when, and how.

CIVIC CULTURE

Democracy relies not only on proper democratic institutions that allow for citizen participation (discussed in Chapter 7) but also on citizens to possess attitudes amenable to the idea that they ought to have a voice and participate in a democracy. In their pioneering work on democracy and political culture, Gabriel Almond and Sidney Verba argued that a democratic political culture—or as they say a "**civic culture**"—relies on citizens knowing about policies and government, feeling positive about how democracy operates, and participating in politics.[1] More than just views of the nuts-and-bolts of democratic governance, a **participatory political culture** requires that people can largely self-govern themselves outside of governmental decision making and in their own interest. The less participatory a society is, the more its people are reliant on or subjected to governmental power to drive the market, define the freedom of preference and movement, or dictate religious and social beliefs.

Three interrelated characteristics help to define a democratic or civic political culture:

1. Democracies require citizens who engage their government and demonstrate high levels of political interest.

2. People have to trust one another in social relations or the vacuum in interpersonal relations among citizens makes deciding who gets what, when, and how in self-governance next to impossible.

3. A large percentage of the people in a democracy must believe they control their own lives rather than be reliant on government or be subjects of fate.

We use indicators from the World Values Survey[2] to compare the United States to different advanced industrial democratic regions whose similar geographic or historical experiences may lead to different beliefs from the United States. This ensures that simply comparing the United States to all other democracies does not paper over important distinctions among the other democracies. The democratic regions include Nordic countries (Finland, Norway, Sweden), northern European democracies (Great Britain, France, Germany, the Netherlands, and Switzerland), southern European democracies (Italy and Spain), former countries of the British

Commonwealth (Canada, Australia, New Zealand), and the Asian democracies of Japan and Korea. There are clearly differences among countries in each of these regions, and citizens of one of these countries likely would object to being placed with what might be a neighbor with whom they have a historical rivalry. The authors beg forgiveness on this count. Nevertheless, these countries generally hold similar enough characteristics to fit together for the ease of presentation.

POLITICAL ENGAGEMENT: POLITICAL INTEREST

Democratic political engagement requires familiarity with the political system in order to participate in voting, party or interest group politics, writing letters to elected officials or bureaucrats, or protesting. It also requires an interest and awareness of the resulting policies that emerge from the political system. One key indicator of a civic culture is **political interest**—it reveals public awareness and engagement with the political system. As Figure 4.1 demonstrates, American political interest ranks highly compared with other advanced industrial democracies. About 60 percent of Americans state that they are very or somewhat interested in politics, and only 39 percent say that they are not very interested or not at all interested. This compares to about 58 percent of Nordic citizens, 53 percent of Northern Europeans, 35 percent of Southern Europeans, 54 percent of Commonwealth, and 51 percent of Asian respondents saying they are very or somewhat interested in politics.

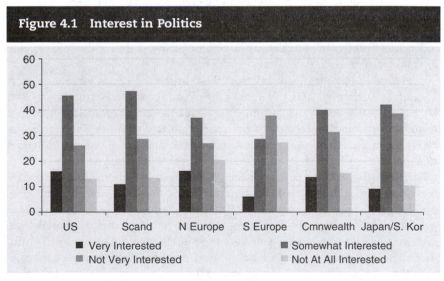

Figure 4.1 Interest in Politics

Source: Data from World Values Survey, http://www.worldvaluessurvey.org.

INTERPERSONAL TRUST, RECIPROCITY, AND SOCIAL CAPITAL

Vibrant citizen interest and participation in social and political life improves democracy because it builds interpersonal trust among citizens. Many scholars refer to this healthy civic culture as a society holding significant **social capital**. That is, citizens join civic groups, social groups, clubs, churches, or even bowling leagues, and this in turn exposes them to broader groups of society than their typical sociodemographic niches. Partaking in civic life improves democracy because it builds *interpersonal trust* and notions of *reciprocity* among citizens.[3] People invest themselves into their community, and like risk-taking in market investments, payoffs to society are greater when more people are invested. Like a bull market increasingly spreads capital to different economic sectors allowing growth across the economy, so too does investment in society and the marketplace of ideas spread benefit throughout society as people get together with citizens of different social stations, learn about differing political views, and participate in self-governance.

In turn, in an unhealthy economic marketplace, if people do not trust one another with capital, no one will loan money, invest in businesses, or trust that a product is safe. The government will have to control the market on the front-end, and consequently, the market becomes less dynamic. Similarly, if people do not trust one another on an interpersonal level, they will not tell their neighbors what they really think about religion or political leaders, and as a result, the marketplace of ideas will shrivel up or be controlled by the government. The warning *caveat emptor*—buyer beware—suggests that people enter the marketplace skeptically and without much trust. It likely reduces purchases and likely leads to a suboptimal marketplace. What a pity it would be if citizens were warned *caveat civis*—citizen beware—prior to joining in collective decision making in society. Therefore, many common democratic cultural attitudes deal with citizens' levels of trust with one another.

Figure 4.2 provides the results from the World Values Survey question "Generally speaking, would you say that most people can be trusted or that you need to be very careful in dealing with people?" The United States ranks relatively high in terms of trust compared to other democracies but far behind the Nordic democracies. Even though a majority of Americans feel most people cannot be trusted (feelings seen in other democracies as well), strong percentages of people think others can be trusted. The interesting case here is Nordic democracies where there are extremely high levels of interpersonal trust, meaning that large numbers of citizens in these countries believe that most people can be trusted (about 65 percent). This may stem from the incredible level of homogeneity in these societies and consociational government (discussed in Chapter 6). It is also interesting that these governments have greater levels of taxation and redistribution than the other democracies, as seen in Chapter 3. Comparatively, in the United States, about 40 percent of people believe that most people can be trusted.

Figure 4.2 Interpersonal Trust

Legend: ■ Most people can be trusted   ■ People can't be trusted

Categories: US, Scand, N Europe, S Europe, Cmnwealth, Japan/S. Kor

Source: Data from World Values Survey, http://www.worldvaluessurvey.org.

POLITICAL EFFICACY: FREE CHOICE AND CONTROL OVER LIFE

Democracy also requires that a civic culture be one where citizens believe that they can participate, and their voices will be heard when they do participate—what is referred to as **political efficacy**. **Internal efficacy** deals with one's confidence in having sufficient knowledge and abilities to influence the political system—that is, the knowledge that individuals know how to and are capable of behaving democratically. **External efficacy** deals with how much the political system is open to influence. The World Values Survey asked whether people "feel they have completely free choice and control over their lives," or whether people "feel that what they do has no real effect on what happens to them." In Figure 4.3, we see how people in different countries rank on these measures. Americans feel as though they have free choice and broad control over their lives and choices (about 60 percent); they are not subjected to fate or denied choice and control by forces such as their government. This level is similar to Nordic and Commonwealth democracies (all about 60 percent), exceeds that of Northern Europe (about 40 percent) and Southern Europe (about 30 percent) by a noteworthy level, and strongly exceeds the feeling of free choice in the Asian democracies (about 35 percent).

Thus, on all measures of civic culture, the United States ranks similarly with some other advanced industrial democracies. This means that out of the gates American citizens are not extraordinarily or inherently more democratic in their beliefs. Americans share common sets of civic cultural beliefs with other advanced industrial democracies, even if these beliefs vary somewhat among regions. This does not mean that American exceptionalism, discussed in Chapter 3, does not lead to many unique political beliefs.

Figure 4.3 Free Choice and Control Over Life?

Bar chart with y-axis from 0 to 70. Categories on x-axis: US, Scand, N Europe, S Europe, Cmnwealth, Japan/S. Kor. Legend: None/Little, Less Choice/Control, More Choice/Control, Great Deal.

Source: Data from World Values Survey, http://www.worldvaluessurvey.org.

DISTINCTION OF AMERICAN CULTURAL BELIEFS

The political culture of the United States shares broad civic cultural features with other advanced industrial democracies but has its own characteristics borne out of its unique formative experiences highlighted in Chapter 3. American exceptionalism is not simply a historical artifact nor should it be equated with a statement of superiority. Instead, it encapsulates a set of political beliefs that Americans have been socialized into over numerous generations and can still be found in their political cultural beliefs today. Further, if politics is about who gets what, when, and how, then Americans have firm beliefs about *how* such decision making *should* occur. The process of democratic decision making in the American case—how they decide who gets what—is biased in a Lockean sense toward protecting and rewarding individual liberties. Compared to the United States, other democracies favor Rousseauian ideas about benefits for the entire society more than individual benefits in decisions over who gets what, when, and how.

As scholar Seymour Martin Lipset (1922–2006) suggests, other societies existed much longer as established political entities, and their national identity typically stems from common historical and cultural ties. Consequently, people in these countries sense that they are "born" a citizen of these countries and from this "common birth" share a mutual blood-relative-type relationship with others in their society. As Lipset notes, "you cannot become un-Swedish." In the United States, on the other hand, there is an ethos that you *become* an American.[4] Not surprisingly, the aspirational component of becoming an American is something Americans feel *he or she has done*, even though most Americans are natural-born citizens. Further, this identity with their nationality and the state differs. If someone asked Americans for their nationality, they may very well say Polish-American, Irish-American, Italian-American, and so on, which would be anathema to most other democratic citizenries. It's an individual identity in the United States, whereas those who are born French, Swedish, Spanish, or Italian have a common identity much more connected to the community or nation. There is often a common language and ethnicity among other democracies. There is no surprise, then, that other democratic citizens connect their political beliefs to what is best for society—or **communitarian values**—that outweigh individualism, since identity is easily defined by common history, culture, and blood. As a result, these countries adopted Rousseau's notion of the "common good" being superior to individual liberties.

Other than particular historical eras or pockets of the American public, individual liberty trumps communitarianism in the United States. This focus on the individual effort leading to reward, self-reliance, and independence, or **individualism**, is the greatest unique feature of American political culture. Americans believe that when making decisions over who gets what, when, and how, the rules and processes need to favor individual liberty. Success in the marketplace—very often where many nongovernmental decisions over who gets what get made—is seen to come from the individual's efforts, so Americans tend to favor that the individual be rewarded. Further, Americans believe there should be little regulation of the marketplace that curbs individual rewards and instead produces or redistributes benefits to the society as a whole—at least when compared to other advanced industrial democracies. As Chapter 3 and Table 4.1 demonstrate, regulating the marketplace of ideas is also less accepted in the United States than other democracies. The United States has far fewer regulations on vacation time or restrictions that hinder firing employees than other democracies. Despite being the world's wealthiest country, the United States also has much more relative inequality compared to other democracies and does not even rank in the middle of all countries on inequality, as seen in Table 4.1.

The United States' focus on individualism also means that our criminal justice system has to overcome a high bar and affirmatively prove someone's guilt, and Americans have to accept a considerable amount of distasteful public expression of hate, racism, and sexism. This is not to say that Americans love hate speech, long work hours, or economic inequality. In fact, the opposite is true. We know because vigilante and old western justice–themed movies often depict a hero chasing down a known guilty criminal, and movies about someone emerging from poverty to make it rich are both solid American film genres. But largely, Americans grudgingly accept these negative aspects of society that come from protecting individual freedom as unfavorable—but nevertheless tolerable—consequences to the American way of life. In fact, Lipset suggests that higher crime, lower political participation, litigiousness (frequency of lawsuits), and poverty are the negative side of American exceptionalism—even though Americans are not ready to trade out their solid faith in individualism in favor of communitarianism, which

Table 4.1 American Individualism and Communitarian Views of Other Democracies

Key Value Areas	Illustrative Responses in Other Democracies
Americans value the rights of the private sector to decide benefits for employees and minimal government involvement in workplace regulation . . .	**In contrast . . .** * Most other democracies require employers to give more paid vacation (sometimes as much as six weeks, with holidays) and cap the number of hours employees work per week (five-day work week in Germany/35 hours per week for many jobs in France). * On a scale of "employment protection," or how costly it is for an employer to get rid of regularly contracted workers as individuals or as a collective, the OECD provides a score for each country, with the United States ranking at the bottom of these developed democracies.[i]

Australia	1.67	Japan	1.37
Austria	2.37	Korea	2.37
Belgium	1.89	Netherlands	2.82
Canada	0.92	New Zealand	1.39
Denmark	2.20	Norway	2.33
Finland	2.17	Portugal	3.18
France	2.38	Spain	2.05
Germany	2.68	Sweden	2.61
Israel	2.04	Switzerland	1.60
Italy	2.68	United Kingdom	1.10

United States   0.26

Avg. 2.00 Standard Deviation 0.71

American emphasis on individualism leads to being more comfortable with higher levels of economic inequality than in other countries . . .	**For example . . .** The GINI Index (higher measure = greater inequality of family income in a country) ranking of income inequality of select countries[ii]

2	South Africa	62.5
4	Haiti	60.8
18	Zimbabwe	50.1
19	Brazil	49.7
25	Mexico	48.2
30	Rwanda	46.8
31	China	46.5
34	South Sudan	46.0
39	Jamaica	45.5

40	Peru	45.3
41	**United States**	**45.0**
45	Iran	44.5
47	Central African Republic	43.6
49	Israel	42.8
52	Kenya	42.5
59	Russia	41.2
78	Yemen	37.9
79	Japan	37.9
94	Spain	35.9
97	India	35.2
101	West Bank	34.5
103	South Korea	34.1
107	Portugal	33.9
113	Ethiopia	33.0
116	United Kingdom	32.4
117	Canada	32.1
125	European Union avg.	31.0
131	Netherlands	30.3
132	Australia	30.3
133	Switzerland	29.5
134	Austria	29.2
135	France	29.2
142	Germany	27.0
143	Norway	26.8
149	Belgium	25.9
151	Sweden	24.9
156	Finland	21.5

*Note: Selection of countries for illustrative purposes to show relation to the United States.

[i] "Strictness of Employment Protection – Individual and Collective Dismissals (regular contracts)," OECD.Stat, Organization for Economic Co-operation and Development, https://stats.oecd.org/Index.aspx?DataSetCode=EPL_OV, accessed June 25, 2018.

[ii] "Country Comparison: Distribution of Family Income—Gini Index," *The World Factbook*. CIA. https://www.cia.gov/library/publications/the-world-factbook/rankorder/2172rank.html, accessed June 25, 2018. The years of information vary per country.

may abate these negative consequences.[5] The point is that they are willing to accept these negative aspects of American-style democracy if it means protecting individualism.

Some scholars suggest that individualism is an even deeper principle to Americans. To them, individualism is a key article of faith in an American **civil religion**. That is, being an American involves a religious-like faith with sacred texts being the Declaration of Independence and the Constitution; key American-biblical prophets being the founding fathers, George Washington, and Abraham

Lincoln; religious symbols being monuments and the American flag; holy days of July 4 and Memorial Day; an exodus from British rule to our holy land; and a view of war as a necessity mechanism—a freedom fight.[6] Consequently, individualism becomes almost a holy virtue that one can imagine is inscribed on national commandments.

Americans, despite their noncommunitarian views, are ironically not anticommunity. In fact, Americans embrace public virtue. Americans' individualist side loves the lone hero in *High Noon*, but Americans also "remember the Alamo." Both demonstrate sacrifice for American justice but one with a lone hero and the other an admired camaraderie of a selfless group willingly and knowingly facing a brutal fate together. Historian Gordon Wood (b. 1933) and political scientist Daniel Elazar (1934–1999) describe the contending components of American political culture as including a strong streak of individualism but also a belief in the commonwealth. That is, Americans hold competing cultural beliefs where self-interest and undivided interest of the whole people can coexist.[7] Americans can embrace the New England Town Meeting model of making collective decisions for the good of society so admired by de Tocqueville. The frontier demanded individual grit but also required neighbors helping each other thrive or even survive (read Laura Ingalls Wilder), building cooperative stores, grain elevators, and community schoolhouses. As Elazar emphasizes, individualism is "tempered" by commitments to community, but it is preferred that nongovernmental avenues are pursued.[8] Some areas of the United States feel less connected to the ideal of community and mistrust government more. Contemporary author and commentator E. J. Dionne has highlighted how Americans have perhaps forgotten the ideal of community from their founding and history relative to contemporary overconcentration on individualism.[9] As Dionne points out, it is perfectly American to be both individualistic and act with civic virtue in community. Chapter 3 provided a chart of governmental spending on social services that rated the United States rather low relative to other democracies. In Figure 4.4, the amount of American social spending is very average when one adds in the private sector social spending, that is, charity. In fact, the United States ranks higher than the OECD (developed countries) average and similarly to social democracies like Sweden.

Other democracies believe in the private sector and have social divisions and inequalities. Their citizens have faith in the free market, pursue individual life goals, and produce incredibly rich capitalist societies. However, because of the common national background that these societies share, there is far less distinction between the community and the state. Further, because the democratic revolutions of these countries very much redefined these governing systems into democracy to provide for social equality, the government is seen as an adequate and preferable mechanism to bring about equality. The government provides commonly accepted social order, so citizens broadly accept that the state should actively participate in the market and redistribute wealth because the social welfare state protects the social order.[10]

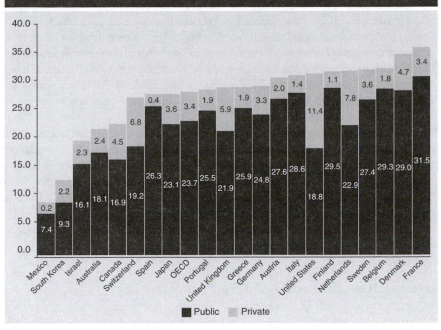

Figure 4.4 Public-Private Social Spending as a Percentage of GDP, 2012

Source: OECED Social Expenditure Update 2016, http://www.oecd.org/els/soc/OECD2016-Social-Expenditure-Update.pdf.

Americans believe in equality as well. However, as Lipset makes evident, Americans believe in **equality of opportunity** not **equality of outcome**, also referred to as equality of result. That is, Americans believe that all individuals should have an equal chance for achievement or to determine their own destinies, and any difference in outcomes or achievements is a result of individual ability. As Table 4.1 illustrates above, Americans often accept inequality of outcome, whereas other democracies place far greater governing value on equality of outcome. In deciding who gets what, when, and how, these democracies prefer that decisions are made in ways that produce equal outcomes—particularly economic outcomes—for the social order. Despite particular moments of protest and reform, Americans have historically been more willing to accept inequalities as long as it seems as if the opportunity for individual achievement has been equal. As political scientists Christine Barbour and Gerald Wright argue, the United States believes in procedural guarantees rather than substantive guarantees.[11] That is, in American political decision making, *the process of deciding who gets what, when, and how must be fair, even if the outcomes are not fair*. In other democracies, citizens want the outcomes of those decisions to be fair as well. Consequently, even when American social service spending occurs, it is process oriented: aimed at trying to make the process fairer rather than focusing on policies that focus on making outcomes fairer. For example, affirmative action attempts to equalize access to educational opportunities for groups formerly discriminated against, but it does not ensure good grades, educational success, or a degree. Public education has a long history dating back to founding father advocates such as Jefferson calling for large government investment designed to provide equal opportunity to the masses, rather than tracking for an elite, and is supported by the majority of Americans. Higher education benefits typically involve access to preferable loans rather than outright tuition payments. Unemployment benefits typically require active pursuit of employment or retraining of skills.

Scholars have established the broad strokes of differences between American political beliefs and other democracies' beliefs, but how do the attitudes of Americans toward individualism and equality fit with other advanced industrial democracies? In other words, how much control should the individual have over her personal fortunes versus how much control should the government have to ensure that outcomes are fair? All democracies should show tendencies toward the individual having control, but Americans favor individual control of outcomes more than other democracies.

INDIVIDUALISM AND ECONOMY

The most common place to see individualism vs. communitarianism play out is in the marketplace. This is because so much of decision making over who gets what, when, and how comes through in markets, and governments involve themselves in efforts to equalize market effects in response to citizen demands. Rather than simply looking at public policies toward the market and redistribution, individualism should become evident through citizens' behavior and attitudes. Individualism is not easy to measure in political or market behaviors because it is not an easy concept to boil down, and it is affected by the incentives that national laws provide. Some marketplace behaviors may demonstrate heavier individual risk-taking. For instance, Europeans tend to invest less frequently in the more risky stock market than Americans compared to other more conservative investment vehicles.[12]

Further, most other advanced industrial democracies have far greater percentages of their workforce in labor unions. Even countries seen to be rather similar to the United States in economic matters such as the United Kingdom and Canada have around a quarter of their workforce belonging to labor unions compared to only around 10 percent of the American workforce being in unions. What's more, social democracies like Belgium, Denmark, Finland, Norway, and Sweden have well over half of their workforce in labor unions. Further, these governments provide a very direct role for labor unions in corporate and public policy in these countries (see Chapter 8). In the United States, the percentage of union workers continues to fall, with even large industrial states like Michigan weakening unions in recent years as well as the Supreme Court ruling in 2018 (*Janus vs. AFSCME*) that public employees do not have to pay union dues to unions

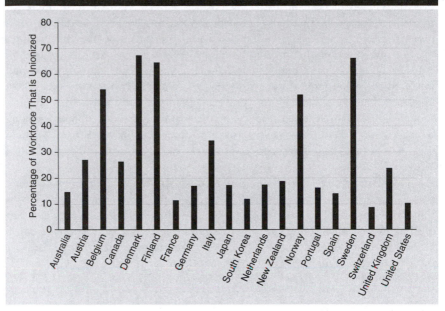

Figure 4.5 Percentage of Labor Force That Is Unionized, 2015–2017

Source: Organisation for Economic Co-operation and Development. "Trade Unions: Trade Union Density in OECD Countries," OECD *Employment and Labour Market Statistics* (2018) 2018. https://stats.oecd.org/Index.aspx?DataSetCode=TUD.

that represent them in collective bargaining. The lack of extreme public outcry in these situations stands in stark contrast to European democracies that would have large-scale strikes shutting down subways, airlines, and industries with far less severe restrictions on unions. For good or for bad, this demonstrates a greater comfort among Americans for individualism within the marketplace rather than binding one's career, labor bargaining, as well as pay and benefits together with others.

More than behaviors and market statistics, the attitudes of Americans demonstrate greater individualism compared to other democracies' greater communalism. In particular, is there a greater acceptance of inequality of outcomes in the marketplace in the United States compared to other democracies? Second, should unequal market outcomes be tied to merit, individual competitive achievement, and hard work? Or should government policies ensure equal outcomes no matter merit, competition, or hard work? We use measures from the World Values Survey Wave 5 to measure attitudes across these democracies.

Table 4.2 (column 1) provides the first glimpse of Americans' acceptance of inequality. Citizens in these democracies were asked their views on income inequality on a scale from 1 (incomes should be made more equal) to 10 (we need larger income differences as incentives for individual effort). Table 4.2 lists the percentage of respondents who rated 6 to 10 on this scale, so on the "need larger income differences as incentives for individual effort" end of the scale. Free markets include the principle of labor being a market and valued differently, so it is not surprising that most democracies' citizens believe that differences in income are necessary. A large difference exists among democratic citizens about the need for income differences as an incentive rather than incomes being more equal. A majority in the United States, Southern Europe, the Commonwealth, and Japan/Korea think large differences provide an incentive for individual effort. Northern Europeans and Nordic citizens are more likely to say that incomes should be made more equal. Americans are the least likely to say that incomes should be made more equal. They are more likely than anyone but the Korean/Japanese cases to say that large differences in income provide an incentive for individual effort.

On a similar ten-point scale, Americans also believe that "competition is good"—that "it stimulates people to work hard and develop new ideas" rather than believing that "competition is harmful"—"it brings out the worst in people," as displayed in Table 4.2. The difference here is typically not as sharp, at least when compared to the Nordic and Commonwealth country cases, but Americans are the most likely to believe that competition is good. That said, all these democracies' citizens generally share a belief in the positive benefits of competition.

Table 4.2 Individualism vs. Collectivism in Competition, Rewards and Success

	Percentage Who Think Larger Income Differences Are an Incentive	Percentage Who View Competition as Good	Percentage Who Think Hard Work Brings Success
United States	65%	87%	78%
Nordic Countries	49%	86%	72%
Northern Europe	41%	74%	60%
Southern Europe	56%	76%	66%
Commonwealth	54%	83%	74%
Japan/South Korea	71%	81%	66%

Note: Figures calculated from World Values Survey Wave 5, variables 116, 119, 120.

Americans also tend to believe that hard work brings success. The World Values Survey asked people to place themselves on a range from 1 (in the long run, hard work usually brings a better life) to 10 (hard work doesn't generally bring success—it's more a matter of luck and connections). The percentage of those who were ranked on the hard work usually brings a better life side of the scale (1–5 on the scale) appear as the percentage of "Hard Work Brings Success" in Table 4.2. Again, Americans are the most common to say that hard work brings success—a very individualistic concept.

Taken together, the findings from Table 4.2 paint the United States as particularly open to competition, hard work, and individual rewards. One can say that citizens in other countries share Americans' views on these indicators of individualism, but Americans are always among the *most individualistic* across all of the measures. Other democratic citizens were high on some of these and low on others. Further, the figures from Table 4.1 indicate that the U.S. economy begins with far fewer regulations empowering workers in the private sector and much more inequality, so the fact that Americans want less equality of outcome than other democracies that begin with much more equality of income is especially noteworthy.

Beyond the more abstract measures on competition, hard work, and pay inequality generally, a more real-life example of how attitudes toward individualism affect what is seen as fair in decisions over who gets what, when, and how may better draw distinctions between Americans and other democracies' citizens. Lipset pointed out one particularly useful question in his discussion of American exceptionalism. The World Values Survey has asked the following question: "Imagine two secretaries, of the same age, doing practically the same job. One finds out that the other earns considerably more than she does. The better paid secretary, however, is quicker, more efficient and more reliable at her job. In your opinion, is it fair or not fair that one secretary is paid more than the other?"

It may seem obvious in a free market system that merit would be rewarded. This is the case in all of these democracies. It is noteworthy, however, that citizens

Table 4.3   Is Merit Pay Distinction Fair for Two Secretaries?

	Fair	Not Fair
United States	91%	9%
Nordic Democracies	72%	28%
Northern European Democracies	80%	20%
Southern European Democracies	73%	27%
Commonwealth Democracies	83%	17%
Japan and South Korea	82%	18%

Source: Data from World Values Survey Wave 5, variable 115, http://www.worldvaluessurvey.org.

in other democracies say such merit reward is unfair two or three times as frequently as do Americans (See Table 4.3).

Americans believe in equality of opportunity, but in decisions over who gets what, when, and how, equality of outcome is significantly less important for Americans as it is elsewhere. On balance, individualism trumps communitarianism for Americans, whereas other democracies have citizens more likely to prefer communal benefits. These attitudes are not merely historical artifacts but play important parts in current democratic expectations and preferences toward decision making. This distinctive political culture spills over into American political ideology, which as a result of these cultural beliefs, includes a narrower set of political ideological viewpoints relative to other democracies.

IDEOLOGY

Like political culture, scholars struggle to clearly explain how political ideology works as well as to provide a definition for the term. The difficulty comes from its broad usage to describe different elements of political thought. Some scholars have used ideology to discuss how ideologues use political ideas as illusions or mysticism to persuade followers to bring about political change or to cling to the status quo, that is, the way things are now.[13] Most political scientists view ideology as a more "value-neutral" concept that describes a shared set of beliefs among a population or group. As public opinion experts Robert Erikson and Kent Tedin define it, **ideology** is a shared "set of beliefs about the proper order of society and how it can be achieved."[14] The simplicity of this definition allows for ideology to reflect a shared belief system among citizens as well as the fact that there can be more than one set of beliefs within a democracy. In fact, ideological beliefs tend to be those ideas that divide groups of citizens in democracies, compared to political cultures, which are those ideas that societies broadly hold in common.[15]

In democracies, the main divide among groups of citizens has historically been viewed as those who are on the left of the political spectrum who favor more government involvement in the economy, and those on the right of the political spectrum who favor less government involvement in the economy. This is due to the fact that the industrial age brought both more democracy to many societies as well as pressure to have governments reign in the dynamic, and at times negative, components of industrial life: changing infrastructure, shifting of wealth from the countryside to the city, worker safety and health, childhood labor laws, wage and housing regulations, social welfare, monopolies, and trade. These terms have stuck, even though new divisions have grown beyond the proper role of the government in the marketplace.

The differential political experience in the United States and other democracies, as outlined in Chapter 3, has led to different types of political debate. Democracies have different types of political divisions based on their histories, but the reasons provided for American exceptionalism are also those that explain why the American ideological debate is narrower than the ideological debates in other advanced industrial democracies. Two broad characteristics about American political beliefs explain why this is the case.

First, Americans share a value-based commitment to liberalism. Again, this is not "liberal" in the context of contemporary left-leaning political ideas in America but the broader notions of liberalism that Americans share from Locke's view of legitimate government as being limited. Americans remain so loyal to this vision of liberalism, and it is so commonly held, that Americans do not recognize it; it is the "natural order of things."[16] Returning to our metaphor from earlier chapters, when they put on green glasses, they can't see anything else. American exceptionalism scholars actually point to this as a potential weakness in the American system. Lipset says this means that Americans—rather than having consensus on contemporary political debates—end up arguing more and sharply about the application of liberal principles that most Americans agree upon.[17] As noted in Chapter 1, Louis Hartz claims that Americans' attachment to Lockean liberalism is absolute and uncritical, and the unanimity of this can be compulsive "Americanism" that leaves the society open to overreaction to other ideological thoughts in the world. For example, in the 1950s, Americans went through the Red Scare, fear of the rise of Communism, which turned into McCarthyism, a witch hunt of sorts led by Senator Joseph McCarthy where suspected communists were spied upon, blacklisted, and even hauled before Congress, as a result of the American fear of the loss of liberalism associated with Soviet Communist threat.[18] In more modern times, after September 11th, many Americans, failing to distinguish between those terrorists who carried out the attacks and the larger Muslim community, reported fear of Muslims in general and a vitriolic dislike of Islam. Hate crimes targeted at Muslim Americans increased 1700 percent in the year after the September 11, 2001, attacks on the United States.[19] Particularly since the 2016 election, fears of multiculturalism and immigration have led to a jump in hate crimes against Latinos and Muslims and more visible and public right-wing supremacy groups. In turn, a fear of the rise of right-wing populist authoritarianism has driven radical leftists to actively disrupt and sometimes physically attack white supremacist followers at rallies. Nationalist parties and socialists are far more prevalent in the mainstream national political debate in other democracies. Whether positive or negative, the American experience of being "locked into Locke" means that American definitions of left and right do not extend very far.

Second, as American exceptionalism scholars have highlighted, Americans' lack of feudalism and socialist movement left the United States without the demand for large-scale government involvement in the economy. This closely relates to the first point, that the United States does not have a significant mainstream left like other democracies. Further, the United States also does not have mainstream far-right nationalism or fascist parties either. While only some democracies have citizens with a nationalist/fascist belief system, its reliance on the primacy of the state as an actor for the people goes well beyond the limited government ideals of Americans. This leaves a narrow band of liberal political beliefs in the United States.

Other democracies have a much broader ideological spectrum. First, the socialist movements that dominated European societies and helped democratize many of these countries means there are many citizens in these democracies who hold political beliefs far to the left of Americans. Communist parties did exist in many of these democracies, but they largely lost steam as the countries succeeded in the free market and the Cold War divisions with communist Soviet-bloc became acute. Most commonly, the socialist movement led most mainstream leftists to identify with Socialist—or often Social Democratic or Labor—parties.

Also slightly to the left of Americans were the mainstream center-right parties such as the Conservative or Christian Democratic parties. Even though these parties serve as the mainstream right of many of these democracies, there is a greater acceptance of social welfare and redistribution on the part of the government among mainstream right parties in other democracies. First, the common brotherhood of these nations meant that for the good of the social order one would not leave their poorer brothers or sisters behind, especially in the cases where parties were built around religious denominations. Second, these parties tended to be made up of the higher classes, who had a sense of *noblesse oblige*— or a sense of responsibility that comes with wealth and privilege—so there was always a greater willingness to use government to provide for less fortunate and lower classes.[20] This sense is not just historical. When visiting the United States shortly following the controversial and vociferous debates about American health care reform inside and outside Congress in 2010, the very conservative—for France—French President Nicolas Sarkozy spoke at Columbia University about the passage of the legislation by saying, "Welcome to the club of states who don't turn their back on the sick and the poor. . . . The very fact that there should have been such a violent debate simply on the fact that the poorest of Americans should not be left out in the streets without a cent to look after them . . . is something astonishing to us."[21]

There is American-style liberal thought in other advanced industrial democracies, but the parties that represent these views tend to be important but minor parties. It is certainly mainstream in those democracies, but it is the *only* mainstream in American political life. In the United States, both parties are liberal parties.[22] Figure 4.6 lays out a theoretical ideological placement of American ideological positions as represented by American parties and the ideological placement of most European parties from left to right. There is not specific quantifiable comparison here, particularly because what Americans think they mean by left and right is different from what other democracies' citizens think is meant by left and right. So, this figure is—at best—a very simplified attempt by the authors to spatially demonstrate the ideological positions of these democracies.

There has been a growing ideological division between the two American parties, but the misplaced accusations of some Americans—including political

	Far Left	Center-Left	Center-Right	Liberal Right	Extreme Right
Ideological Space in Other Advanced Industrial Democracies	Communist	Social Democratic Socialist Labor	Christian Democratic Conservative	Liberal	Nationalist/ Fascist
Ideological Space in United States			Democrats Republicans		

Note: We "wall off" the extreme right to keep it from appearing as if the mainstream American parties even approach this belief system. The Nationalist-Fascist ideologies in these democracies are distinct from the typical left-right debate and trend not to be in the mainstream of those democracies.

leaders and news commentators—against their political opponents as "socialists" or "fascists" lack any accuracy. A European social democrat would laugh off the suggestion that an American Democratic Party member was socialist, and a European nationalist/fascist would reject an American Republican Party member as a sell-out to their nation.

Scholars of American political ideology have suggested that Americans are pragmatic and not very ideological, even if Americans fight like cats and dogs over public policy. Political scientist Philip Converse (b. 1928–) found that Americans' views on issues shifted frequently because American political beliefs were not constrained due to the fact that Americans were "innocent of ideology" and that their only belief systems were "folk ideologies" at best.[23] This means that Americans shift their positions on issues because they are not very well differentiated from each other or anchored in a firm differentiated ideology—at least there lacks an ideology beyond the common belief system of liberalism. Thus, Americans commonly believe that government should be limited in the marketplace and individuals' lives. Even when the government does provide social services, much of these are provided by the private sector that receives grants from the government rather than a government entity providing the benefit directly (see Figure 4.4). Americans prefer that a lot is left to the private sector. Americans reading this book may be students at a public university. While that institution is funded by a state (and has comparatively large tuition costs relative to other democracies), the university is accredited by a private not-for-profit accreditation body. This means state governments do not have authority to say whether or not the degrees their universities provide are certified. Further, these public institutions often—and increasingly—rely on private donations to keep their doors open.

Thus, Americans tend to be to the ideological right of other democracies' citizenries. They prefer less government control over who gets what, when, and how. In decisions over who gets what, when, and how, the government typically has a moderate footprint in free economies. Yet, ownership of business was something pushed for by the socialist movement and the successor center-left parties in Europe, often referred to as social-democratic or labor parties. So, a greater history of government-owned businesses has existed in other democracies with less resistance to it than one would find in the United States.

The World Values Survey asked people to rank from 1 (private ownership of business and industry should be increased) to 10 (government ownership of business and industry should be increased). We have collapsed these into four categories for ease of presentation, with full private ownership (answer of 1 or 2), some private (answer or 3, 4, or 5), some public (answer or 6, 7, or 8), and more public (answer of 9 or 10). As Figure 4.7 illustrates, Americans are far more likely than other countries' citizens to say that businesses should be privately rather than publicly owned. Only a tiny fraction of Americans believe in public ownership of business. While other countries prefer private ownership as well, the divide between private and public ownership is not nearly as stark as it is in the United States.

Though not as dramatic as public vs. private ownership, when people were asked on the same 10-point scale whether 10 "the government should take more responsibility to ensure that everyone is provided for" versus 1 "people should take more responsibility to provide for themselves," Americans again emerge as more likely to prefer that people take more individual responsibility compared to all other democratic regions except Commonwealth countries (see Figure 4.8).

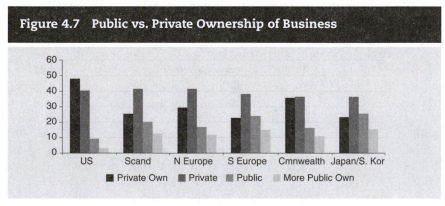

Figure 4.7   Public vs. Private Ownership of Business

Source: Data from World Values Survey, http://www.worldvaluessurvey.org.

Figure 4.8   People or Government Should Take More Responsibility

Figure 4.8   People or Government Should Take More Responsibility

Legend: ■ People take more   ■ People   ■ Government   Government take more

Source: Data from World Values Survey, http://www.worldvaluessurvey.org.

These categories are broken into four groups for ease of presentation with "government takes more" responsibility (values of 10, 9, or 8), "government" (values of 7 or 6), "people" (values of 5 or 4), and "people take more" responsibility (values of 3, 2, or 1). The difference may appear marginal, but it is important to remember that the American government is far less involved in the marketplace as highlighted in Chapter 3 and in Table 4.1. So, in context, the greater likelihood that Americans prefer private ownership even given that they already have it, makes this finding stronger.

CONCLUSION

When examining political culture and ideology, the United States is in some ways very similar to its cousins in other advanced industrial democracies; yet on key indicators, the United States is quite exceptional, or different. When examining political culture, or shared norms and beliefs, scholars emphasize how important it is for a democracy to have a civic culture, or an engaged and trusting citizenry who knows how to and believes in their ability to influence politics. On measures such as interest in politics and trust of fellow citizens, the United States is on par with other democracies; while it doesn't always have the highest levels of trust, and displays more interest than many other democracies, it is certainly not outside the norm. In terms of political efficacy, the United States also ranks similarly to other democracies.

This chapter also highlighted the aspirational aspects of "being American." American focus, some would say even religious-like adherence, on individualism has led American political culture to deviate from other democracies in important ways. For example, Americans prefer private solutions to social problems rather than government, or public solutions, more than other democratic citizenries. American individualism also causes its citizens to be more in favor of competition and less likely to support income redistribution than citizens in other democracies.

Finally, American ideology is different than other countries' ideological beliefs. The United States has a much more truncated ideological spectrum compared to other democracies. American Democrats and Republicans are both liberal parties and occupy a much smaller ideological space than parties in other countries. This stems in part because of the very different historical experiences that shaped political debate and ideology in the United States compared to other democracies. Thus, Americans are ideologically further to the right than publics in other democracies, causing Americans to favor economic policies such as private ownership of business and to place greater value on personal responsibility.

POINTS TO REMEMBER

- Political culture is the shared political norms, values, and beliefs of a citizenry about politics. The term *political culture* refers specifically to attitudes toward the political system and attitudes toward the role of citizens in the system.

- A participatory political culture requires that people can largely self-govern themselves outside of governmental decision making and in their own interest and implies that citizens understand how to influence government and the outputs of democratic government.

- Three interrelated characteristics help to define a democratic or civic political culture. First, democracies require citizens who engage their government and demonstrate high levels of political interest. Second, people have to trust one another in social relations or the vacuum in interpersonal relations among citizens makes deciding who gets what, when, and how in self-governance next to impossible. Third, a large percentage of the people in a democracy must believe they control their own lives rather than be reliant on government or subjects of fate.

- Americans report high levels of interest in politics, similar to other advanced industrial democracies.

- In terms of trust and free choice, Americans rank similarly to citizens of other advanced democracies.

- Americans place greater emphasis on individualism while other democracies place greater emphasis on communitarianism. This is illustrated by the fact that social spending is similar across democracies, but where the United States has more private (or charitable) spending, an individual endeavor, other countries have much higher levels of public, or governmental, social spending.

- American emphasis on individualism also causes American citizens to place more emphasis on individual responsibility and private ownership of industry than citizens in other democracies.

KEY TERMS

Civic culture 54
Civil religion 61
Communitarian values 59
Consolidated
    democracies 53
Equality of
    opportunity 63

Equality of
    outcome 63
External efficacy 57
Ideology 68
Individualism 59
Internal efficacy 57
Noblesse oblige 70

Participatory political
    culture 54
Political culture 53
Political efficacy 57
Political
    interest 55
Social capital 56

REVIEW QUESTIONS

1. What is political culture? What is civic culture?

2. What is social capital, and how is it related to interpersonal trust? How is this similar in the United States and other democracies?

3. In what ways is American political culture similar to the political culture in other advanced industrial democracies? Different?

4. How is American individualism manifested in attitudes toward fellow citizens, government, and personal and government responsibility? How is this similar or different than what is seen in other countries?

5. Describe the ideological orientation of Americans. How does the ideological space occupied in the United States differ from the space occupied in other democracies?

6. What are the negative consequences of American individualism? How is this manifest on your campus/in your life today? What are the benefits?

SUGGESTED READINGS

Almond, Gabriel, and Sidney Verba. *The Civic Culture: Political Attitudes and Democracy in Five Nations*. Princeton, NJ: Princeton University Press, 1963.

Barbour, Christine, and Gerald Wright, with Matthew J. Streb and Michael Wolf. *Keeping the Republic: Power and Citizenship in American Politics*, 3rd ed. Washington, DC: CQ Press, 2006.

Converse, Philip E. "The Nature of Belief Systems in Mass Publics." In *Ideology and Discontent*, edited by D. E. Apter. New York, NY: Free Press, 1964.

Elazar, Daniel. *American Federalism: A View from the States*. New York, NY: Thomas Y. Crowell, 1973.

Etzioni, Amitai. *The Spirit of Community: Rights, Responsibilities, and the Communitarian Agenda*. New York, NY: Crown, 1993.

Lipset, Seymour Martin. *American Exceptionalism: A Double-Edged Sword*. New York, NY: W. W. Norton and Company, 1997.

Putnam, Robert. *Bowling Alone: The Collapse and Revival of American Community*. New York, NY: Touchstone Books, 2001.

NOTES

1. Gabriel Almond and Sidney Verba, *The Civic Culture: Political Attitudes and Democracy in Five Nations* (Princeton, NJ: Princeton University Press, 1963).

2. We use World Values Survey Wave 5 (2005-2008). R.C. Inglehart et al., *RWorld Values Survey: Round Five-Country-Pooled Datafile* Version: http://www .worldvaluessurvey.org/WVSDocumentationWV5.jsp (Madrid: JD Systems Institute, 2014). World Values Survey Wave 6 does not have all country databases available at the time of this edition's writing.

3. Robert Putnam, *Bowling Alone: The Collapse and Revival of American Community* (New York, NY: Touchstone Books, 2001).

4. Lipset, *American Exceptionalism: A Double-Edged Sword* (New York, NY: W.W. Norton and Company, 1997), 31.

5. Lipset, *American Exceptionalism*, 26.

6. See Robert Bellah, "Civil Religion in America," *Journal of the American Academy of Arts and Sciences* 96, no. 1 (1967): 1–21; Raymond Haberski, "War and America's Civil Religion," Huffingtonpost.com, July 2, 2012, http://www.huffingtonpost .com/raymond-haberski-jr/war-and-americas-civil-religion_b_1638152.html.

7. Daniel Elazar, *American Federalism: A View from the States* (New York, NY: Thomas Y. Crowell, 1973).

8. Elazar, *American Federalism*, 97.

9. See Elazar for discussion of the individualistic political culture concerning the limited and transactional view of government; see Lipset, *American Exceptionalism*, 21, for disdain of authority; E. J. Dionne, *Our Divided Political Heart: The Battle for the American Idea in an Age of Discontent* (New York, NY: Bloomsbury, 2012); Gordon Wood, *The Idea of America: Reflections on the Birth of the United States* (New York, NY: Penguin Books, 2013) talks of the long-standing balance of individualism and ethic of Republican engagement; also read Amitai Etzioni's call for a new communitarianism in Amitai Etzioni, *The Spirit of Community: Rights, Responsibilities, and the Communitarian Agenda* (New York, NY: Crown Publishers, 1993).

10. Lipset, *American Exceptionalism*, 33–36.

11. Christine Barbour and Gerald Wright, with Matthew J. Streb and Michael Wolf, *Keeping the Republic: Power and Citizenship in American Politics*, 3rd ed. (Washington, DC: CQ Press, 2006).

12. See Julie Cruz, "Why Don't Germans Invest in Stocks?" *Bloomberg Businessweek*, September 30, 2010, http://www.bloomberg.com/news/articles/2010–09–30/ why-dont-germans-invest-in-stocks-businessweek-business-news-stock-market -and-financial-advice; also see Luigi Guiso, Michael Haliassos and Tullio Jappelli, "Household Stockholding in Europe: Where Do We Stand and Where Do We Go?" *Centre for Studies in Economics and Finance*, University of Naples, Italy, 2002.

13. See John Jost, Christopher Federico, and Jaime Napier, "Political Ideology: Its Structure, Functions, and Elective Affinities." *Annual Review of Psychology* 60 (2009): 307–337; also see Terence Ball and Richard Dagger, *Ideals and Ideologues*, 6th ed. (New York, NY: Pearson, 2006).

14. Robert Erikson and Kenneth Tedin, *Public Opinion*, 8th ed. (New York, NY: Longman, 2011).

15. Barbour and Wright, *Keeping the Republic*.

16. Dominic Tierney, "Why Are Americans So Ideologically Unified?" *The Atlantic*, August 23, 2011. http://www.theatlantic.com/national/archive/2011/08/why-are -americans-so-ideologically-united/243951.

17. Lipset, *American Exceptionalism*, 25.

18. Louis Hartz, *The Liberal Tradition in America* (New York, NY: Harcourt, Brace and World, 1955), 6–13.

19. Mussarat Khan and Kathryn Ecklund, "Attitudes toward Muslim Americans Post-9/11." *Journal of Muslim Mental Health* 7, no. 1 (2012): 1–16; J. Cherie Strachan and Michael Wolf, "Party Polarization and Separate Worldviews: Attitudes toward Muslim-Americans and the 2010 Elections." Paper presented at the Midwest Political Science Association, April 2012.

20. Lipset, *American Exceptionalism*, 21.

21. Steve Benen, "Sarkozy on Health Care Debate: 'It's Hard to Believe.'" Political Animal column, *The Washington Monthly*, March 30, 2010, http://www .washingtonmonthly.com/archives/individual/2010_03/023111.php.

22. Lipset, *American Exceptionalism*, 32.

23. Philip E. Converse, "The Nature of Belief Systems in Mass Publics," in *Ideology and Discontent*, ed. D. E. Apter (New York, NY: Free Press, 1964).

CHAPTER FIVE

CIVIL LIBERTIES AND CIVIL RIGHTS

In 1977 and 1978, pro-Nazi groups existed in the United States and the United Kingdom, like they do today. In the United States, the National Socialist Party of American wanted to march in uniform in Skokie, Illinois, which had a predominantly Jewish population. The Village of Skokie charged the National Socialist Party of America with a $350,000 bond to issue a park permit for the march. In effect, this was meant to price the Nazis out of marching. Officials also protested the plan for the marchers to wear Nazi uniforms, claiming it might lead to excessive violence. Illinois courts allowed an injunction against the march until the U.S. Supreme Court ruled that the Nazi Party's First Amendment rights had been violated because the Illinois courts had not provided sufficient procedural appellate review. Ultimately, the Nazi's First Amendment rights provided them choices of where to march, and they moved the march to Chicago. Meanwhile, the National Front, a neo-Nazi group, wanted to march in different sections of London in 1978. The Metropolitan Police Commissioner of London and the government's Home Secretary banned all marches or processions by the National Front for a number of months based on the fear of violence.[1] As a result, Nazis did not march in London.

While both the United States and United Kingdom protect political speech, and both localities wanted to ban the Nazi marches, constitutional protections differ between these liberal democracies. The U.S. Constitution provides much more latitude to freedom of speech—even hateful speech—relative to public safety and the sensibilities of the general public than what we see in most other democracies.[2]

Democracies always struggle with questions of individual liberties versus public good. As this chapter will demonstrate, the United States tends to provide its citizens with more civil liberties protections but fewer protections for their civil rights. The reasons for this have everything to do with differing political values that previous chapters have highlighted. The United States is not more pro-Nazi; nor do Americans love the often violent and nasty scenes that such marches by extremists bring with them. The pictures from the "unite the right" white nationalist rally in Charlottesville, Virginia in August 2017 would make anyone cringe. Interestingly, the mayor of Charlottesville tried to move and restrict the rally out of fear that it would turn violent. Unfortunately, an awful vehicular attack by a white supremacist ended up killing one protestor, Heather Heyer, and injuring dozens more. This is the ugly side of individual freedom of expression. What are the positive sides to such expansive individual freedoms?

CIVIL RIGHTS AND CIVIL LIBERTIES

All democratic societies share considerable **civil liberties** or rights and freedoms that governments cannot take away from their citizens. As Chapter 2 discussed, civil liberties are the basis of what defines a society as free. They provide the ability for people to make decisions over who gets what, when, and how outside of government influence. Such decisions over who gets what, when, and how, as well as what they can say in public, what they can buy, and even what god they believe in—or not—are what defines a **civil society**.

A civil society is at the center of the idea of the social contract, that governments both protect citizens but also limit themselves to provide for citizens' freedoms. Thus, people are ensured protection *by* the government and protection *from* the government, which leads to the very confusing situation of trying to define when government should step in to protect people from ripping each other off or discriminating against each other versus when the government stepping in takes people's rights away. **Civil rights** are citizen freedoms that governments proactively protect against being taken away by regional governments, institutions, employers, or social groups. When should the government decide that our civil liberty to express something hateful goes too far and takes away someone else's civil rights?

A core distinction between civil liberties and civil rights centers on how active government is in providing those rights. Civil liberties tend to be thought of as **negative rights**, or those rights that are protected because a government is not permitted to take action. While all democratic societies share a core set of civil liberty protections like freedom of speech, freedom of expression, freedom of association, freedom of religion, freedom against imprisonment without due process, and press freedoms among others, there are relatively significant differences among democracies about just how extreme the things that you can say are or whether you can associate with groups with extreme beliefs or hatred toward others.

Positive rights are civil rights that people receive by government taking action to protect them against other governing bodies, institutions, social groups, or employers. Free societies always have discrimination in civil society since we have pluralism of thought. Such discrimination can hurt society if it is unfair to social groups or if it hurts the workings of a free market or has a chilling effect on the marketplace of ideas. When should a government step in? Governments tend to act when groups or important social values are threatened in civil society.

Democracies differ on what rights they want government to defend. Most democratic governments will act to protect against discrimination based on race, religion, gender, age, sexual orientation, or gender identity. Some also protect social and economic rights like ethnic and linguistic rights as well as health care and medicine, housing, wages, social security, educational rights, the right to work and the right to leisure, and environmental and internationally recognized rights of dignity. In fact, for most democracies besides the United States, these positive rights are extensive. As comparative law and human rights scholar Mary Ann Glendon notes about a European legal historian's "basic inventory" of rights that are accepted in "most Western countries," "The list includes, first and foremost; human dignity; then personal freedom; fair procedures to protect against arbitrary government action; active political rights (especially the right to vote); equality before the law; and society's responsibility for social and economic conditions of its members. An American reader of this list is apt to be struck both by the omission of property rights, and by the inclusion of affirmative welfare obligations."[3]

For most democracies, the distinction between positive rights and negative rights is not as stark as it is in the United States. The United States provides its society with extensive civil liberties, whereas most other advanced industrial democracies ease civil liberties to protect the social order when in conflict with individual freedoms. This should not be a surprise given the findings from Chapter 4 and the intense individualism that Americans support in public policies and in dealing with social welfare.

This same individualism has an ironic but understandable counter effect concerning civil rights. Because of individualism and the American belief of equal opportunities over equal outcomes, the American political system does not provide for as many civil rights as do the governments of other advanced industrial democracies. So, core notions of government action to protect race, religion, gender, age, and sexual preference and gender identity exist in the United States, but other democracies include social, cultural, and economic well-being rights that compel government action to secure citizens' social security, educational, housing, labor, health, environmental, and even internationally defined rights.

These distinctions in what government has to do proactively to protect core rights of citizens are a big deal. It is one thing to highlight the policy preference distinctions among democracies and the United States, but the distinctive way the United States protects some rights but does not proactively protect others is a dramatic example of how our political culture, political values, and core political beliefs differ on the most fundamental relations citizens have with their government: what rights should government protect and how.

EXPLAINING DIFFERING LEVELS OF CIVIL RIGHTS AND LIBERTIES

What affects the balance and levels of civil liberties and civil rights in democracies centers on a number of fundamental principles that will be highlighted in the following sections. They drive the high number of negative rights in the American political system and the relatively low number of positive rights articulated by the American Constitution. These principles have been touched on in earlier chapters but stand as important interrelated drivers of American civil liberties, and civil rights are somewhat out of balance with other democratic societies.

American Exceptionalism

Not surprisingly, American exceptionalism plays a large role in explaining why the United States has relatively broader levels of civil liberty protections as well as less proactive protection of some civil rights that are both recognized and explicitly protected elsewhere. Many of the political cultural beliefs highlighted in Chapter 4 aid in this explanation. Individualism means citizens have a strong sense that liberties should not be trespassed upon, even if it means complications for the social order. For instance, freedom of speech and assembly means that hate groups and people with beliefs completely aberrant to American social norms can meet, protest, and voice their hate. Religious freedoms led to a plethora of religious practices and beliefs that some may find peculiar or even creepy. It also frustrates many Americans that their kids cannot pray in school or that religious symbols like the Ten Commandments or a nativity scene may be banned from government property unless contextualized with other religious displays.

Americans also dislike how difficult it is for police to arrest someone for a crime that police and the public are circumstantially sure someone committed. Even more, the public hates when a guilty person goes free because of an unconstitutional goof up in the seizure of evidence. The United States' assumption of innocence and broad protections from unreasonable searches and seizures create genuine difficulties in solving crimes. Many Americans also describe some vivid cruel and unusual punishments they would like to commit against those accused of heinous crimes, and they are disturbed that the accused retain an assumption of innocence.

Even with these critiques, most Americans appreciate the rights ensured by the American Bill of Rights. The belief in individualism and individual rights means that the restrictions on government relative to citizen rights are understood, even if frustrating. Americans do not believe there is a constitutional crisis when a guilty crook goes free due to a bad search or when accused criminals are not forced to testify against themselves.

The lack of civil rights as positive rights protections written into the U.S. Constitution comes from the path-dependent argument laid out in earlier chapters. The idea that bridged the American Revolution to the emergence of American sovereign democracy was the social contract that limited government's action. Further, the lack of feudalism and the socialist movement never drove an extension of explicit government action for the protections of economic and social security rights. As a result, Americans never expected their government to proactively provide much relative social policy or social spending. This is clear from the evidence from Chapter 4.

Therefore, there is less of a push for explicit government extension of civil rights beyond ensuring equal opportunities for particular groups.

Timing of a Country's Constitution

The timing of the writing of a country's constitution and what it says about the government's belief about what a legitimate government should do affects the balance of negative and positive rights in democratic societies' constitutions. Given the conditions it faced during the colonial period, the United States drew its influence from Locke and firmly sided on the legitimacy of government coming from its relative limitation when weighed against the civil liberties of its citizens. Government that trespassed on citizens' rights to life, liberty, or property (pursuit of happiness) would lack legitimacy and need to be replaced. So, the U.S. Constitution was a product of its time, as were other democracies' constitutions. As we discuss in Chapter 6, other countries developed their constitutions later and placed much more emphasis on the need for the common good over individual liberties when in conflict. Scholars of civil rights and liberties discuss the extension from negative rights to positive rights in democratic constitutions as coming due to successive generations of constitutions.[4]

First generation rights are political rights and civil liberties that came in the first constitution of the modern democratic world, the Magna Carta, which was the first primary document limiting government for civic power. The generation is really demarcated with the Declaration of Independence and the Constitution of the United States but also includes the French Declaration of Rights of Man of 1789. The key to this generation of rights is that they defined negative rights in constitutions. For instance, the Declaration of the Rights of Man added to the American Declaration of Independence's explicit call that a legitimate government would not take away a citizen's life, liberty, and property. It says, "The aim of all political association is the preservation of the natural rights of man. These rights are liberty, property, security, and the resistance to oppression."

Because of individualism and the American political culture, the U.S. Constitution and Bill of Rights remains a document that shields rights from government more than other democratic societies' constitutions.[5] As we will see, the French later updated their constitutional principles a number of times, and with each update, added positive rights protected by the government. The United States Constitution has not extended beyond its core protection of political rights. This leaves issues of economic rights and social rights not explicitly defined in American constitutional documents.

Newly forming or reforming democracies following World War II added positive rights to their constitutions that recognized economic and social rights as obligations the state needed to protect. Such rights include social security, food, housing, healthcare, public education, and wage security.[6] These **second generation rights** create proactive obligations on governments to protect rights. Not surprisingly, American political culture and individualism do not see such responsibilities as relevant for government. It is not just that the constitutions were written during this era. It is that the welfare state was already set well ahead of these countries' constitutions. A deeply rooted set of beliefs from the Rousseauian social contract, familial-like citizenship identity, and a communitarian political culture led to positive government obligations to provide food, work, and welfare to citizens.[7] So, most other social democracies have the policies and values highlighted in Chapter 4 not because they are "welfare states," but they are welfare states based on their views of core rights a government needs to provide citizens.

Third generation rights are associated with countries that have written constitutions in the post-Soviet era and have been heavily influenced by international legal norms. These constitutions often compel the government to protect rights to a clean environment and natural resources, human dignity, and sometimes even the application of international human rights conventions on domestic political governance.[8] It is not surprising that those societies emerging from repressive governments, and overly industrialized or dependent on extractive resources, would craft constitutions that directly addressed human dignity and so-called "green rights." The South African Constitution is the model of this era's rights. Many European democracies revisited and updated their constitutions to include environmental rights as well. Americans' view of civil rights and liberties remains rather comfortably situated where it began in the late eighteenth century: protecting civil liberties and not actively addressing civil rights.

Institutional Responsibilities over Civil Liberties and Civil Rights

The institutional structure and powers of a democracy also affect its ability to provide civil rights and liberties. Chapter 7 will discuss the broad differences between the judicial system of the United States and most other advanced industrial democracies. It will show that the American judiciary is designed to protect the civil liberties of individual citizens far more than other democracies, whose judicial institutions aim to protect the social order more than the individual.

Beyond this institutional analysis, the United States is also unique in how much power it provides the judiciary—the Supreme Court—over decisions of constitutionality. The United States' judiciary has the substantial power of **judicial review**.[9] Judicial review, also discussed in Chapters 6 and 7, means that the U.S. Supreme Court and at times lower Federal Appellate Courts can declare a law unconstitutional or how the executive branch is executing a law unconstitutional because the law or its execution infringes on citizens' civil liberties. Other democracies have **political constitutionalism**, where the legislative branch has the ultimate authority over whether the laws they write are constitutional. This so-called legislative supremacy or **parliamentary sovereignty** means a country's legislature has the ultimate authority to write or rewrite legislation without an official ability of the judiciary to stop it. Some countries have a judicial body that can suggest whether the laws written by the legislature fit the constitution, but they cannot stop the legislation.

Ultimately, this means that other democracies lack the power of the Supreme Court to cease legislation. It is not that these democracies disregard civil liberties and protections, it is that they trust that their legislature will consider the constitutional ramifications of legislation prior to passing it.[10] It is also foreign to those democracies that a judicial body of nine people—like the United States Supreme Court—could ultimately decide against popularly elected officials.[11]

This is particularly important because this biases American judicial constitutional decisions toward protecting individual liberties because the Supreme Court has the U.S. Constitution and Bill of Rights as its main playbook. Other democracies' judiciaries lack this relative power. It also means that civil rights protections are not well defined in American politics because the judiciary cannot write positive rights into the Constitution.

Explicit and Implicit Negative Rights and Positive Rights in Country's Constitution

Finally, the particular balance between how to protect the social order versus safeguarding civil liberties is known as **proportionality**. Proportionality of civil liberties is the proportion that a government may go in pursuit of public policy objectives for the common good of society that may infringe on an individual's liberty.[12] What does the constitution say directly or indirectly about how much the government can infringe on citizens?[13] Not surprisingly, the American system is far less proportional in the balance between civil liberties and the social order and weighs significantly toward civil liberties. Further, the American Constitution and Bill of Rights do not state that the protections of the Bill of Rights should be weighed against the needs of broader society. Other democracies situate such individual civil liberties against the need to balance individual civil liberties proportionately against the broader needs of society and the social order.[14]

For instance, Box 5.1 lists many countries' constitutional statements about balancing individual liberties against the public good. These initially spell out the need for an ordered society to protect the public good using words like *society, public, order, peace*, and so on that balance in some proportion those individual liberties. The American Bill of Rights makes no generalized statement about primary civil liberties—speech, assembly, press freedoms, and the rights of the accused—being weighed against anything. The U.S. Constitution begins with "We the People of the United States, in Order to form a more perfect Union, establish Justice, insure domestic Tranquility, provide for the common defense, promote the general Welfare, and secure the Blessings of Liberty to ourselves and our Posterity, do ordain and establish this Constitution for the United States of America." This phrase discusses broad goals for all of society, but it does not connect these to individual liberties directly.

BOX 5.1

Proportionality: Constitutional Clauses That Limit Civil Liberties

German Basic Law

Every person shall have the right to free development of his personality insofar as he does not violate the rights of others or offend against the constitutional order or the moral law.

Every person shall have the right to life and physical integrity. Freedom of the person shall be inviolable. These rights may be interfered with only pursuant to a law.

Canadian Charter of Rights and Freedoms

The *Canadian Charter of Rights and Freedoms* guarantees the rights and freedoms set out in it subject only to such reasonable limits prescribed by law as can be demonstrably justified in a free and democratic society.

Denmark

The citizens shall without previous permission be entitled to assemble unarmed. The police shall be entitled to be present at public meetings. Open-air meetings may be prohibited when it is feared that they may constitute a danger to the public peace.

France

Article 4

Liberty consists in being able to do anything that does not harm others: thus, the exercise of the natural rights of every man has no bounds other than those that ensure to the other members of society the enjoyment of these same rights. These bounds may be determined only by Law.

Article 10

No one may be disturbed on account of his opinions, even religious ones, as long as the manifestation of such opinions does not interfere with the established Law and Order.

Article 11

The free communication of ideas and of opinions is one of the most precious rights of man. Any citizen may therefore speak, write and publish freely, except what is tantamount to the abuse of this liberty in the cases determined by Law.

Italy

The Republic recognizes and guarantees the inviolable rights of the person, both as an individual and in the social groups where human personality is expressed. The Republic expects that the fundamental duties of political, economic, and social solidarity be fulfilled.

Spain

Freedom of ideology, religion, and worship is guaranteed, to individuals and communities with no other restriction on their expression than may be necessary to maintain public order as protected by law.

In fact, the U.S. Constitution begins by laying out the institutional powers of the federal government. While section nine of Article I discusses the rights of *habeas corpus* (right to face quick trial) and no bills of attainder (passing a bill finding someone guilty of a crime and punishing them for that guilt) or ex *post facto* bills (a bill that makes someone retroactively guilty of a crime before laws were written making it illegal), they are very far removed from the broad statements about the "general welfare" of the United States. Further, the **Bill of Rights** that states very directly the civil liberties of American citizens is very distant in text from the discussion of the general welfare—so much so that it is a different document ratified two years later. So, the weight of the civil liberties does not have proportional statements about how to limit them relative to the general welfare of society like other advanced industrial democracies.

This means that the Supreme Court or even federal appellate courts are left to decide the balance of social order versus individual liberty. The constitutional decisions on these set **precedence** for later decisions, meaning they set the general rules for balancing the interests of the social order/public good versus individual liberty[15] Further the Supreme Court does not formally limit individual liberties for three reasons:

1. They are not formally expressed (written) as a constitutional amendment.

2. They are often well-intended but confusing when applied.

3. Precedent on these issues often changes as social norms, technology, and the culture of the Supreme Court change.

There are only three amendments to the U.S. Constitution that curtail liberties for the public. The first, the Thirteenth Amendment, is hardly controversial in that it takes away the right to own slaves or indentured servants but, in fact, opened up the rights for former slaves. The second is the Eighteenth Amendment that prohibited the manufacturing or sale of alcohol. That was repealed just under fifteen years later. The third is a restriction on salary increases for Congress until after elections and the seating of a new Congress, which had been the original Second Amendment but was not ratified until 1992.

The balance of when to curtail liberties is not always an easy decision for the Supreme Court. As Box 5.2 demonstrates, some of the constitutional precedence "tests" for proportionality for freedom of politically unpopular speech and freedom of religion are not entirely clear. How far should the government allow an antigovernment speaker to go in a time of war? How much free speech should we allow racists, bigots, or sexists to have when they offend so many and may bring an overly vigorous response to their presence? The Supreme Court has established a "clear and present danger" test that has shifted over time because no clear proportionality is stated in the Constitution or Bill of Rights.

BOX 5.2

American Proportionality: Constitutional Precedence Tests

The U.S. Constitution does not directly delimit proportionality, a constitutional balance between social order and civil liberties, as do other democracies' constitutions. Deciding when a particular civil liberty may be limited is more difficult as a consequence. The Supreme Court tries to create evaluative standards of proportionality through decisions and the precedence those decisions provide, which may include suggested measures of when the civil liberty may be limited for the public good. Two examples deal with First Amendment civil liberties of freedom of speech/expression and the prohibition against the establishment of religion.

The First Amendment states, "Congress shall make no law respecting an establishment of religion, or prohibiting the free exercise thereof; of abridging the freedom of speech, or of the press; or the right of the people peaceably to assemble, and to petition the Government for a redress of grievances." But what is the establishment of religion, and what are the limits to the freedom of speech?

Clear And Present Danger

The Supreme Court is loath to limit First Amendment's freedom of expression, particularly political speech, and has said expression can be limited when it poses a **"clear and present danger."** Justice Oliver Wendell Holmes provided a colorful analogy for when free speech would be limited: "The most stringent protection of free speech would not protect a man in falsely shouting fire in a theatre and causing a panic." Americans have held on to this broad notion, but the Supreme Court has shifted its definition of clear and present. The Supreme Court rejected the precedent set by the case associated with Holmes's quote, where it said that the First Amendment did not protect a Socialist party official from being convicted under the Espionage Act for printing a flier that tried to get Americans to not be drafted into the military during World War I.[16] That substantial limitation on freedom of expression was eased, and now the precedent comes from the *Brandenburg v. Ohio* (1969) case where clear and present danger is defined much more narrowly: "the constitutional guarantees of free speech and free press do not permit a State to forbid or proscribe advocacy of the use of force or of law violation except where such advocacy is directed to inciting or producing imminent lawless action and is likely to incite or produce such action."[17]

Lemon Test

In an era when the Supreme Court decided that public schools could not allow prayers in school, *Engel v. Vitale* (1962), it also had to decide on other educational laws about religion. One decision, *Lemon v. Kurtzman* (1971), surrounding whether states could pay the salaries of private religious school teachers, provided the Supreme Court an opportunity to develop a standard to determine when a government violated the First Amendment against the establishment of a religion. Like the prohibition against prayer in school, the Supreme Court was not suggesting that states were "establishing" a religion. Instead they were trying to evaluate whether laws supporting religious organizations—schools in this case—were unfairly promoting a religion. In the *Lemon v. Kurtzman* decision, the Supreme Court set a standard about "excessive entanglement" between church and state (U.S. federal government or state/ local governments). In particular, the Court said that laws infringe on the First Amendment's "Establishment Clause" if they violate any of three tests. The decision states, "Every analysis in this area must begin with consideration of the cumulative criteria developed by the Court over many years. Three such tests may be gleaned from our cases. First, the statute must have a secular legislative purpose; second, its principal or primary effect must be one that neither advances nor inhibits religion, *Board of Education v. Allen*, (1968); finally, the statute must not foster "an excessive government entanglement with religion," *Walz, supra,* at 397 U. S. 674."[18]

Clear Tests?

The question that Americans may face when considering the limitation of particular civil liberties is whether these tests are sufficiently clear. For instance, can you tell when advocacy of something will incite imminent lawless action AND is likely to incite such action? What if you are a loser and incite violence, but no one listens? Then are you not a clear and present danger? Second, these tests may serve as precedent for subsequent decisions, but they can also be overturned by subsequent decisions. Or Justices might not prefer to view the test as a proper limitation—or too limiting of individual liberty. About *Lemon*, Justice Antonin Scalia wrote in *Lamb's Chapel v. Center Moriches Union Free School District* (1993), "As to the court's invocation of the Lemon test: Like some ghoul in a late-night horror movie that repeatedly sits up in its grave and shuffles abroad, after being repeatedly killed and buried, Lemon stalks our establishment clause jurisprudence once again, frightening the little children and school attorneys of Center Moriches Union Free School District."

Social change also brings changes to constitutional precedence. Often the Supreme Court wants to avoid changing precedence because it may be seen to undermine its power to set constitutionality if such constitutional definitions were to change frequently. This has unfortunately left some bad precedence as constitutional, such as the *Plessy v. Ferguson* (1896) decision that allowed for discrimination in public institutions (schools, etc.) and in accommodations (workplace, restaurants, hotels, transportation, sports leagues) until undone six decades later by *Brown v. Board of Education* (1954). Other times, precedence can change rather quickly, like the *Lawrence v. Texas* (2003) overturning of the constitutional anti-homosexual sodomy laws seven years after they had been deemed constitutional or the *Citizens United v. FEC* (2010) decision, which rejected limits set on issue advocacy advertisements that had been deemed constitutional less than a decade before in *McConnell v. FEC* (2003). Precedence is far more slippery than expressed constitutional civil rights protections in other democracies' constitutions.

Overall, it is clear that the United States provides more negative rights than positive rights. The U.S. Constitution is very defensive of civil liberties and curtails government action that would threaten such liberties. In turn, the American Constitution is largely silent on positive rights, or civil rights that require government action to protect citizen rights. As a result, fewer civil rights protections exist in the United States relative to other democracies.

CIVIL LIBERTIES IN PRACTICE

American civil liberties were codified in the Bill of Rights and again eight decades later with the passage of the **Fourteenth Amendment**, which applied federal civil liberties protections to state and local governments. Because many areas of public policy that deal with civil liberties happen at the state and local level, like policing and prosecuting suspected criminals, equal protection of voting and access to education, and transportation policies that do not discriminate, civil liberties have expanded in practice since the ratification of the Fourteenth Amendment 150 years ago. The process of applying the constitutional rights in the Bill of Rights to states and localities is referred to as incorporation: the **incorporation** of federal civil liberty protections to states and localities through Supreme Court decisions.

This has meant that civil liberties have expanded in practice over time in American political history. For example, the rights of the criminally accused were expanded with the *Miranda v. Arizona* (1966) decision that required police to make the accused aware of their Fifth Amendment rights and by Gideon v. Wainwright (1963), which stated that states were required by the Sixth Amendment to provide accused criminals with defense counsel. *Heller v. District of Columbia* (2008) expanded the Second Amendment right to bear arms as an individual right, which broke from earlier more restrictive interpretations that limited gun rights.

How do these expanded American civil liberties—negative rights—generally compare to other advanced industrial democracies? They share general principles of freedom of speech, assembly, religion, rights of accused, and so on. However, the American protections go further than the civil liberties of other advanced industrial democracies. While all core civil liberties could be viewed comparatively, we'll focus on the First Amendment for clarity. While the American Bill of Rights is not a definitive menu of rights, and the First Amendment is only one of many, it should be intuitive to many observers of American politics, and many scholars have used it as a reasonable measuring stick on comparative democratic civil liberties.

First Amendment: Freedom of Speech, Expression, Press, Association, and Religion

Hate Speech

The freedom of speech and expression is multifaceted and distinct in the United. There are multiple ways this plays out, including protecting hate speech. As previously highlighted, the United States allows such speech, even when offensive and even when such controversial speech may spark vivid counter protestation and conflict. Recently, American universities were criticized when they canceled speeches by right-wing extremists or white supremacists or tried to keep the speakers away from their campuses. The University of California at Berkeley canceled a speech by right-wing polemicist Milo Yiannopolous when riots broke out and caused over $100,000 in damage. Michigan State University was criticized for trying to disallow white supremacist Richard Spencer's talk at the university. The university relented following a lawsuit, though they shifted the schedule for the event to Spring Break and chose a rather remote venue away from the main campus. Michigan State had argued that it denied the white supremacist's petition based on consultations with law enforcement and significant concerns for public safety due to the violence that occurred after the white nationalist rally in Charlottesville, Virginia.[19] The free speech interests of the supremacist won out over the will of the university and concerns about violence that ended up occurring.

This is not to say that Americans' freedom of expression and speech have not been limited in ways people would find remarkable today. As discussed previously, a century ago in *Schenk v. United States* and *Debs v. United States*, Socialist party officials were jailed due to violating the Espionage Act of 1917, due to their promotion of avoiding the draft during World War I. Generally, however, the United States has protected such speech more than other democracies. There are many examples of other democracies disallowing hate speech for the tighter regulations on public statements. For example, Holocaust denial is not allowed in Germany, something Americans may find repugnant but is still protected speech.

Support for Antigovernment or Violent Groups

Another point of friction between freedom of speech promotion and maintenance of the social order occurs when citizens support an enemy of their state.

The United States allows verbal and symbolic support more than other democracies. Safya Roe Yassin posted numerous pro–Islamic State (ISIS) tweets in Buffalo, Missouri during the time the United States was fighting the Islamic State in Iraq and Syria in 2015. She was not arrested for her support of ISIS until she specifically mentioned a backpack potentially disrupting an anti-Muslim protest in Phoenix.[20] Meanwhile, French authorities arrested a comedian who made an apparent supportive reference on a Facebook post to an Islamic extremist gunman who murdered four people at a Paris kosher market in 2015.[21] Germany made it illegal to distribute any ISIS propaganda or display ISIS symbols because these political expressions were a threat to public security.[22] France, Britain, and most other democracies can prohibit marches, speeches, or other actions that may threaten or provoke the public.[23]

The key difference between the United States and other democracies likely stems in legal language, such as the United Kingdom's Public Order Act of 1986, which stated a person is guilty of provocation of violence if the person uses "threatening, abusive or insulting words or behaviour, or distributes or displays to another person any writing, sign or other visible representation which is threatening, abusive or insulting, with intent to cause that person to believe that immediate unlawful violence will be used against him or another by any person, or to provoke the immediate use of unlawful violence by that person or another, or whereby that person is likely to believe that such violence will be used or it is likely that such violence will be provoked." France, too, uses the notion of provocation, and the government can disallow a group's speech by decree.[24]

Free Speech Rights of Media

The American media has far fewer restrictions on what it may report than other advanced industrial democracies.[25] In the United States, media outlets face little threat of being sued for libel (publishing falsehoods that damage a person's reputation) following the landmark *New York Times v. Sullivan* (1964) case. L. B. Sullivan, a Montgomery, Alabama, public safety commissioner, sued the *New York Times* after an advertisement included some inaccurate information about Montgomery's arrests of Martin Luther King Jr. and other civil rights activists. Sullivan said that the moderately inaccurate accusations had hurt his reputation. The Supreme Court decided unanimously against Sullivan and argued the First Amendment protected all published information, even false information about public officials, unless this information was made with actual malice. Actual malice means not only did the press publish false information that may have injured the person's reputation but also that the media published the false and defamatory information knowingly or with "reckless disregard for the truth."[26]

In other democracies, avoiding libel lawsuits requires the media to report things truthfully. It is also often incumbent on the press to prove the accuracy of the reporting rather than on the accuser to prove that the reporting was erroneous and defamed a person.[27] French libel laws have permitted French politicians to sue publications rather frequently. Marine Le Pen, leader of France's National Front Party, a French nationalist party with strong anti-immigrant positions, sued philosopher Bernard-Henri Levy due to his statements in a newspaper linking her nationalist positions to an assault on three young Jews in France in 2012.[28] French politicians even sue each other. For good measure, then-candidate, now-French President Emmanuel Macron filed a defamation lawsuit against Le Pen for suggesting he had a secret offshore bank account shortly before the presidential election in 2017.[29] French hero Charles De Gaulle brought 350 defamation suits against the media in nine years of his presidency.[30] In the United Kingdom as well there is a greater concentration on the importance of not damaging someone's dignity or reputation in reporting. Consequently, members of the media, book authors, or movie makers are frequently sued in the United Kingdom for defamation or libel, and they often lose.[31]

To Americans, such legal focus on the media's and politicians' accuracy in order to avoid punishment for defamation would seem bizarre given the vitriolic attacks that politicians hurl at each other in American elections or on Twitter and the extraordinary if not conspiracy theoretical things that editorial writers or cable news use to challenge politicians. Legal accuracy and penalties for not telling the truth in political campaigns also seem peculiar to Americans. In *Trump v. Hawaii* (2018), the Supreme Court itself said it did not have to consider the truthfulness or accuracy of presidential statements.[32] Such large distinctions in the protection of the American media compared to other democracies' media affects the overall freedom to report forcefully on political or public figures. Where being wrong in reporting or damaging someone's reputation may keep the press from openly reporting on political figures, this has a substantial effect on how much information the public may have on politicians. Granted, the information may be wrong and may damage someone's reputation in the United States where it would not elsewhere. But it also provides a more vigorous check due to the freedom in the pursuit of a story by American media.

Freedom of Religion: Establishment of Religion

Most European and commonwealth democracies have had substantial downturns in the number of people who are religious. Meanwhile, the religiosity of Americans remains very high. As Box 5.2 demonstrated, the American people and courts have often struggled when dealing with the entanglement of politics and religion. Supreme Court cases have dealt with whether states or the government favored particular religions, and in doing so, infringed on the free exercise of others' religions or forced religious beliefs on nonbelievers. In most of these cases, the constitutionality falls on protecting individuals' religious beliefs rather than preservation of the public order. In rare cases, the common good outweighs religious practice, but this is not common. For example, the Supreme Court found that the free exercise of two Oregonian Native Americans' religious beliefs to smoke peyote did not outweigh the state of Oregon's drug laws because the law was not written to curtail religious practice even if it had this effect.[33] Typically, individuals' religious beliefs trump social restrictions.

Therefore, it would be implausible to picture a staff member or professor at an American public university demanding that a female Muslim student remove a hijab (head scarf) or burqa (face cover). Indeed, fellow students would likely object to a state official infringing on an individual student's religious practice. Yet in France, since 2004, women are not allowed to wear any face veils in public universities or schools. Crosses, turbans, and yarmulkes were also banned. A broader ban outlawed full-face veils favored by many Muslim women since 2010.[34] Similar laws limiting wearing of these veils in public places have been adopted in Belgium and the Netherlands, and many German states have banned teachers from wearing religious veils on their heads or faces.[35] The banning of the Muslim headscarf was justified because France is constitutionally a secular country, and it has constitutional protections for secular values and gender equality.[36] So the social norms outweighed the individual religious rights of French Muslim women.

In addition to the First Amendment examples, the rights of the accused are far more extensive in the United States than other democracies. For example, some democracies have majority verdicts rather than unanimous verdicts to establish guilt. While many democracies ensure that defendants do not have to testify in their own defense, some allow the judge or jury to consider that lack of testimony in their decision of guilt.[37] As discussed in Chapter 7, judges in other democracies are most frequently not neutral constitutional actors as in the United States but tend to work in a three-judge panel that investigates, interrogates, and often either directly decides guilt or innocence or deliberates directly with a jury on such decisions.[38] The court can admit voluntary confessions even if defendants were not cautioned of their rights, and illegally seized evidence may be considered as well.[39] All of these show how the individual liberty protections against government encroachment outweigh the common good in the United States, where the individual liberty would have far less relative weight in other democracies.

CIVIL RIGHTS IN PRACTICE

Concerning civil rights, many democracies explicitly spell out what rights they will protect for citizens in their constitutions. These may include government assurance that they will protect the rights of racial or ethnic groups, social security and economic rights, rights to health care and medicine, right to dignity, environmental rights, and so on. These civil rights—or positive rights—oblige the government to act to protect citizens' rights when dealing with government agencies (including regional and local governments), corporations, and social groups.

The United States does not even have an affirmative expression of core rights we associate with democracy, like an explicitly written right to vote. The Equal Rights Amendment attempts to grant equal rights based on sex in the United States, but as discussed in Chapter 6, has not yet been ratified. Public schools are

Table 5.1   Positive Civil Rights in Other Democracies: Employment and Labor Rights

Constitution of the Italian Republic Article 32	The Republic protects work in all its forms and practices. It provides for the training and professional advancement of workers. It promotes and encourages international agreements and organizations which have the aim of establishing and regulating labor rights. . . . and protects Italian workers abroad.
Denmark Section 75	In order to advance the public weal efforts should be made to afford work to every able-bodied citizen on terms that will secure his existence.
France, Preamble to Constitution of 1946	Each person has the duty to work and the right to employment. No person may suffer prejudice in his work or employment by virtue of his origins, opinions or beliefs.
Constitution of Spain Section 35	All Spaniards have the duty to work and the right to work, to the free choice of profession or trade, to advancement through work, and to a sufficient remuneration for the satisfaction of their needs and those of their families.
France, Preamble to Constitution of 1946	All men may defend their rights and interests through union action and may belong to the union of their choice. All workers shall, through the intermediary of their representatives, participate in the collective determination of their conditions of work and in the management of the work place
German Basic Law Article 9 (3)	The right to form associations to safeguard and improve working and economic conditions shall be guaranteed to every individual and to every occupation or profession. Agreements that restrict or seek to impair this right shall be null and void; measures directed to this end shall be unlawful.
Constitution of Spain	Trade unions and employers' associations contribute to the defense and promotion of the economic and social interests which they represent. Their creation and the exercise of their activities shall be free in so far as they respect the Constitution and the law.

(Continued)

Table 5.1 (Continued)	
Constitution of Japan Article 27 & 28	All people shall have the right and the obligation to work. Standards for wages, hours, rest and other working conditions shall be fixed by law. Children shall not be exploited. The right of workers to organize and to bargain and act collectively is guaranteed.

not constitutionally mandated to provide equal funding according to the Supreme Court because there is no fundamental right to education in the U.S. Constitution.[40] The United States certainly has no statement about providing economic rights or protecting citizens' social security, economic welfare, labor rights, or environmental rights as are detailed in other democracies' constitutions.

Table 5.1 lists the constitutional protections for work and labor laws in a few sampled democracies. The American Constitution says nothing about work, wages, or the assurance to be able to collectively bargain. Indeed, the Supreme Court recently weakened public sector unions in *Janus v. AFSCME* (2018). While other countries protect union membership in their constitutions, it would be hard to imagine an individualistic political culture like the United States' would want a constitution to force the government to get deeply involved in private-sector hiring relationships, even if one supports labor union advocacy and collective bargaining rights.

Most democracies also explicitly ensure healthcare and social welfare rights in constitutions (see Table 5.2). Chapter 4 highlighted how Americans value equality less than other democracies, particularly equality of outcome. It also showed how this leads to very different social policies as well as social inequality. Those findings are closely connected to the values of citizens who both want those policies but also want a constitutional system that demands that their government provide such policies. The United States does have social welfare programming and the Affordable Care Act, also known as Obamacare, which extended healthcare insurance to millions of Americans who had not previously had it. Yet, both sets of policies, social welfare programs and Obamacare, have been cut back with Republican control of Congress and with President Trump's election. Other democracies' constitutions oblige their governments to provide such programs due to citizens' rights.

Finally, Table 5.3 lists environmental rights from a sample of other democracies' constitutions. While many Americans view environmental protection as a human right, it is not a positive constitutional right. Further, many opponents of environmental regulations believe such regulations take from their property rights or their freedoms generally.

Taking Tables 5.1, 5.2, and 5.3 together, it is clear that other democracies constitutionally require their governments to pursue many policies to satisfy positive rights that most Americans would likely not consider constitutional rights.

France, Preamble to Constitution of 1946	It shall guarantee to all, notably to children, mothers and elderly workers, protection of their health, material security, rest and leisure.
Constitution of the Italian Republic Article 32	The Republic safeguards health as a fundamental right of the individual and as a collective interest, and guarantees free medical care to the indigent.
Constitution of the Netherlands Art 22	The authorities shall take steps to promote the health of the population.
Constitution of Spain Section 43	It is incumbent upon the public authorities to organize and watch over public health by means of preventive measures and the necessary benefits and services. The law shall establish the rights and duties of all in this respect.
Constitution of the Italian Republic Art. 38	Every citizen unable to work and without the necessary means of subsistence is entitled to welfare support.
France, Preamble to Constitution of 1946	All people who, by virtue of their age, physical or mental condition, or economic situation, are incapable of working, shall have to the right to receive suitable means of existence from society.
Denmark Section 75 (2)	Any person unable to support himself or his dependents shall, where no other person is responsible for his or their maintenance, be entitled to receive public assistance, provided that he shall comply with the obligations imposed by Statute in such respect.
Constitution of the Netherlands Article 20; (1, 3)	It shall be the concern of the authorities to secure the means of subsistence of the population and to achieve the distribution of wealth. Dutch nationals resident in the Netherlands who are unable to provide for themselves shall have a right, to be regulated by Act of Parliament, to aid from the authorities.

(Continued)

Table 5.2 (Continued)

Constitution of Spain Sections 40; 47	The public authorities shall guarantee, through adequate and periodically updated pensions, a sufficient income for citizens in old age. Likewise, and without prejudice to the obligations of the families, they shall promote their welfare through a system of social services that provides for their specific problems of health, housing, culture and leisure The public authorities shall maintain a public Social Security system for all citizens guaranteeing adequate social assistance and benefits in situations of hardship, especially in case of unemployment. All Spaniards have the right to enjoy decent and adequate housing.
Constitution of Japan Article 25	All people shall have the right to maintain the minimum standards of wholesome and cultured living. In all spheres of life, the State shall use its endeavors for the promotion and extension of social welfare and security, and of public health.

Other democracies' constitutions even provide data protection rights of citizens. Americans have not always been entirely opposed to providing some positive rights. President Franklin D. Roosevelt proposed a Second Bill of Rights in his 1944 State of the Union address, where he claimed that because the United States lacked many economic rights, the nation lacked sufficient political rights of equality and the pursuit of happiness. As a result, he laid out many rights that should be in a Second Bill of Rights such as work, adequate food and housing, medical care, and education.[41] In fact, his proposal sounds considerably like other democracies' constitutions. These changes to the Constitution never moved forward, and even in the heyday of the New Deal system, it would be difficult to imagine such a stark constitutional shift toward positive rights occurring. There were expansions of other civil rights for race, gender, national origin, and for workers as well as environmental regulation in the 1960s and 1970s. But these expansions were during one Supreme Court period, and many were rolled back later.[42]

The expressly written civil rights in the U.S. Constitution are narrow and date from specific historical moments. The Thirteenth Amendment prohibits slavery, and the Fifteenth Amendment prohibits the denial of voting based on race. The Nineteenth Amendment prohibits the denial of voting based on sex, and the Twenty-Sixth Amendment prohibits the denial of voting to those eighteen or older. These are the sole distinctions on race, gender, age, or other social stratification that compels the government to protect against discrimination. Importantly, the Fourteenth Amendment mandates that no state can "deprive any person of life, liberty or property, without due process of law; *nor deny to any person within its*

Table 5.3 Positive Civil Rights in Other Democracies: Environmental and Data Privacy Rights

France Charter for the Environment, Constitution of 1958 (revised 2008)	Each person has the right to live in a balanced environment which shows due respect for health. Each person has a duty to participate in preserving and enhancing the environment. Each person shall, in the conditions provided for by law, foresee and avoid the occurrence of any damage which he or she may cause to the environment or, failing that, limit the consequences of such damage. Each person shall be required, in the conditions provided for by law, to contribute to the making good of any damage he or she may have caused to the environment.
Constitution of the Netherlands Article 21	It shall be the concern of the authorities to keep the country habitable and to protect and improve the environment
Constitution of Spain Section 45	Everyone has the right to enjoy an environment suitable for the development of the person, as well as the duty to preserve it. The public authorities shall watch over a rational use of all natural resources with a view to protecting and improving the quality of life and preserving and restoring the environment, by relying on an indispensable collective solidarity.

jurisdiction the equal protections of the law" (our emphasis added). These are expressly stated positive civil rights, but they do not provide an entirely explicit set of what equal protection means and interpretation has been left up to the Supreme Court.

The Supreme Court relies on other actors to bring cases forward before action is taken. Further, the Supreme Court only really actively considers *some* cases of discrimination depending on who is affected by the discrimination. When a law discriminates—or treats people differently—the Supreme Court is likely to consider the constitutionality of such discrimination when the people affected are in a **suspect classification**. The term ironically comes from the decision in *Korematsu v. United States*, where the court rejected the civil rights of a Japanese American against being detained with other Japanese nationals and Japanese Americans during World War II. In the case, the Supreme Court wrote, "It should be noted, to begin with, that all legal restrictions which curtail the civil rights of a single racial group are immediately suspect. That is not to say that all such restrictions are unconstitutional. It is to say that courts must subject them to the most rigid scrutiny."[43] Regarding this last point, rigid scrutiny is a heightened scrutiny the court gives to some discrimination.

The hierarchy of scrutiny the Supreme Court will give to laws that treat people differently depends on who is affected by the laws. **Strict scrutiny** is the highest level of review, meaning the Supreme Court will study the laws very closely when it affects people differently based on *race, national origin, religion, and (in some cases) alienage (citizen vs. noncitizen status)*. The test of constitutionality in these cases is whether the state can prove there is a **compelling state interest** in discrimination for it to be constitutional.

A notch below strict scrutiny, the Supreme Court will bring an **intermediate standard of review** to laws or actions that treat men and women differently. For such laws to be constitutional, the government has to demonstrate that it is an **important state interest** but not compelling for the law to treat people differently based on sex. Finally, the **rational basis scrutiny** affects other classes of people being treated in society, which means that there is a rational reason—rather than a compelling or important reason—for the government treating people differently. Of note, the Supreme Court has become more attentive and scrutinized laws based on age discrimination and discrimination against homosexuals (gay marriage, for instance) in recent years.

The lack of expression of positive rights and the need for the Supreme Court to interpret equal protection from the Fourteenth Amendment—and develop standards of interpretation of suspect and nonsuspect classes of people—has meant that actually protecting civil rights has taken considerable time. Discrimination in the private sector is not addressed by the equal protection clause in the Fourteenth Amendment, because it states that "No *State* shall . . . deny to any persons within its jurisdiction the equal protection of the laws." [44] That does not mean companies and private institutions can simply discriminate against others based on race, national origin, gender, age, or so on because Title VII of the Civil Rights Act of 1964 "makes it illegal to discriminate against someone on the basis of race, color, religion, national origin, or sex."[45] Subsequent civil rights legislation has also protected Americans with disabilities, pregnancy, age, and genetic information.[46] While these laws protect private sector civil rights, this does not mean they are constitutionally protected. The laws could be changed tomorrow, and the executive branch, which is given the power to execute this law, may not be as proactive in its execution For civil rights protections of race, color, national origin, religion, and sex discrimination in private sector employment in the United States, the **Equal Employment Opportunity Commission** (EEOC) is empowered to investigate claims of discrimination.[47] Studies have shown that the EEOC has pursued civil rights protections more aggressively under Democratic presidential administrations than Republican presidential administrations.[48]

Beyond employment and civil rights protections, other positive rights guaranteed in other countries' constitutions are left to other executive branch departments, agencies, or commissions in the United States. Courts cannot proactively force the executive branch to say that someone's rights are being injured. This means that executive agencies often have to take charge to protect rights. For example. the Environmental Protection Agency can force companies who pollute to stop or to even clean up damaged environments. Also, the Securities and Exchange Commission can bring suits against investment or insurance companies, and the fines that result go to the injured. The Consumer Financial Protection Bureau Safety compensates consumers injured by an action by a company. The National Highway Traffic Safety Administration can bring cases of dangerous vehicles or parts to the courts to win civil penalties against companies that have injured people. The Social Security Administration can make decisions on worker disability, and state-level agencies that deal with unemployment decide eligibility for unemployment insurance pay. It is up to Congress or state legislatures to write legislation for investors, consumers, drivers, disabled workers, or the unemployed, and it is up to the discretion of these executive agencies to interpret the execution of such laws. Thus, the lack of constitutionally expressed civil rights in the U.S. Constitution, relative to other democracies' constitutions, means that evaluation of when the government should proactively protect positive civil rights remains connected to political decisions rather than constitutional decisions.

Finally, even when positive rights have been pursued by the U.S. government, these often are limited to the public sector rather than private sector. For example, affirmative action programs have tended to concentrate on hiring in government agencies at federal, state, and local levels, as well as to public-sector contracts and university admissions. There is no legislation to compel the private sector to implement affirmative action hiring, contracting, or other actions. As far as race, national origin, gender, and age, the Supreme Court has frequently ruled that the United States has a compelling state interest in diversity in education, in particular for affirmative action programs to exist, but the court often finds the mechanisms to bring about such affirmative action programs unconstitutional in practice. Universities cannot bring diversity—a compelling state interest— through quota systems or points systems. Certainly, corporations may have such programs in the interest of diversity, but the EEOC is meant to evaluate when corporations or institutions are violating racial, gender, age, disability, national origin, pregnancy, and other classes of people, not to evaluate whether they are proactively making corporate hiring or contracting decisions.

International Law and Civil Rights

A final influential component of civil rights protections in societies comes from the pressures from international human rights law on domestic constitutional civil rights protections. The European Union's (EU) European Convention on Human Rights has had enormous influence on national governments' civil rights. To be in compliance with EU rights, many member states have shifted their domestic constitutional protections to match the higher EU standards. The United Nations'

Universal Declaration of Human Rights has also effectively pressured democracies to make positive rights fit broader international rights since 1948. Many democracies have explicit statements in their constitutions to evaluate or even to adopt international norms of positive rights into their constitutions. The United States often does not ratify human rights documents that could pressure it to ensure more positive rights.[49]

CONCLUSION

This chapter explained the similarities and differences among the civil liberties and rights in the United States and other democracies. The United States provides more negative rights and fewer positive rights compared to other democracies. In other words, the United States protects civil liberties from government interference more extensively than it extends its power to protect citizens' rights from others who may violate their rights in society.

The main reasons for this go back to American exceptionalism and the individual political cultural ideals Americans hold relative to other democracies' more communitarian political cultural beliefs. Relatedly, the timing of the adoption of constitutions affects the constitution's generation of positive rights. The U.S. Constitution is first-generation rights, which are strictly negative rights (civil liberties). The second-generation rights are the social welfare, healthcare, and economic rights that arose in the twentieth century. Third generation rights include environmental rights and human dignity rights, typically included in post–Cold War constitutions.

POINTS TO REMEMBER

- All democracies provide citizens core civil liberties, which are negative rights, meaning the government cannot take them away from citizens except in substantial conditions.

- Civil rights are citizen rights that governments proactively protect from infringement by regional governments, institutions, employers, or social groups. Because they require government action, they are known as positive rights.

- The social contract, political cultural beliefs of individualism, and American exceptionalism have led to more civil liberties protections and fewer civil rights protections for Americans relative to other democracies.

- The timing of the American Constitution has meant that the Constitution provides substantial negative rights—or civil liberties—because of the time of its writing in the first generation of rights. Other democracies' constitutions were written in the second or third generation of rights, which means they provide more positive rights such as economic, social welfare, and environmental rights.

- When there is a question of constitutionality, the Supreme Court decides the constitutionality of American civil liberties and American civil rights due to its power of judicial review. The Supreme Court has expanded many civil liberty protections for American citizens through the incorporation of the Bill of Rights to states and localities through the Fourteenth Amendment. The Supreme Court has not expanded civil rights consistently or as much because it relies on other actors to brings civil rights cases to the court.

- Other democracies' legislatures or other political actors have political constitutionality—that is they have sovereign authority to pass legislation affecting positive or negative rights.

- Other democracies provide more proportionality in their constitutions This leaves the Supreme Court to interpret liberties and rights and set precedence on the relative positive and negative rights for Americans.

- Some countries adopt civil rights protections from international human rights conventions and documents. The United States has not signed on to many of these and resists adopting positive rights from international conventions on human rights.

KEY TERMS

Bill of Rights 87
Civil liberties 80
Civil rights 80
Civil society 80
Clear and Present Danger 88
Compelling state interest 100
Equal Employment Opportunity Commission 100
First generation rights 83

Fourteenth Amendment 90
Important state interest 100
Incorporation 90
Intermediate standard of review 100
Judicial review 84
Lemon Test 89
Negative rights 80
Parliamentary Sovereignty 84

Political constitutionalism 84
Positive rights 80
Precedence 87
Proportionality 85
Rational basis scrutiny 100
Second generation rights 83
Strict Scrutiny 100
Suspect Classification 99
Third generation rights 84

REVIEW QUESTIONS

1. What are the differences between civil liberties and civil rights?

2. How do positive rights and negative rights relate to civil liberties and civil rights?

3. Why does the United States have differing levels of civil liberties and civil rights compared to other democracies?

4. What are the different generations of rights? What does this mean for democratic rights and liberties?

5. How are other democracies' constitutions more proportional than the U.S. Constitution? How does that affect rights and liberties?

6. What institutional limitations does the Supreme Court face that limit the provision of positive civil rights for American citizens? What other actors play a vital role in defining American civil rights?

7. Discuss why suspect classification and levels of standards of constitutional review limit the extension of civil rights.

SUGGESTED READINGS

Gardbaum, Stephen. "The Structure and Scope of Constitutional Rights." In *Comparative Constitutional Law*, edited by Tom Ginsburg and Rosalind Dixon. Cheltenham, UK: Edward Elgar, 2013

Glendon, Mary Ann. "Rights in Twentieth-Century Constitutions." *University of Chicago Law Review*, Vol. 59, 1 (1992).

Kramer, Daniel. *Comparative Civil Rights and Liberties*. Lanham, MD: University Press of America, 1982

Sunstein, Cass. "Why Does the American Constitution Lack Social and Economic Guarantees?" *University of Chicago Public Law and Legal Theory Working Paper* no. 36 (2003).

Tushnet, Mark. *Weak Courts, Strong Rights: Judicial Review and Social Welfare Rights in Comparative Constitutional Law*. Princeton: Princeton University Press, 2008

Tushnet, Mark. *Advanced Introduction to Comparative Constitutional Law*. Cheltenham, UK: Edward Elgar, 2014, 72.

NOTES

1. David Barnum, "Freedom of Assembly and the Hostile Audience in Anglo-American Law," *The American Journal of Comparative Law*, 29, 1 (1981): 59–96.

2. Daniel Kramer, *Comparative Civil Rights and Liberties* (Lanham, MD: University Press of America, 1982) 37–38.

3. Mary Ann Glendon, "Rights in Twentieth-Century Constitutions," *University of Chicago Law Review*, 59, 1 (1992): 523. Glendon refers to the "basic inventory" of rights established by Franz Wieacker, "Foundations of European Legal Culture," *The American Journal of Comparative Law*, 38, 1 (1990).

4. Stephen Gardbaum, "The Structure and Scope of Constitutional Rights," in *Comparative Constitutional Law*, ed. Tom Ginsburg and Rosalind Dixon (Cheltenham, UK: Edward Elgar, 2013); Mark Tushnet, *Weak Courts, Strong Rights: Judicial Review and Social Welfare Rights in Comparative Constitutional Law* (Princeton: Princeton University Press, 2008), iv–17; Mark Tushnet, *Advanced Introduction to Comparative Constitutional Law* (Cheltenham, UK: Edward Elgar, 2015), 63–69; Cass Sunstein, "Why Does the American Constitution Lack Social and Economic Guarantees?," *University of Chicago Public Law and Legal Theory Working Paper* no. 36, 2003.

5. Stephen Gardbaum, "The Structure and Scope of Constitutional Rights," 388.

6. Stephen Gardbaum, "The Structure and Scope of Constitutional Rights."; Mark Tushnet, *Weak Courts, Strong Rights*; Mark Tushnet, *Advanced Introduction to Comparative Constitutional Law*, 63–69; Cass Sunstein, "Why Does the American Constitution Lack Social and Economic Guarantees?"

7. Mary Ann Glendon, "Rights in Twentieth-Century Constitutions," 524.

8. Mark Kende, "The South African Constitutional Court's Embrace of Socio-Economic Rights: A Comparative Perspective," *Chapman Law Review*, 123 (2003); Mark Tushnet, *Weak Courts*, iv–17; Mark Tushnet, *Advanced Introduction to Comparative Constitutional Law*, 63–69; Cass Sunstein, "Why Does the American Constitution Lack Social and Economic Guarantees?"; Stephen Gardbaum, "The Structure and Scope of Constitutional Rights."

9. Mark Tushnet, *Advanced Introduction to Comparative Constitutional Law*, 44–45.

10. Tushnet, *Advanced Introduction to Comparative Constitutional Law*, 44–45.

11. Seymour Martin Lipset, *American Exceptionalism: A Double-Edged Sword* (New York, NY: W. W. Norton, 1997).

12. Stephen Gardbaum, "The Structure and Scope of Constitutional Rights," 390.

13. Mark Tushnet, *Advanced Introduction to Comparative Constitutional Law*, 72.

14. Stephen Gardbaum, "The Structure and Scope of Constitutional Rights"; Mark Tushnet, *Weak Courts*, iv–17; Mark Tushnet, *Advanced Introduction to Comparative Constitutional Law*, 63–69.

15. Stephen Gardbaum, "The Structure and Scope of Constitutional Rights," 389.

16. Trevor Timm, "It's Time to Stop Using the 'Fire in a Crowded Theater' Quote," *The Atlantic*, November 12, 2012; Eugene Volokh, "Shouting Fire in a Crowded Theater," *The Washington Post*, May 11, 2015.

17. *Brandenburg v. Ohio* transcript, "Landmark Cases," C-SPAN, http://landmarkcases.c-span.org/Case/23/Brandenburg-v-Ohio, accessed July 1, 2018.

18. *Lemon v. Kurtzman* transcript, Justia U.S. Supreme Court, https://supreme.justia.com/cases/federal/us/403/602/case.html, accessed July 1, 2018.

19. David Jesse, "MSU Sued by Richard Spencer's White Supremacist Group for Refusing Space on Campus," *Detroit Free Press*, September 3, 2017, https://www.freep.com/story/news/local/michigan/2017/09/03/msu-sued-richard-spencers-white-supremacist-group-refusing-space-campus/630355001.

20. Thomas Gounley, "Neighbors Never Saw Her, But Buffalo Woman Arrested by FBI Was 'Well-known in the ISIS Twitter Scene," *Springfield* (Missouri) *News-Leader*, February 25, 2016, https://www.news-leader.com/story/news/crime/2016/02/25/safya-roe-yassin-well-known-isis-twitter-scene-fbi-arrested-buffalo-missouri-terrorism-woman/80621154.

21. Krishnadev Calamur, "Controversial French Comedian Arrested over Facebook Post on Paris Attacks," *National Public Radio*, January 14, 2015, https://www.npr.org/sections/thetwo-way/2015/01/14/377201227/controversial-french-comedian-arrested-over-facebook-post-on-paris-attacks.

22. Kashmira Gander, "ISIS Crisis: Islamic State Banned in Germany," *The Independent*, September 12, 2014, https://www.independent.co.uk/news/world/europe/isis-crisis-islamic-state-banned-in-germany-9730289.html.

23. Daniel Kramer, *Comparative Civil Rights and Liberties*.

24. Kramer, *Comparative Civil Rights and Liberties*.

25. Kramer, *Comparative Civil Rights and Liberties*.

26. Roy Gutterman, "The Landmark Libel Case, *Times v. Sullivan*, Still Resonates 50 Years Later," *Forbes*, March 5, 2014, https://www.forbes.com/sites/realspin/2014/03/05/the-landmark-libel-case-times-v-sullivan-still-resonates-50-years-later/#25853d5f585a.

27. Dominique Mondoloni, "Legal Divisions: French versus English Libel Laws," *X Index on Censorship*, Sage Journals, June 11, 2014, http://journals.sagepub.com/doi/full/10.1177/0306422014537174.

28. Sara Yasin, "French Politician Marine Le Pen Sues Writer for Libel," *X Index*, June 11, 2012, http://www.indexoncensorship.org/2012/06/french-politician -marine-le-pen-sues-writer-for-libel.

29. Sam Meredith, "France's Macron Takes Legal Action over Le Pen 'Defamation' Debate Days before Elections," *CNBC*, May 5, 2017, https://www.cnbc .com/2017/05/05/macron-le-pen-france-election-debate-fake-news-legal-action -bank-bahamas.html.

30. Daniel Kramer, *Comparative Civil Rights and Liberties*, 86.

31. Ari Shapiro, "On Libel and the Law, U.S. and U.K. Go Separate Ways," *Weekend Edition Saturday, National Public Radio*, March 21, 2015, https://www.npr.org/ sections/parallels/2015/03/21/394273902/on-libel-and-the-law-u-s-and-u-k-go -separate-ways.

32. Supreme Court of the United States, *Trump v. Hawaii*, No. 17-965, https://www .supremecourt.gov/opinions/17pdf/17-965_h315.pdf, accessed July 8, 2018.

33. Pew Research Center, "The Smith Decision," *Pew Research Center Religion & Public Life*, October 24, 2007, http://www.pewforum.org/2007/10/24/a-delicate -balance6.

34. Matthew Weaver, "Burqa Bans, Headscarves and Veils: A Timeline of Legislation in the West," *The Guardian*, May 31, 2018, https://www.theguardian.com/ world/2017/mar/14/headscarves-and-muslim-veil-ban-debate-timeline.

35. Weaver, "Burqa Bans."

36. Angelique Chrisafis, "Nicolas Sarkozy Says Islamic Veils Are Not Welcome in France," *The Guardian*, June 22, 2009, https://www.theguardian.com/ world/2009/jun/22/islamic-veils-sarkozy-speech-france.

37. Daniel Kramer, *Comparative Civil Rights and Liberties*, 239, 261.

38. Kramer, *Comparative Civil Rights and Liberties*, 266.

39. Kramer, *Comparative Civil Rights and Liberties*, 237–239.

40. "*San Antonio Independent School District v. Rodriguez* (1973)," Oyez, https://www .oyez.org/cases/1972/71-1332, accessed July 1, 2018.

41. Franklin Roosevelt, "State of the Union Message to Congress," January 11, 1944, *Franklin D. Roosevelt Presidential Library*, http://www.fdrlibrary.marist.edu/ archives/address_text.html.

42. Cass Sunstein, "Why Does the American Constitution Lack Social and Economic Guarantees?"

43. *Korematsu v. United States* decision, *Legal Information Institute*, Cornell Law School, https://www.law.cornell.edu/supremecourt/text/323/214#writing-ZS, accessed July 4, 2018.

44. Lenora Lapidus, Emily Martin, and Namita Luthra, *The Rights of Women: The Authoritative ACLU Guide to Women's Rights* (New York: NYU Press, 2009), 1–3.

45. U.S. Equal Employment Opportunity Commission, "Laws Enforced by the EEOC," https://www.eeoc.gov/laws/statutes/index.cfm, accessed July 2018.

46. EEOC, "Laws Enforced by the EEOC."

47. EEOC, "Laws Enforced by the EEOC."

48. B. Dan Wood, "Does Politics Make a Difference at the EEOC?" *American Journal of Political Science*, 43, 2 (1990): 503–530.

49. Mary Ann Glendon, "Rights in Twentieth-Century Constitutions," 526.

CHAPTER SIX

CONSTITUTIONAL ARRANGEMENTS

I magine a dusty room in Philadelphia, with members from the infant American government and Revolutionary War leaders in attendance. Their country was on the verge of collapse. The Articles of Confederation were not working, and a new constitution needed to be drafted. The framers had many options. The majority, known as "Federalists," put forth what was known as the Virginia Plan. This was a plan that laid out a constitutional government based on proportional representation among the states by population. That is, each state would be represented in a governing body by representatives, and the number of these representatives would be based on the population of the state. The "old patriots" had different ideas. They advocated what is known as the New Jersey Plan, a constitution that was motivated by a strict adherence to federalism and allowed each state to have equal representation. There was deadlock. In what is known as the Connecticut Compromise, the framers worked out a plan that gave us the constitution we know today and allowed both ideas to work together. (We'll see the Federalist ideas in the House of Representatives and the Anti-Federalists in the Senate in Chapter 7). While the Connecticut Compromise solved one of the largest problems, other controversies arose over slavery and including rights in the main, original document. Eventually, a constitution was drafted and went to the states for ratification. Some states refused to ratify because the Constitution did not talk about rights. They were afraid the new government could end in tyranny. It was agreed that the Bill of Rights would be taken up immediately by the First Congress under the new constitution, allowing ratification to proceed.

The U.S. Constitution born of this compromise in 1787 is the backbone of American democracy. It has been amended only twenty-seven times in the 230 years it has been in existence. One of these times was to outlaw slavery, an issue debated since its inception and settled by a bloody war. Five amendments provided voting rights to African Americans, women, and eighteen-year-olds; Electoral College votes to Washington, DC; and nondenial of voting rights for not paying poll or other taxes. Four amendments deal with the election or succession of presidents, another for the direct election of Senators, another permits the income tax, and yet another considers congressional pay raises. Two amendments cancel each other out due to Prohibition and then the reinstatement of alcohol rights.

This leaves a couple amendments dealing with the extension of federal civil liberties to states (discussed in Chapter 5) and judicial powers that were added to the first ten amendments in the Bill of Rights. Thus, very few substantive constitutional changes have occurred since 1789. By comparison, the German constitution (known as the **Basic Law**), mainly written by the Allies and put in place in 1949 after World War II has been amended 50 times. When Germany unified East and West in 1990, there was talk of drafting a brand new constitution. This idea was thrown out, however, in favor simply revising the Basic Law to incorporate the East into the West.

A country's constitution is the blueprint for how to run the government. Just as blueprints tell builders where to place a bathroom or how large to make a walk-in closet, a constitution tells lawmakers and citizens who gets what, why, and how in politics. Thus, a **constitution** is a body of fundamental principles and precedents according to which a state is governed. It defines citizen rights as well as the institutions of government. Not all democratic constitutions are the same, and the variation is stark. Some of these consequences of constitutional variation we've talked about in other chapters—like positive rights, protection of liberties, and judicial review. In this chapter, we focus on three main nuts-and-bolts ways in which the U.S. Constitution is exceptional—longevity, its degree of majoritarianism, and its vertical organization of power.

No single constitutional element trumps others. Instead, a democracy's institutions must match the nature of a country's society and political culture. If democracy was a "one-size-fits-all" approach, when the United States spent most of the 2000s and early 2010s trying to build democracies in Iraq and Afghanistan, why wouldn't the United States just have set up carbon copies of its own institutions in these countries? Why didn't the United States set up constitutional arrangements in Japan or Germany after World War II that mirrored what we see in the United States? After all, the arrangement in the United States has worked fairly well for over 200 years. Very few people would suggest that the political cultures, or the nature of society in Iraq and Afghanistan or Germany and Japan, were anything like the United States—or each other for that matter—so simply transferring democratic institutions from one context to another will not ensure success elsewhere. In fact, political observers and maybe even this book's readers would chuckle at the notion that democratic institutions could be interchangeable.

CONSTITUTIONAL ARRANGEMENT: CONSTITUTIONAL LONGEVITY

The United States' Constitution has been in place since its ratification in 1788. It is the oldest constitution in the world still in use today. While it has been modified through amendments (see Chapter 5 for a discussion of the Bill of Rights, the first ten amendments to the U.S. Constitution negotiated during the Constitutional

Convention), the first three articles, laying out the legislative, executive, and judicial branches, respectively, remain in force today. Article IV of the U.S. Constitution governs the relationship between states and the central government, establishing a system of federalism as discussed later in the chapter. The framers, knowing that a constitution likely would need updating in the future, included Article V to allow for the U.S. Constitution to be amended and a new constitutional convention called. (This has not been used, although there are statewide movements to call for a new convention). Article VI sets forth the Constitution as the law of the land, and Article VII refers to ratification. More than 230 years later, these seven articles have remained the backbone of the U.S government.

Thus, we would refer to the U.S. Constitution as **rigid** and not flexible. It is difficult and arduous to change the Constitution. An amendment may be proposed either by the Congress with a two-thirds vote in both the House of Representatives and the Senate or by a convention of states called for by two-thirds of the state legislatures. The last amendment to the U.S. Constitution was the Twenty-Seventh Amendment in 1992, which requires any change to the rate of compensation for members of the U.S. Congress to take effect only after the subsequent election in the House of Representatives. In other words, Congress can't vote a raise for itself, only subsequent Congresses. Some hope that the Equal Rights Amendment (ERA), which would constitutionally codify women's equality with men, will be the Twenty-Eighth Amendment. The ERA was passed by Congress in 1972 and sent to the states for ratification. Currently, the ERA has been ratified by thirty-five states but has been stalled for over twenty years. There is a new push as of 2018 to get three more states to ratify (resulting in three-fourths ratification). Alabama, Arizona, Arkansas, Florida, Georgia, Illinois, Louisiana, Mississippi, Missouri, Nevada, North Carolina, Oklahoma, South Carolina, Utah and Virginia have yet to ratify. Five states—Nebraska, Tennessee, Idaho, Kentucky, and South Dakota—originally ratified but voted to rescind their ratifications. Since Article V only talks about making an amendment and not rescinding, this likely does not hold legally.

Students may think that the statute of limitations has run out on the ERA as it has been over forty-five years since it was originally introduced. While the Fifth Amendment lays out the process for amending the U.S. Constitution, it says nothing about time limits. Two court cases, *Dillon vs. Gloss* and *Coleman vs. Miller* ruled that ratification must happen in a reasonable time and affirmed Congress's right to affix a time limit for ratification of amendments. The Eighteenth Amendment, prohibition, was fixed with a seven-year time limit, but the Nineteenth Amendment, women's suffrage, went forward with no time limit. The seven-year limit was placed in the Twentieth, Twenty-First, and Twenty-Second Amendments but was not found in the Twenty-Third, Twenty-Fourth, Twenty-Fifth, and Twenty-Sixth Amendments. The Twenty-Seventh Amendment certainly did not have a time limit attached to it as it was proposed in 1789 and ratified in 1992! Thus, even if the ERA were to be ratified fifty years after it was proposed, it would still be constitutionally viable under Article V of the U.S. Constitution.

In contrast to the U.S. Constitution, France is on its fifth republic and has had fifteen constitutions since its first one in 1791. The most recent French constitution dates from 1958 and has been modified seventeen times. In fact, since 1791, the date of the first French constitution, France has been governed by five democratic republics with differing constitutional arrangements and multiple constitutions, two empires, three monarchies, a revolutionary government, and a fascist puppet state. The United States looks boring in comparison. France, however, is not an outlier. On average, democratic constitutions have lasted seventeen years since 1791.[1] This is a short life span considering constitutions ought to express guiding national principles, establish basic rules, and limit the power of government—things that you expect need longevity and stability. Most democracies' constitutions date from the 1800s when positions of monarchies were renegotiated to provide more democracy (Norway, Netherlands, Belgium, etc.), the post–World War II era (Germany, Japan, France), and in the 1970s after democratic transitions in the Iberian Peninsula (Portugal, Spain).

If the French constitutional system seems chaotic to readers of this book, then the British system is likely even more bizarre. This is because the British do not have a single written constitution. You can visit the U.S. Constitution in the rotunda of the National Archives building in Washington, DC and see with your own eyes John Hancock's John Hancock on the Declaration of Independence and the Constitution of the United States, but there is not one codified document the British can point to as their constitution. The Magna Carta was a broad charter of rights for the aristocracy from the crown 800 years ago that established a general sense of liberties but lacked any institutional definition. The British Constitution is the sum of laws and principles that make up the body politic of the nation and pulls from four sources. First, there is **statute law**, laws passed by the legislature (parliament). The concept of **parliamentary sovereignty**, that the parliament is supreme over other governmental institutions, has been in place in the U.K. since 1688. Second, there is **common law**, laws established through court judgments. Third are **parliamentary conventions**, or norms of behavior, which means that political actors know to stay in their lane and not overreach their authority. The final component is **works of authority**, which are writings by constitutional scholars. For example, the concept of the **rule of law**, the authority and influence of law in society, was introduced into the British constitution through the writings of Albert Ven Dicey in 1885. All of these elements create an integrated recognized constitutional culture even if it remains a literal unwritten rule.

CONSTITUTIONAL ARRANGEMENT: MAJORITARIAN AND CONSOCIATIONAL DEMOCRACIES

We mentioned in the introduction to this chapter that constitutions cannot just be transferred with name changes from one country to the next. When new democracies are forming, they can't just go grab a constitution off the shelf and call it good.

Why? If politics is about who gets what, when, and how, political institutions tend to be the mechanism through which governments make these decisions, and constitutions lay out how these institutions ought to be imagined. Particular institutions that may accomplish this for certain social and cultural conditions would fail miserably in other social settings and particularly in differing political cultures. The institutions also have to produce social order, ensure the citizenry's ability to drive government policy, decide the best way to produce the common good while protecting civil liberties, and do so meshing with that society's political culture. How the institutional design best produces this hinges on how diverse or homogenous a country's society is. Imagine we are building a house on two different lots. One lot is flat with little tree cover, and the second is a sloped at 45 degrees and covered in massive pine trees. Could we take a blueprint off of a shelf and build the same type of house on both lots? The answer is no; we would need to modify the blueprint to fit the lot. In the same way, we can't take a constitution off of a shelf (so to speak) to lay the foundation for democracy. The blueprint of democracy, the constitution, has to fit the country with which it is matched.

A country with a high level of ethnic, religious, linguistic, and regional **homogeneity**, or similarity, has an easier time keeping the political system and society unified. When decisions over who gets what, when, and how are made, they are unlikely to set off strong resistance because the outcome will not likely lead to great social division, so the governing institutions do not have to be designed as much to keep the peace as well as they do to decide who gets what. In societies with high ethnic, religious, linguistic, and regional diversity, governing institutions must both work out ways to decide who gets what, when, and how and also be designed to do so in ways that do not lead to particular ethnic, religious, linguistic, or regional groups feeling like the system is stacked against them.

One preeminent institutional scholar, Arend Lijphart (b. 1936–), classified democracies into two types, **majoritarian** and **consensus** (or **consociational**), based upon the predominant institutional configurations codified in the institutional designs.[2] Those institutional designs stem from the diversity of the society and are typically codified in constitutions. Each type—majoritarian and consensus—is an **ideal type**, meaning that no country perfectly embodies majoritarianism or consociationalism.

The United Kingdom best fits institutional features of the majoritarian institutional system, and Lijphart even refers to the ideal example of the majoritarian systems as **Westminster systems**, a reference to London's city center where the government is located. Majoritarian democracies have more homogenous societies ethnically, religiously, linguistically, and regionally. Consequently, the institutions typically have election and party systems that leave a single party in control of government, and few institutional checks on the ability of that party to easily translate their majority status into public policy. The attraction of majoritarian democracies rests on the argument that decisive government is good government. With fewer internal social divisions, there can be fewer players involved in the policy-making process in a majoritarian system because there are fewer social groups and people to appease and fewer people to derail certain policies. Consequently, majoritarian governments produce a greater number of laws because of the streamlined policy-making process.[3]

Consociational democratic systems have deep social divisions, usually along the ethnic, linguistic, religious, or regional distinctions highlighted above. Institutions must spread power across different sectors of society to keep a balanced order among social groups. In contrast to majoritarian institutions, consociational institutions lean toward producing multiple competitive parties, which leads to more than one party controlling the legislation and execution of law. This, along with powers provided to regional governments, means that parties and political leaders must compromise and that public policies are the product of a *consensus* developed from numerous quarters of society. Such efforts take time and involve less efficient policy making compared to majoritarian systems, even if they provide governing representation to more sectors of society.

The basic argument for consensus democracies builds around the idea of representation. Scholars have argued that proportional representation in consensus democracies provides better minority representation.[4] In short, consensus democracies allow more players at the proverbial table and more voices heard when drafting policies. They accomplish this by adopting election rules that encourage more parties and governing rules that provide more seats to disparate social groups as we'll see in Chapters 10 and 11. As a result, minority voices do not feel disenfranchised from the policy-making process.

The specific construction of democratic governing institutions in countries will be looked at in more depth in Chapter 7. The blend of these institutional arrangements—particularly how much power regional governments have in making their own policy decisions, how election rules encourage or discourage numerous political parties to compete for office (see Chapter 9), as well as how much power is concentrated in a single party or person in the executive branch—differentiates democratic governments on a scale between the ideal types of majoritarian systems versus consociational systems. Lijphart developed scales to measure levels of majoritarian versus consensus institutional features on two dimensions. One measures the power of regional governments versus the national government in making public policy, referred to as the **federal-unitary** dimension.[5] In effect, this dimension looks at the relative power distribution regionally in a country. Majoritarian systems typically have institutions that concentrate power in the national government. Consociational systems tend to have institutions that provide regional governments with key public policy powers because those regions may reflect a particular ethnic, religious, linguistic, or regional group that prefers to craft policies that fit its own culture rather than the majority national culture.

A second dimension, called the **executive-parties** dimension, looks at the representational nature of the political system in terms of the number of political parties that compete and share power in the legislative and executive

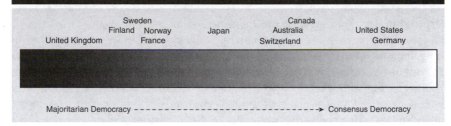

Figure 6.1 Spatial Representation of Democracies Based upon Lijphart's Majoritarian/Consociational Criteria

Source: Adapted from Arend Lijphart's *Patterns of Democracy: Government Forms and Performances in Thirty-six Countries, 2nd ed* (New Haven: Yale University Press, 2012).

branch, the dominance of the executive branch over policy, and the degree to which interest groups are formally or informally represented in government. Majoritarian systems tend toward governing efficiency and stability by having institutions that promote a single party controlling both the legislature and executive branches and strong executive control over policy. Consociational institutions promote multiple parties competing and winning seats in the legislature, and the executive branch tends to have to build a coalition among different parties to function. This ensures that different sectors of society have a voice in governing policy, which should ward off social divisions transitioning into political strife.

Countries typically hold majoritarian or consociational institutions consistently across both the federal-unitary and executive-parties dimensions. Figure 6.1 illustrates where countries fall along a continuum of majoritarianism and consociationalism based upon the two dimensions, executive-parties and federal-unitary. This is merely meant as an illustration for the reader, and a country's positioning along each continuum should not be treated as absolute. Nevertheless, differing democratic institutions can conclusively produce decisive government from elections in majoritarian systems compared to furnishing diverse social representation and policy consensus in consociational systems.

The United Kingdom's institutions tend to lead to one party dominating legislative elections, producing a strong, single-party executive that easily passes and executes policy with few checks. It tends to be a model of decisive policy making born of a majority election victory. Thus, it is *majoritarian* on the executive-parties factor. The United Kingdom's national government has **sovereignty**, that is, right of rule, over the entire country, so it is *majoritarian* on the federal-unitary factor as well. This means that legislation can pass quickly. When one party (or a party acting in coalition) controls the legislature, there is less of a check on policy making.

In contrast, the United States, with its majority and minority parties and intricate system of committees is much slower at getting policy through the legislative branch of government.

Switzerland demonstrates the consociational case well. Switzerland has three large ethnic/cultural/linguistic groups that tend to be concentrated in particular regions, one French-speaking, one Italian-speaking, and one German-speaking. To not slight any of these ethnic, linguistic, and regionally divided groups, the Swiss institutions promote multiple parties for the legislature and executive branch. Eleven parties won seats to the Swiss National Council in the last election—its main legislative body—with six of those parties winning double-digit seats in the 200-seat legislative body. The Swiss Federal Council heads the executive branch. In contrast to the U.S. president who leads the executive branch as a single person, there are seven people in the Federal Council from numerous parties to reflect the diversity of Swiss society. On the executive-parties factor, Switzerland, then, is extremely *consociational* in order to ensure that all sectors of its very ethnically and linguistically divided society have representation in the legislature and executive.

Further, the Swiss are highly *consociational* on the federal-unitary factor. Each regional government (there are twenty-six cantons) is given far-reaching policy-making power on issues like education, public safety, and social welfare. The cultural preferences of these differing groups can be expressed in policy and not subject to a singular majority policy preference.

As you would expect given the comparison of American political culture to other democracies, the U.S. institutional structure shares many features with other democracies, but it also has very unique features. In the two previous examples, it shares some key features with Britain on the executive-parties factor. It provides many more checks and balances than the British system does, however. In turn, it also shares many features of the Swiss federal-unitary factor. Not surprisingly, this is an exceptional, and some would say somewhat strange, mix.

Most advanced industrial democracies are either majoritarian along both dimensions or consociational along both dimensions. The United States, however, is majoritarian on the executive-parties dimension and consociational on the federal-unitary dimension. The Scandinavian countries are nearly the mirror opposite of the United States, with high consociationalism on the executive-parties dimension and majoritarian in terms of the federal-unitary dimension, a mixture much more common among advanced democracies if a country is going to have a mixing among dimensions.

Whether or not a country is majoritarian or consensus is more than just an academic exercise. There is a debate when constructing new types of government as to which type of institutional configuration is best. As we noted, the basic argument for consensus democracies builds around the idea of representation of different social groups in government, while the argument for majoritarian government comes from its decisive election result, public policy connection, and ability to quickly make and execute policy. What is most important is that what is best for one society might lead to policy failure, ineffective governance, or even

Table 6.1 Majoritarian versus Consensus Traits

Institutional Design	Majoritarian	Consensus
Executive Power	**One party and bare majority cabinets and majority party control of cabinet** = one political party (the one with the most votes) controls the executive and that party also controls the cabinet; power is not shared	**Executive power sharing in broad coalition cabinets and balance between legislative and executive branches** = more than one political party controls executive, and cabinet is made up of people from many parties; power is shared
Party System (see Chapter 9 for discussion of party systems)	**Two-party system** = two main political parties; although smaller parties may exist, they do not garner enough votes for seats	**Multiparty system** = numerous political parties, each with a chance of gaining enough votes for seats in the legislature meaning that often they must operate in coalition
Elections (see Chapters 10 and 11 for discussion of elections)	**Disproportionality of Elections** = one party controls nearly all government positions as long as it gains a plurality, the most, of the votes	**Proportionality of Elections** = parties share positions and power in proportion to the amount of votes they receive
Interest Groups (see Chapter 8 for discussion of interest groups)	**Pluralist** = there are many different types of groups with competing policy preferences; no formal structure for influencing policy	**Corporatist** = there are fewer groups, and groups have a formal seat at the table when negotiating government policy
Vertical Organization of Authority	Unitary structure	Federal structure
Houses of Legislature (see Chapter 7 for a discussion)	Unicameral	Bicameral
Constitution	**Constitutional flexibility** = constitution can be easily adapted and changed; usually by the legislature	**Constitutional rigidity** = it is a difficult and arduous process to change the constitution

(Continued)

Table 6.1 (Continued)

Judiciary (see Chapters 5 and 7 for a discussion)	**No judicial review** = judiciary does not pass judgment on constitutionality of laws, merely enforces laws enacted by the legislature	**Judicial review** = judiciary passes judgment on the constitutionality of laws passed by the legislature
Central Bank	**Executive control of central bank** = the appointing of lead bankers and making of monetary policy is at the discretion of the executive branch	**Independence of central bank** = the central bank operates independently from any of the branches of government and sets its own monetary policy

Source: Adapted from Arend Lijphart, *Patterns of Democracy in Thirty-Six Countries* (New Haven, CT: Yale University Press, 2012).

civil war in other social settings. The connection between a country's political culture and its political institutions is tight, and it is a reason why the American constitution is very unlike other countries' constitutions.

Table 6.1 details Lijphart's (1984, 2012) constitutional traits along with other important components—institutions, party systems, interest groups, and elections—talked about in subsequent chapters. Democracies differ greatly; one clear conclusion that can be drawn is that the United States has a constitutional system that is exceptional.

VERTICAL ORGANIZATION OF GOVERNMENT: UNITARY, FEDERAL, AND CONFEDERAL SYSTEMS

The two factors that Lijphart developed to differentiate democratic institutional systems explain how much power is concentrated or spread within the government and across the country regionally. These factors can be translated into the vertical organization of government and the horizontal organization of government. **Vertical organization** of government refers to layers of government from **national** (center) to **subnational** (below the center), which relates to the federal-unitary factor discussed above. The parties-executive factor relates to the **horizontal organization** of government, or to the relationship between the legislative, executive, and judicial branches of government at any level (discussed in Chapter 7).

Vertical organization refers to how many layers of government a country has and how the country distributes governing power across those layers of government (see Figure 6.2). As highlighted previously, many democracies are **unitary systems**, where all significant legislative and executive power is vested in a single national (sometimes referred to as central) government with little to no independent power vested in lower levels of government. In unitary systems, lower levels of government exist *"at the will of"* the central government. This means that sovereignty rests with the central government, and the central government can create administrative units at lower levels but can also abolish these units.

Federal systems provide two or more layers of government, which means a country has regional or local units of government with authority and powers independent of those of the national government. The fact that they have independent powers is important. Unitary systems may have regional or local offices, but as noted, they do not have independent policy-making powers. Federal systems provide regional governments with significant power over many essential governmental policies that may involve public safety, education, social welfare, transportation, and even taxation.

Whereas unitary states concentrate sovereignty in the central government, and federal states have independent sovereignty in lower levels of government, **confederal** states are those where sovereignty is vested in lower levels of government, with lower levels having more authority than the central government. This is where confederal differs from federal. In federal systems, lower levels of government have independent sovereignty, but substantial, if not superior, power rests with the national government. In confederal systems, it is the opposite; the lower levels of government is where the power lies. Students of American history will recall the Confederate States of America, the southern states, which among other things, were fighting for the idea that sovereignty should lie in the states and not the national government during the Civil War years in the United States. Confederal systems are not common in the world and especially not common among advanced industrial democracies. Switzerland and Belgium—the two closest democracies to a confederation—both have aspects of a confederation, but they are more similar to a federal system than a confederal system. The European Union and the United Nations are confederations. Their success comes from member states banding together for mutual interests. Their failure comes when member states, based on their sovereignty, refuse to follow through on the organization's goals, which would devastate a country were it to have this governing structure. Indeed, the problems of the United States under the Articles of Confederation will be highlighted later in the chapter.

The United States has a federal organization of government. It is important to differentiate between the American federal government—the national government—and federalism as a system of government. In this chapter, **federal** means a country in which local units of government have powers independent of those of the national government and in which authority is divided between the different levels of government. The independent policy-making powers that state and local governments have in American federalism include public safety and policing; primary, secondary, and higher education; transportation and infrastructure; social welfare; and economic development. These powers play out in very different forms throughout the United States, with different states and localities choosing very different ways to fund government, distinct definitions and laws about social order and decency, and regulations of individuals' lives. Americans live a very different life relative to government depending on where they live.

Figure 6.2 Vertical Organization of Government: Federal, Unitary, and Confederal

Confederal

States

Federal

States ↔ Central Government

In a federal system, states and the central government share power, or sovereignty.

Unitary

Central Government

Central Government

States

In a confederal system, states (or lower levels of governmnet) grant sovereignty, or power to the central government.

In a unitary system, the central government grants sovereignty, or power to states (or lower levels of government).

Take the authors' hometowns as examples. One of us lives in the city of Flagstaff, in Coconino County, Arizona. The other lives in Fort Wayne, situated in Allen County, Indiana. Beyond sharing a common president and vice president, the authors have dozens of separate executive and legislative officials at the state, county, and city level, not to mention governing bodies such as water districts, fire districts, or solid waste districts. One author pays an Indiana state income tax of 3.4 percent compared to Arizona's income tax of 4.54 percent, but Fort Wayne has passed a local income tax of 1.35 percent that Flagstaff does not have. Flagstaff has a city minimum wage of $15/hour; Fort Wayne does not. Until one grand day in 2018, Hoosiers could not buy beer on Sunday, forcing some in Fort Wayne to drive the short distance to Ohio should they have not warehoused enough for the weekend. In Arizona, there has been no such "problem."

Other differences among localities are even starker. It is not hard to imagine that Las Vegas and Salt Lake City have very different standards of decency concerning exotic dancing, and citizens in Arizona would be infuriated if the state government had to inspect their jalopy for road worthiness each year as is the case in neighboring California. Bars close early or late, marijuana can be or not be smoked, speed limits differ in rate and enforcement efforts, and codes exist or do not regulating whether people can have a bath tub as a flower planter in their front yard. The president will not dispatch the FBI on these matters; they are left up to local laws and local enforcement. Other advanced industrial democracies with federal systems include Canada, Germany, Australia, Belgium, Switzerland, Austria, and New Zealand (which switched to a federal system in the 1990s). While there are some differences between these countries, what they have in common is that all have lower levels of government with independent decision-making authority.

A federal structure of government is not a superior way for all countries to vertically organize a country, but it was the best way for the United States. It particularly made sense for a country where the original colonies were independent, as well as geographically and economically isolated from one another. After the American Revolution, the former colonies turning over their sovereignty to a central authority was not going to happen—it seemed too much like giving authority to the recently thrown-off king. Even after the Articles of the Confederation failed because they led to tyranny of the majority, the individual states still were distrustful of having too strong of a central government. Further, James Madison noted in *Federalist 10* that tyranny would best be checked at the federal government level because the diverse interests of these states would lead them to seldom, if ever, agree enough to get a majority vote in the U.S. Congress. Tyranny of the majority is solved not by controlling the tyrannical potential of human nature but by colliding parochial interests of states. Given the history and political culture in the United States, a federal system made the most sense in order to protect against tyranny of the majority from unchecked democracy or tyranny from a single individual.

Additionally, a federal system enhanced self-government, something that was key to the framers in 1787 drafting the U.S. Constitution. How is self-government enhanced in a federal system? As noted above, the distinctive patchwork of laws in different states in the United States allows citizens of each state to make rules and flavor their policies based on their population rather than being imposed from a national government. At the time of our founding, the federal structure was a unique experiment. It has been an experiment that has worked and has since been emulated by other democracies preferring consociational institutions on the unitary-federal factor. That said, a federal system is not the only way to organize a government, and it is not appropriate for all democracies.

While the United States' federal system is familiar to an American student reading this book, a student in France would likely react with puzzlement. Indeed, many democracies, like the United Kingdom, France, Italy, Japan, Spain, and the Scandinavian countries are unitary systems. Many of these countries are social democracies with a generally homogenous population that identifies itself strongly as a nation. The national government tends to be trusted as a force for producing the common good for society. Further, the administrative efficiency of one legislature and one executive making and executing laws in such a society trumps the frequent inefficient replication or complicated hodgepodge of policy-making efforts that can exist in federal systems. Centralization of authority can create efficiency and uniformity. There was a time in France, for example, that a first-grade student in a public school at 3 p.m. on Monday, anywhere in the country, would be learning the exact same thing. This has relaxed somewhat, but educational standards are still decreed centrally. For example, all children in their last year of high school are required to take a year of philosophy and the same written exam.

In these countries, regional governing offices tend simply to be administrative units of the national government. When lower levels of government have any policy-making power, it can be broadened or narrowed at the will of the central government, or delegated through **devolution**.

BOX 6.1

Devolution in Great Britain

Devolution means the decentralizing of power, or the granting of power from a central state to a lower level of government. The United Kingdom, also called Great Britain, is a unitary state made up four constituent parts—Scotland, Wales, England, and Northern Ireland—that each has a degree of autonomous devolved power. In Scotland, there is the Scottish Parliament and in Wales, the National Assembly. In Northern Ireland, there is the Northern Ireland Assembly. This power, however, is only devolved and delegated by the central government, or the Parliament of the United Kingdom. The central government can roll back devolution. (It has abolished the Northern Ireland Assembly four times—2000, twice in 2001, and from 2002 to 2007. Since January 2017, there has been no power-sharing Executive in place in Northern Ireland. As of September 2018, talks to restore power-sharing in Northern Ireland continue). The devolved governments cannot challenge the Parliament of the United Kingdom. Devolution can mean that regional governments get more and more authority. The Scottish, who by far have the most devolved power of all the constituent parts of Great Britain in their Scottish Parliament, went to the polls in September 2014 to determine if they should completely break away and become independent from Great Britain.

In polling just before the election, it looked as if the "No" and "Yes" votes were neck and neck. As election results rolled in on the morning of September 19, 2014, it became clear that in answering the question "Should Scotland be an independent country?" approximately 55 percent of the voting population

Photo by Nick Poloni, NDOTP Photography, www.ndotp.com.

▶ **Photo 6.1** Parliament, United Kingdom

(ages 16 and above) voted "No." This is not to say that results were uniform across the country. In the city of Glasgow, approximately 54 percent of the voting population actually voted "Yes" for independence. The exact ramifications of this hard-fought campaign for independence will be seen in the coming years, and it is certain that there will be an increased push for additional devolution. In fact, there is a special chairman to oversee further devolution to Scotland. After Brexit (British break with the EU), there is renewed talk in Scotland of an independence referendum.

CONCLUSION

While the Unites States has a constitution that has been in place for over 230 years, this is rare. We saw in our discussion that most constitutions are much shorter lived. While the blueprints for your house may have called for no running water in 1787 or avocado green countertops in 1970, it doesn't mean you are stuck with them forever. You can amend your house, like you can amend a constitution. The United States has done this only seventeen times since the ratification of the Bill of Rights nearly 230 years ago. However, maybe you no longer like your starter home from 1787; maybe you have outgrown it and want to move to a modern, larger home with more conveniences. Many countries do just that, changing their constitution as their society changes, not just through amendments but also by getting an entirely new constitution. They have constitutional flexibility. The United States, on the other hand, has chosen to keep the farmhouse from 1787 with just a few updates. This gives it the oldest constitution in the world, but it is also a function of constitutional rigidity in the United States. To critics, this constitutional rigidity means that American government often cannot respond to social problems until they become genuine crises.[6] To others, rigidity may sound harsh, but this was at least partially intended by the framers. In Washington's Farewell Address, he pleaded to preserve the constitutional structure and to "resist with care the spirit of innovation upon its principles, however specious the pretexts."[7]

In other societies, the design of democratic constitutions differs based on whether countries prefer majoritarian or consociational institutions based on their social and political cultures. Institutions do not pop up on their own and would not be easily imported or exported unless the nature of ethnic, religious, linguistic, and regional differences were extremely similar. Societies with large divisions choose institutions that represent differing sectors of society, whereas homogenous societies tend toward more efficient institutions of majoritarian democracies. Countries have set up institutions vertically and horizontally in ways to produce efficient (majoritarian) or consensus-based decision making. The United States has a unique blend of institutions.

For instance, the United States shares a federal structure with some democracies, like Germany, but this differs from the vertical organization of power in other countries, which have a more unitary structure. In this regard, we saw that the United States shares characteristics with some of its democratic cousins, but it has some very unique features that make categorizing the United States along the majoritarian or consociational system very difficult. In sum, the constitution of a country reflects the unique aspects of that country, which in turn shape how that country is governed, a topic we turn to in the next chapters.

POINTS TO REMEMBER

- The United States has the oldest constitution of any democracy in the world.

- The U.S. Constitution is distinguished by its rigidity. It has been modified much less often than other countries' constitutions, and modification is a difficult and slow process.

- Vertical organization of government refers to layers of government from national to subnational, or below the level of the central, national government.

- Horizontal organization refers to the relationship between governmental entities, or branches, at a single level of government.

- In a federal system, states, or lower levels of government, have sovereign power over some areas of policy and share power with the national level of government.

- In a unitary system, power is centralized in the national level of government, and any lower levels of administration exist at the will of the national government.

- Democracies can be classified as being either majoritarian or consensus (consociational) along two dimensions—executive-parties and federal-unitary.

- Elections tend to be the decisive element for policy making in majoritarian systems. In consociational systems there is a lot of post-election bargaining to establish who governs and the policy-making process. The United States also has more checks and balances, so post-election political bargaining is important as well.

- Majoritarian parliamentary systems tend to have one party that dominates the executive and legislative branches. Coalition parliamentary systems tend to have multiple parties in the executive and legislature branches to bring consensus to policy making among diverse groups in society.

KEY TERMS

Basic Law 110
Common law 112
Confederal 119
Consensus 113
Consociational 113
Constitution 110
Devolution 122
Executive-parties 114
Federal 119
Federal systems 119
Federal-unitary 114

Homogeneity 113
Horizontal
    organization 118
Ideal type 113
Majoritarian 113
National 118
Parliamentary
    conventions 112
Parliamentary
    sovereignty 112
Rigid 111

Rule of law 112
Sovereignty 115
Statute law 112
Subnational 118
Unitary systems 118
Vertical
    organization 118
Westminster
    systems 113
Works of
    authority 112

REVIEW QUESTIONS

1. What is the difference between a unitary and federal structure of government?

2. What is devolution?

3. What does vertical organization of government refer to? What does horizontal organization of government refer to?

4. What variables describe a majoritarian system? A consociational system?

5. When we say a country can be majoritarian or consociational along two dimensions, what does this mean? What do the two dimensions measure? How does the United States compare to other democracies?

6. If you were to design the U.S. constitution today, what would you keep? What things would you change?

7. What might be some advantages and disadvantages of a rigid constitution? Of a flexible constitution?

SUGGESTED READINGS

Lijphart, Arend. *Patterns of Democracy in Twenty-One Countries*. New Haven, CT: Yale University Press, 1984.

Lijphart, Arend. *Patterns of Democracy in Thirty-Six Countries*, 2nd ed. New Haven, CT: Yale University Press, 2012.

NOTES

1. See https://www.law.uchicago.edu/news/lifespan-written-constitutions.

2. See, for example, Arend Lijphart, *Democracy in Plural Societies: A Comparative Exploration* (New Haven, CT: Yale University Press, 1977); Arend Lijphart, *Patterns of Democracy in Thirty-Six Countries*, 2nd ed. (New Haven, CT: Yale University Press, 2012); G. Bingham Powell, *Elections as Instruments of Democracy: Majoritarian and Proportional Democracies* (New Haven, CT: Yale University Press, 2000).

3. A. L. Lowell, *Governments and Parties in Continental Europe* (Boston, MA: Houghton Mifflin, 1896); George Tsebelis, "Veto Players and Law Production in Parliamentary Democracies: An Empirical Analysis," *American Political Science Review* 93, no. 3 (1999): 3.

4. See, for example, Lijphart, *Patterns of Democracy in Thirty-Six Countries*.

5. The federal-unitary dimension is a factor scale comprised of the following variables: federalism-decentralization, bicameralism, constitutional rigidity, judicial review, and central bank independence.

6. Walter Dean Burnham, *Critical Elections and the Mainsprings of American Politics*, New York: W.W. Norton & Company, 1977.

7. George Washington "Farewell Address, September 17, 1796," *Library of Congress*, https://www.loc.gov/resource/mgw2.024/?sp=229&st=text, accessed July 9, 2018.

CHAPTER SEVEN

GOVERNING INSTITUTIONS

When Americans think of the British, what likely comes to mind is drinking tea, good manners, and the Queen. They do not picture fist pounding and jeering as typical of British manners, unless they have a chance to watch the British prime minister respond to questions by members of the opposition party in the legislature. The prime minister is often met with jeers, boos and hisses as he or she must defend his or her policies against an unsympathetic opposition. One could not imagine the United States Congress erupting into similar levels of rowdiness when the president makes his yearly State of the Union Address, where the president typically receives numerous standing ovations, and the largest display of disagreement members of the U.S. opposition make is not to clap when the president lays out accomplishments and goals to the Congress. In fact, when Republican Joe Wilson yelled "you lie" at President Barack Obama at Obama's address before a joint session of Congress in 2009, Americans were somewhat shocked that a congressional representative would disrespect the office of the president in such a way. In Britain, such outbursts would not only seem common but could be expected. Why? The United States and Britain not only have different political cultures, but they have very different political institutions.

This chapter digs deeper into the similarities and differences in the political cultures between liberal and social democracies highlighted in previous chapters to demonstrate how differing beliefs about government translate into differing governing structures in the United States and other advanced industrial democracies. Chapter 4 highlighted how distinct American political culture is compared to the political cultures of other countries. This difference, combined with a different historical trajectory, led the United States down an institutional path that was distinct from other democracies. Chapters 5 and 6 set the stage for how these differences translated into different constitutional arrangements, enshrining rights and liberties into blueprints for democracy. Interestingly, the United States shares some institutional similarities with many democracies, but the features do not line up with particular countries in any consistent manner. For instance, the United States is not the only liberal democracy in the world, but most other liberal democracies do not have presidents. Like other democracies with high levels of ethnic and sociodemographic diversity, American political institutions keep any one social group or political interest from easily controlling government.

The extensive American system of **checks and balances**, where three branches of government can each constitutionally limit the power of the others, is complicated, confusing, and unique to the United States. Conversely, the British system promotes the parliament (or legislature) above all other branches of government (as explained in more detail in later sections of this chapter).

NATIONAL GOVERNING INSTITUTIONS

Countries need their institutions to do three functional things: to legislate law, to execute law, and to adjudicate whether laws have been violated or whether the laws are just. These functions tend to be separated into three branches: the legislative, the executive, and the judicial branch of government, respectively. There are two main reasons governments split up these functions. First, a division of labor helps the efficiency of these functions. Second, the separation of powers ensures that no single person or group can be creator, prosecutor, judge, and jury over society's rules.

As the majoritarian-consociational ideal types showed in Chapter 6, there are significant differences among democracies about the efficiency of policy making coming from concentrated power versus providing diverse sectors with representation in policy. Lijphart's second factor emphasized separating institutions in majoritarian and consociational democracies focused on the number of competing parties in the executive and legislature of national governments, as well as how streamlined the policy-making process is for the executive branch. Some societies, particularly consociational democracies, provide key institutional checks to make sure power is distributed rather than concentrated in any department. Compared to the United States, however, these checks tend to come within the executive branch. This means that oppositional political parties "check" the power assertion of the party in power. In the American system, checks come strongly within and *between* branches of government. That is, each branch of government provides a "check" on the power asserted by other branches of government

American students can likely recall the mantra of "checks and balances" as being key to a democracy. While the idea that one branch of government "checks" the power of another branch of government is key to the organization of government in the United States, it is not like this in every democracy. Thus, while other democracies have three branches of government as well, the relationship between these branches is different in the United States. This is in part why American politics textbooks present legislative, executive, and judicial branches of government in different chapters. When we look at these institutions comparatively, however, it makes little sense to separate them. We'll see in the next few sections that in most democracies there is not a firewall between branches of government like in the United States but that they derive from each other and should be looked at cohesively.

This chapter will focus on institutions at the national level. While all democracies, and particularly federal democracies, have well-developed institutions of government at local levels, discussing institutions at these levels is beyond the scope of this book.

THE LEGISLATIVE BRANCH

The **legislative branch** of government is responsible for writing and crafting laws. The United States is a **republic**, where representatives of the people are elected to make laws on their behalf.[1] In the United States, these laws are made in a **bicameral** legislature. This means there are two legislative chambers. The House of Representatives, designed to represent the people, and the Senate, designed to give representation to the states. As Madison explains in *Federalist 39* "The House of Representatives will derive its powers from the people of America. . . . The Senate, on the other hand, will derive its powers from the States, as political and co-equal societies; and these will be represented on the principle of equality in the Senate."[2] When a bicameral system affords relatively equal power to both chambers of the legislature, we refer to this as **symmetrical bicameralism**. Recalling from Chapter 6, the bicameral nature of the U.S. legislature derives from the Connecticut Compromise, which allowed representation based on population proportionality (House of Representatives) advocated by the Federalists and equal numbers of votes per state (Senate) advocated by the Anti-Federalists.

A bicameral legislature is not the only type of legislature the United States could have chosen. Many advanced democracies (like New Zealand, Denmark, Sweden, Spain, and Israel) have **unicameral**, or one chamber, legislatures. These legislatures can pass legislation much quicker and more efficiently than the slow process of American bicameralism. That said, most democracies have bicameral legislatures like the United States, however, they are examples of **asymmetrical bicameralism**, meaning that the two chambers do not share equal legislative power, as they do in the United States.

In asymmetrical bicameral systems, scholars confusingly refer to the more powerful chamber as the "lower house" and the weaker chamber as the "upper house." The lower house received this name because historically, it was "below" the upper house, or the house that was supposed to represent the nobility or upper classes. Over time, the lower house has evolved in all democracies to be the more powerful of the two houses and the one closest to the people. The lower house tends to actually write the legislation, and the upper house may have some powers to review, delay, or advise on legislation but has no real role in crafting legislation. Further, in prime ministerial systems (see the following discussion of the executive), the prime minister is elected to and chosen by the lower house and, as noted, ends up dominating the agenda and writing of legislation. So clearly, the lower house is where the action is.

In some countries, asymmetrical bicameralism fits well with their political cultures, because checks within the legislative branch in symmetrical bicameral systems like the United States diminish the ability of democracy to provide the common good through legislation. In an asymmetric system, you do not have gridlock and can more easily achieve the goal of the public good that stems from a more Rousseau vision of democracy. The United States' symmetric bicameral legislature fits the Locke-based limited government American vision.

The U.S. Congress does have power inequalities between the two chambers but only in so far as they involve checks on the president. The more sober U.S. Senate provides advice and consent to presidential appointments to the executive and judicial branches, including Supreme Court Justices, and ratifies treaties. But on the main role of Congress—legislation—both chambers must pass legislation with exactly the same language. This is not how bicameralism works elsewhere when one chamber writes legislation with typically only token oversight by the other chamber.

The internal checks that Congress provides frustrate the American public. Americans have high expectations of businesses in the marketplace and would never accept a business that was inefficient and often never achieved its goals. Due to **congressional gridlock**, otherwise known as deadlock or political stalemate, this is common practice in the United States Congress. Yet, when considering congressional gridlock, people dislike it but do not work to overthrow the Congress. It is a situation where the alternative would be worse. A Congress that quickly kicked out legislation with few internal checks might move legislation that ended up being unpopular or even encroach on people's liberties. Thus, while we can think of policy making in other democracies like a fast race horse, policy making in the United States is more like a plow horse, slow and plodding.

Representation

As stated previously, advanced industrial democracies are republican forms of government. This does not mean that Donald Trump's policies rule the day; it means that these governments are representative governments. **Representation** is the efforts of elected officials to look out for the interests of those who elect them, that is, working on behalf of their **constituency**, or the voters who elect the legislator. How closely should leaders reflect public views? At a broad level we can contrast the trustee model of representation in legislatures with the delegate model of representation.

In the **trustee** model, representatives are entrusted with the autonomy to deliberate and act in favor of the common good and national interest, even if this means going against the short-term interests of their own constituencies. In the trustee model, trustees consider a policy issue, listen to all sides of debate, and use their own judgment to make a decision about what should be done. Philosophers Edmund Burke (1729–1797) and J. S. Mill (1806–1873) championed this model. Burke in 1774 is quoted as saying *"[Y]ou choose a member, indeed; but when*

you have chosen him, he is not member of Bristol, but he is a member of Parliament."
Burke incidentally was not reelected after championing this approach. Mill took
things further and thought that while everyone had a right to be represented, not
all political opinions had equal value. He argued for a trustee system where constituents would receive votes based upon their level of education.

The **delegate** model is based on the idea that constituents elect their representatives as delegates for their constituency who act as a mouthpiece for the
wishes of their constituency and have no autonomy from the constituency. Burke
also developed this idea of representation in his effort to contest it and promote
the trustee model. In the delegate model, a representative would only make decisions as wanted by their constituents, not necessarily considering the common
good. In practical terms, we can see this in terms of populist legislation, such
as **pork barrel spending**. This is focused project spending in a representative's
particular district that will not likely benefit the country as a whole. In a country
with single member electoral districts (see Chapter 9 for a further discussion), it is
easier to fall into the delegate model. The Unites States, particularly in the House
of Representatives, often seems more like a delegate than trustee model while the
Senate, by design, has more features of the trustee model with longer terms and
older age requirements for membership. Though other democracies that have
at-large elections (see Chapter 10) also tend toward the trustee model.

Research shows that the more the trustee style is emphasized within parties,
the more positively the performance of liberal democracy is evaluated.[3] Trustee
representatives and parties are better able to integrate and serve heterogeneous
interests. On the other hand, delegate systems are associated with more negative
views of democracy. One reason why this may be is that protest parties (like far-
right populist parties) are more likely to emphasize the delegate style. This style
fits with these parties' ideas and populist messaging of reverting to the "will of
the people" against the political establishment. Thus, protest parties and candidates mobilize as well as fuel the discontent of voters.[4] This is something that
has been seen with Donald Trump's presidency in the United States. The afore-
mentioned discussion notwithstanding, there is strong critique about the trustee/
delegate.[5] Nevertheless, the trustee/delegate dichotomy persists in the literature,
likely because it gets to the core of representation—who is represented by whom.[6]

Legislative Elections

Elections are discussed in a bit more detail in Chapter 10, and this section
will focus specifically on the way in which legislative elections in Untied States are
exceptional. Primarily, the uniqueness of American legislative elections has to do
with **primaries** and **midterms**.

Primary elections are the process by which political parties select who runs
for office. In response to party machine abuses that ripped off American cities
through public projects and the party spoils systems in the 1800s in the United
States, where partisan supporters were given federal bureaucratic positions based

on loyalty rather than competence, most states changed the laws of nomination to political parties during the Progressive Era (1900–1929). In other countries, candidate selection is usually an internal party negotiation, which keeps power centralized with the party. In the United States, members of the same party compete against each other to decide who will represent their party in the general (or main) election. There are some exceptions to this rule. In California, for example, only the top two vote getters, regardless of party, move forward to the **general election**. Primary elections have the benefit of strengthening general election candidates and cluing the electorate into politics. On the downside, this is one more thing Americans must turn out for (see Chapter 11 for a discussion of how often Americans vote), and a particularly hard fought primary election could result in a candidate appearing as "damaged goods" in a general election. Other critics point out that ideologically extreme candidates end up winning legislative primary elections, which has made the U.S. Congress much more polarized.

Midterm elections take place between, or in the midterm, of presidential elections. Every House of Representative member runs in the midterm and in presidential election years, as they are elected every two years. Since Senators serve for six years, one-third of Senators are up for election in midterm election years. This is unique to the United States. Since most other democracies are parliamentary or mixed systems, their elections happen all at the same time. In the United States, we also see the phenomenon of the **midterm loss** where the party of the sitting president loses seats in Congress during the midterm election. This has happened in nearly every midterm election since the inception of the United States.

The reason for midterm loss stems from the surge of voters who support a particular presidential candidate. With that president's electoral success comes congressional "coattails"—or legislators from the president's party who receive votes because of the presidential candidate's popularity. Two years later, the president is not on the ballot, so some of his supporters have a decline in turnout, whereas the party who does not control the presidency is mobilized by their opposition to the president and his agenda.[7] This surge and decline phenomenon is familiar to congressional candidates. Consequently, many incumbent members of Congress of the president's party may decide to retire if they think they could lose in a midterm election. Second, many up-and-coming potential congressional candidates of the president's party decide not to run in an unfriendly environment while the out-party's superstars have likely waited for this very moment to run.[8] In other words, due to strategic decisions by these candidates, the president's party has fielded their J.V. team while the opposing party has fielded their varsity team, which further sets the table for midterm loss.

This brings a volatility to the American Congress that does not exist in other democracies. In other countries, where we see operation by party government, we don't have the midterm loss phenomenon but instead power would shift between parties in the parliament at the regular election. This furthers the lurching nature of American congressional lawmaking compared to the typically much smoother making of policy by other legislative bodies.

Party Government in the Legislature

Political parties (discussed in Chapter 9) play a more fundamental practical governing role in most other democracies relative to the role they play in the United States. The primary reason for this is that citizens in other democracies view democratic representation as something that occurs through political parties rather than being carried out by specific elected representatives, as is the case in the United States.[9] Therefore, citizens evaluate their electoral behavior and evaluations of government policy making through the lens of political parties. In fact, many democracies have citizens vote for a party on their ballots rather than any specific individual candidate. This places direct electoral and representative expectations in the hands of a political party. In contrast, in the United States, many candidates run for office specifically emphasizing their independence from their party's positions on key issues, and citizens view their elected official as their vehicle of representation (in a delegate model) rather than simply acting as a partisan figure.

The American view of parties has typically been that the two major parties are made up of very diverse sets of groups, which requires intense internal party bargaining. This leads to a very Madisonian view of policy making where differing internal party divisions must be worked out in the governing process, along with deal making with the opposing party, in order for legislation and policy to move forward. In this classic view of party roles, parties do not completely and uniformly drive the political agenda but rather they work to build **consensus** among their diverse members.[10] In other democracies where representation takes place through parties and political leaders are considered agents of these parties, parties control the policy agenda. The term *party government* is used to discuss how these democracies operate. For these democracies, party competition in elections provides the representation and mandate for public policy. There tends to be few institutional inhibitions for parties to implement their agenda after an election, and this substantial control over policy means that parties will be held directly accountable at subsequent elections for their policies, successes, and failures. In these democracies, political parties provide voters with very explicit policy promises in party platforms and translate them into actual policy when elected.[11]

Elected officials remain loyal to their party in voting on these policies out of recognition that this is the currency of representation in these democracies but also because party rules tend to provide party leaders with extreme power over their governing representatives. In most democracies, party loyalty is ensured because party leaders select who represents the party in government. As Chapters 10 and 11 demonstrate, electoral institutions and ballots differ across democracies, but in democracies that have party candidates who run in a district, party organizational leaders recruit and select the candidates who will be on their party's ballot line. If party members do not support their party in the British House of Commons, for instance, they will be left without any mechanism for advancement in government, receive no electoral support in future elections, or may even be expelled from their party. In those democracies where voters vote for a party rather than an individual candidate—the **party list systems**—the party leadership either recruits and selects the people who will appear on the list for the voters to choose, or the party simply fills out the list of people without public knowledge. Either way, the party organizational leaders provide strong incentives for their members to follow the party positions loyally or be left off the ballot and out of office.

For institutional, legal, and historical reasons, American parties lack the ability to bring about party government. First, the separation of powers system in the United States provides firm divisions across the legislative and executive branches that do not exist in most other democracies as highlighted throughout this chapter. Unlike prime ministers, presidents have few institutional tools to force their fellow partisans to support their agenda and rely on old-school persuasive techniques. Unfortunately for presidents, no one agrees with them all the time, and members of their party in Congress may even be rewarded for not agreeing with their president.

Second, most states changed the laws of nomination to political parties during the Progressive Era (1900–1929). This means that for many, if not most offices, candidates run for a party's nomination independently of the party organization. Discussed further in Chapter 9, this brings internal party divisions, can weaken a party's message, hurt its chances at the general election, and even leaves party officials with a candidate that does not represent the party's position on issues or will not demonstrate any loyalty to the party.

Third, the historical mistrust that Americans have had for parties means that they prefer electoral competition to strong parties that appoint people to office. The U.S. electoral system is much more candidate-centered in comparison to the more party-centered elections in other democracies and even in other eras of American electoral history.[12] American party scholars discuss the nineteenth century as the era of the strongest party organizations because parties that won the presidency used the spoils system to fill the federal bureaucracy with party loyalists, while states and large cities were dominated by party machines that chose who would be on the preprinted party ballot, and the party doled out social services based on party loyalty. While the corruption that came along with these practices was particular to that time and place, the organizational power that parties had is far more comparable to what other party organizations have in other contemporary democracies than it is to the American party system today.

Further, Americans vote for dozens of offices with elections for president; House of Representatives; U.S. Senate; and state gubernatorial elections along with a handful of other state executive offices that are not appointed by the governor; representatives to two state legislative chambers; and multiple county, township, city, town, or village legislative and executive offices. In other democracies, the party would appoint nearly every executive position in regional government and likely would not have any legislative body at such lower levels, which thereby provides parties with real governing control.

THE EXECUTIVE BRANCH

The executive branches of most countries tend to have two main offices: head of government and head of state. A **head of state** is a ceremonial position that carries with it little to no real decision-making power. The Queen of England would be the example of a head of state (see Box 7.1). A **head of government**, the state's chief political officer, is responsible for presenting and developing policies and has decision-making authority. The British prime minister would be an example of a head of government.

In constitutional monarchies, the positions of head of state and head of government are held by two different people, with the head of the royal family occupying the position of head of state and an elected chief executive occupying the position of head of government. Other advanced industrial democracies other than the United Kingdom and Commonwealth countries (more on these later) with a ceremonial monarch as head of state include Belgium, Denmark, Japan, Luxembourg, Netherlands, Norway, Spain, and Sweden. In other republics, like Germany, there is a dual executive, but the head of state is not a hereditary position passed down through a royal family but rather is indirectly elected.

BOX 7.1

The Role of the Queen of England

In constitutional monarchies and kingdoms that are advanced industrial democracies, the monarch serves as head of state. Currently in the United Kingdom and for all other Commonwealth countries, this is Queen Elizabeth II. The queen serves a largely ceremonial role as a figurehead and symbol of the state. She does not hold any real political power. Although, convention does maintain that the head of government in the United Kingdom seeks permission from the queen to form a government and notifies her before elections. The queen retains certain constitutional powers over the military and other areas of lawmaking, but since the United Kingdom and all other Commonwealth countries operate as constitutional monarchies, the queen only acts upon advice of the elected prime minister in each country. In fact, the queen's speech each year before parliament sets out the prime minister's policy goals and is written by the prime minister's office.

Photo from NASA, www.nasa.gov.

▶ **Photo 7.1** Queen Elizabeth II, head of state in the United Kingdom and other Commonwealth countries.

(Continued)

(Continued)

When we say that the queen is head of state to not only the United Kingdom, but to **Commonwealth countries** as well, this refers to the countries that were one time part of the United Kingdom. Commonwealth countries outside of the United Kingdom with Queen Elizabeth as their head of state include Antigua and Barbuda, Australia, Bahamas, Barbados, Belize, Canada, Granada, Jamaica, New Zealand, Papua New Guinea, Saint Kitts and Nevis, Saint Lucia, Saint Vincent and the Grenadines, Solomon Islands, and Tuvalu.

In the United States and France, the positions of head of state and head of government are held by one person, the chief executive, or the president. This may seem like a bonus for the American president, and it does provide some important benefits to be the unifying figure representing the entire United States. In times of national crisis or national pride, people often rally around the president, likely less due to his policies than as an embrace of the head of state. Many of the most beloved American presidents are viewed through history by their strong roles as head of state as much or more than their policies. Historians refer to the Kennedy White House as Camelot because of the near-Royal family-type presence the handsome Kennedy family projected. The rugged actor Ronald Reagan had a personal approval rating that was always higher than his job approval. Views of presidents historically do not translate into contemporary presidential power, however. Juggling both roles can be difficult for presidents because the president must play both roles simultaneously or be judged negatively.

On one hand, the president was elected by supporters who want him to aggressively champion the policies upon which he ran. The president's political opponents can aggressively criticize the president, but presidents must take more measured stances toward their opposition or be accused of not acting "presidential"—or, in other words, not properly acting with the respect expected of a head of state. To go with our example earlier, the British prime minister does not have this same burden and can unleash cutting criticism of his opponents and give full-throated advocacy to his or her positions without having to act like the queen. We are seeing a change in this in the United States. Donald Trump is the first president to excessively tweet in office, often sending out biting and rude messages to his opposition. This has led many, including members of his own party, to criticize President Trump for his unpresidential conduct rather than the substance of his policies.

In turn, the president also has to warmly receive people as head of state with whom he would likely prefer to argue. Bill Clinton presented a Kennedy Center Honor for lifelong achievement to Charlton Heston, who at the time headed the National Rifle Association (NRA), which strongly opposed Clinton's gun control policies. In a speech before the NRA, Heston said, "Mr. Clinton, sir, America didn't trust you with our health-care system. America didn't trust you with gays in the military. America doesn't trust you with our 21-year-old daughters. And we sure, Lord, don't trust you with our guns."[13] George W. Bush had to present the same honor to Elton John just weeks after Elton John said, "It's a nightmare. Bush and this administration are the worst thing that has ever happened to America."[14] So while the president may have some benefits from holding both roles, it often ties one hand behind his back. Donald Trump has somewhat broken the mold in this regard, refusing to attend the White House correspondents' dinner (where the president and his administration are routinely roasted) and calling out professional sports figures for disagreeing with his politics.

The greater role of the president is as head of government, or head of the **executive branch** of government that "executes" the laws passed by the legislative branch of government. In the United States, the president is the chief executive. The president tends to be referred to as the most powerful person in the world, so it seems like the U.S. president should have considerable governing power within the United States. In actuality, the powers of the president have risen and fallen over time because Article II of the Constitution is somewhat vague on the explicit powers of the president. Why? The founders, only a decade earlier, had fought a "tyrannical" king who threatened their liberty. In turn, the Articles of Confederation were ineffective because they provided no executive branch and insufficient power to stop tyranny of the majority. So in the drafting of the Constitution, the framers recognized the need for a vigorous executive and provided for legislative checks, but they did not want to specify all details of presidential power because the controversy could have been a deal breaker for the Constitution. They had an ace up their sleeve in that they knew that George Washington would be the first president and set the precedent for following presidents. Washington did not seek power like other political actors. In fact, he took the presidency out of duty more than out of ambition. Consequently, he was the proper person to set a limited office.

However, not having explicit and exhaustive presidential powers enumerated in the Constitution has meant that presidents have been incredibly strong relative to Congress in some eras but undeniably weak relative to Congress in other eras. The balance of checks and balances and presidential power remains unclear, leaving presidents to struggle to control their agenda and often claiming that the Constitution not specifically denying them a certain activity means they could in fact do it.

In other words, the framers designed a system with an independent executive branch so that the branches could balance each other through a system of "checks and balances," and considered "executive power" to be distinct from the "legislative power" given to Congress. The "balance" of these checks may favor or disfavor the president at different times and is specifically vague in the Constitution because the framers needed to get the Constitution ratified. This is not to say that the presidency is unhinged or unlike other executive positions in democracies. In fact, the type of government that separates the legislative and executive powers is known as a **presidential system** (Figure 7.1 and Box 7.2), named because the independent executive is led by a popularly elected president.

Figure 7.1 Presidential System

Executive Branch

Electorate → elects → President → appoints → Cabinet

Electorate → elects → Legislature → approves → Cabinet

Legislative Branch

In the presidential system, the citizens elect a president who appoints his or her cabinet. The **cabinet** is a body of advisers to the president, composed of the heads of the executive departments of the government, who with the president and vice president compose the executive branch. In a separate election, citizens elect a legislature that often has to approve the president's cabinet but also has control over legislation. Each branch of government provides a check on the other branch's authority. The adoption of a presidential system makes the United States stand out from other advanced industrial democracies. While there are other presidential systems around the world, the United States is the *only* advanced industrial democracy with this system of government. Presidents in other advanced industrial democracies govern in "mixed presidential systems" highlighted later. This makes the American brand of presidential government unique. Students should be cautioned on one point: while the U.S. president certainly is a powerful figure and occupies a powerful governmental position, at least in the U.S. context, the presidential system does not imply presidential dominance. No one would suggest that the U.S. Congress is also not a very assertive and powerful branch of government. In fact, relative to other executives, the American president may be more tightly checked by other branches.

BOX 7.2

Presidential System

In the presidential system, the electorate elects a president who appoints his or her cabinet. This is the executive branch. In a separate election, the electorate elects a legislature who provides approval for the president's cabinet. This is the legislative branch. There are "firewalls" between the executive and legislative branches. The United States has a presidential system.

Figure 7.2   Parliamentary System

Electorate → elects → Parliment → appoints → Prime Minister and his/her cabinet

Legislative Branch   Executive Branch

BOX 7.3

Parliamentary System

In a parliamentary system, the electorate elects a parliament (legislative branch), and the parliament provides majority support for the prime minister and his or her cabinet (executive branch). The legislative and executive branches are said to be "fused" because the executive comes out of the parliament. "Provides majority support" means that the prime minister (or chancellor) comes from the majority party or majority coalition in the parliament. Most democracies other than the United States have a parliamentary system with fused legislative and executive branches of government.

We can contrast the presidential system of government found in the United States with the **parliamentary system** (Figure 7.2 and Box 7.3), a system much more common among advanced industrial democracies. Every advanced industrial democracy besides the United States, Portugal, France, and the Czech Republic has a parliamentary system of government. In the parliamentary system, the executive and legislative branches of government are *fused*. The executive is composed of two units, a monarch or figurehead president who is head of state and a prime minister (also sometimes called a chancellor or premier) and cabinet that is *selected by and responsible to the parliament*. The cabinet is also often frequently called "the government." Most often the prime minister and cabinet are chosen from members of the legislature. In a comparative sense, this would be like the U.S. House of Representatives choosing the president and cabinet from among its members. There are two very different types of parliamentary systems depending on whether a country is a majoritarian or consociational democracy.

In consociational systems, numerous parties receive seats in the legislature and so choosing the prime minister and cabinet requires bargaining among two or more parties (a handful in some systems like the Netherlands or Israel) to appoint a **coalition government**. The coalition may include parties that disagree on many policies, and parties that have strong positions on some policy area may demand the relevant cabinet position leading that governmental department in the bargaining to build a government. (This concept will be discussed in more detail in Chapter 11). This reflects consociationalism because the parties must come to *consensus* among many different partisan voices on any policy, which increases representation of voices in society but decreases the efficiency of policy making. In fact, the government may not push particularly important issues for fear it could drive a wedge in the coalition and lead to the end of the government.

This differs from majoritarian parliamentary systems that typically occur in what is normally a two-party system like the United Kingdom. In these systems, one party tends to win a majority of legislative seats and gets to appoint the prime minister and all executive cabinet positions. In these cases, the prime minister ends up dominating the legislation and execution of law. The prime minister commands loyalty from his or her party members in the legislature because they control nominations for election and only select loyal partisans to the cabinet. In some systems, the ballot lists only parties and not candidates, so the public votes for parties, and the party gets to create a list of party members who will go to the legislature and/or be in a cabinet position. Either nomination for election or presence on a list requires loyal party voting.

To use the American case as an example again, this would be as if the party that won a majority in the House of Representatives selected the U.S. president and his or her cabinet from among themselves and then allowed the president to write all legislation while providing the president enormous power to command party loyalty in voting. The primary example of such a majoritarian parliamentary system is the United Kingdom, where prime ministers have long dominated the legislative process. Interestingly, in 2010, no single party won a majority in the United Kingdom so the Conservative Party joined in a coalition with the Liberal Democrats. This is rare, however, as the most recent previous example of a British coalition government was Winston Churchill's World War II coalition government. Other democracies have a similar type of limited coalition partnership where a large party only requires a "junior partner" to control the cabinet and the legislative process. Germany tends to follow this model. The German chancellor in this case largely controls the policy agenda and his or her party's legislative support thereof. (Both types of cases will be discussed in more detail in Chapters 10 and 11.)

The fusing of the different branches does not mean there are no checks on the prime minister, even in majoritarian parliamentary systems. In all parliamentary governments, the chief executive (prime minister or chancellor) may not serve his or her entire term. If a controversy or controversial issue saps support for the government, the parliament can dissolve itself and hold new elections before a term is up. These votes are called **votes of no confidence** or **confidence votes**. Not surprisingly, they occur far more frequently in consociational parliamentary systems because a coalition of parties may divide on a large issue. In fact, in Italy, Israel, and other consociational parliamentary systems with multiple parties, the coalition may disband and recreate itself in order to avoid a vote of no confidence and not have to hold elections. This demonstrates the fragility of such consociational parliamentary systems, but it also shows the real checks they provide through political parties for multiple interests in society.

It is far more rare for a vote of no confidence to occur in a majoritarian parliamentary system. The last British vote of no confidence was in 1979 when Prime Minister James Callaghan's Labour government lost a confidence vote by one vote, ushering in the Conservative Party's nearly two-decade dominance. The previous such vote of no confidence was in 1924, so it is rare indeed because members of the prime minister's own party would have to oust him or her and their cabinet and themselves face the public. Checks on authority come at election time when the public can choose to continue with the government's platform or vote in a new party, thus changing the course of governmental policy. Further, British prime ministers can call for elections whenever they wish within a five-year window, so they often choose the moment of their highest approval to gain further governing power. So like the American president, prime ministers mainly enjoy a fixed term of office unless there are favorable electoral conditions. In the United States, even in cases of resignation (like with Richard Nixon in 1974) or death (like with John F. Kennedy in 1963), the vice president carries out the remainder of the term until the regularly scheduled election.

There is a third system of government, which is a hybrid of the presidential and parliamentary systems. We call this system the **mixed** (or semipresidential) **system** of government (Figure 7.3 and Box 7.4) because it carries both elements of the parliamentary system and the presidential system. Like the presidential

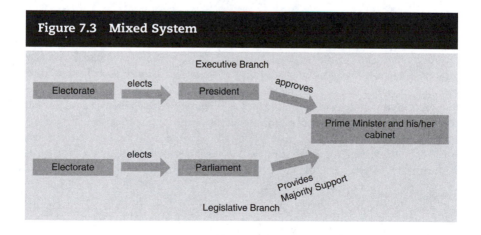

Figure 7.3 Mixed System

system, the executive and legislative branches hold separate elections; however, like with the parliamentary system, the executive must have the support of the parliament in order to stay in power. In mixed systems, we see a dual-executive where usually a prime minister and a president share executive power. The prime minister (or premier as he is called in France) is the head of government, yet shares some of these responsibilities with the president who is head of state. The president's powers go well beyond being a figurehead. In semipresidential systems, the president selects the prime minister to lead the parliament, but the prime minister must be acceptable to the parliament. Consequently, the president and prime minister share executive authority, and they must **cohabitate** as executives. The cohabitation is peaceful when the president and prime minister are from the same party but can be volatile when they come from different parties. Different worldviews and personalities can affect how well they work together, too. Advanced industrial democracies with mixed systems include France, Portugal, and the Czech Republic. Although not considered a liberal democracy, Russia also has a mixed system.

BOX 7.4

Mixed System

Mixed, or semipresidential, systems combine elements of presidential and parliamentary systems. There are separate elections for the executive and legislative branches, yet there is a dual executive. The prime minister (called premier) is technically the head of government, but he shares responsibility with the president, who is both head of government and head of state. In the mixed system, the president is usually the more powerful position. France and Austria have this sort of system.

While presidential and parliamentary systems are certainly different, there is no evidence that one is "better." Further, there are considerable differences among parliamentary systems based on whether they require a coalition within the executive branch or one major party dominates. What the "better" system is depends on the underlying homogeneity or diversity of the society, as well as key political cultural factors that lead to the public's view that a government is legitimate. A parliamentary system that carries a homogenous society's wishes quickly into policy is better for that country. That does not mean that it would work elsewhere, even given its efficiencies. Would other institutions work in the United States, and what might they be like? Table 7.1 and Box 7.5 demonstrate some of the upsides and downsides to majoritarian parliamentarism versus presidentialism and what the United States would be like as a majoritarian parliamentary

Table 7.1	Positives and Negatives of Presidential and Parliamentary Systems	
	Presidential System	**Parliamentary System**
Upsides	–Stability: fixed term to govern, not easily removed by legislature –Independence: compete for executive functions in election separate from fortunes of legislative elections –Checking power: executive branch power checks legislative branch –Cooperation: requires branches and parties to compromise to govern	–Clear mandate: election results translate public wishes into public policy –Easy to hold leaders/parties responsible: it's clear to electorate whom to punish for policy failures or reward for good governance –Can remove unpopular executive: legislature can quickly ditch prime minister, government, and legislature in bad times
Downsides	–Can be left with unpopular president: elections at set intervals making president entrenched unless legislature takes difficult action like impeachment –Limited authority on legislation: often can only veto what the legislature has passed –Lack of governing mandate: separate place on ballot and time provides no definite message for policy from elections –Voters struggle to hold officials responsible: presidents can blame legislature and vice versa for problems or both can take credit for good times, leaving the public without clear electoral target	–Instability of executive: lacking a set term, public can sack prime ministers and governments in bad times and may do so repeatedly—making it hard for leaders to adopt change that hurts in the short term but benefits society in the long term –Indirect selection of executive and government: head of government not directly chosen by the public –Government may be built postelection: coalition governments chosen by elite bargaining rather than by vote –Lack of executive checks: prime minister largely controls legislation and execution of laws

government. What should be clear is that in most other democracies, thinking of the legislative and executive branches separately is tricky, as they are fused into one parliamentary system, and thus, you can't really talk about the legislative branch without also bringing up the executive and vice versa. This is why we deal with them in one chapter in this book.

BOX 7.5

What If the United States Were a Parliamentary System?

In the latter half of 2013, pundits across the country were asking a similar question: Should the United States switch to a parliamentary system? Why the sudden interest in the structure of American institutions? The United States was in the throes of yet another looming government shutdown, with the two houses of Congress and the president unable to reach agreement on the budget. Unable (or unwilling) to enact legislation that would appropriate funds for fiscal year 2014, the federal government shut down from October 1 to 16, 2013. Hundreds of thousands of federal workers were furloughed without pay, and the dollar dropped immediately against foreign currency. Additionally, this shutdown threatened to once again lower the U.S. credit rating and (if you listened to some commentators) spin the world in to economic Armageddon. Was it time, some asked, to ditch the presidential system in favor of another model? The romanticism with the parliamentary system had to do with frustration over American gridlock between executive and legislative leaders, something you do not see in a parliamentary system since the branches of government do not check each other's power, yet are fused.

If the United States had a parliamentary system, you would not have seen the "great shutdown crisis" of 2013. This is because you would not get a situation where the executive branch leader is in a standoff with the legislative branch. In a parliamentary system, the president would have support from the majority party in the legislative branch. In the case of the 2013 shutdown, Barack Obama would have either led a majority of Democrats in the House, or more likely, John Boehner would have been prime minister, as leader of the majority party (the Republicans) in the legislature. With the Republicans in charge of both the legislative and executive branches, they would be able to pass their budget. The Democrats, as the opposition party, could scream and yell all they wanted about cuts to programs, but they couldn't derail the legislative process. If the situation were flipped, with Barak Obama as head of a Democratic legislative majority, the budget of the president would have been passed amidst much Republican protestation, but the Republicans would not have been able to stop it. In short, since the executive leader would command support from his or her party in the legislature, in a parliamentary system, you would not have a president at loggerheads with the legislative branch, leading to a shutdown. The executive and legislative branches would have been controlled by either the Republicans or Democrats, enabling the party in power to fully enact its platform.

If, say, the Republicans controlled the legislature in coalition with another political party (maybe the Tea Party), there could have been the chance that the coalition would have broken apart over the budget negotiation. In that case, a new negotiation would have taken place to find a new coalition partner, maybe the libertarians. Or, there could have been a "**snap election**" called, which is an election when no election has been previously scheduled. In this case, the voters would have settled the matter of the budget in short order, either electing the Democrats and Barack Obama into power or affirming the Republican budget with a stronger majority.

Thus, parliamentary systems avoid standoffs and gridlock, something that was seen at its worst in the United States at the end of 2013. This does not mean that parliamentary systems are without their problems and would fit the American political culture. First, in public opinion polls, a majority of Americans prefer divided government and its checks over one-party rule. Second, parliamentary systems can bring their own gridlock in the government formation process. For example, in Belgium, where there is a parliamentary system, a meltdown of the coalition led to new elections and nearly a year passed before a government could be formed to command support. In Greece, a country facing economic crisis, elections had to be called within a month of each other because a government could not be formed. The presidential system avoids such instability in government.

As a result, as pundits (and students and readers of this book) ponder a switch from the presidential to parliamentary system for the United States, they need to weigh the problems associated with gridlock that eventually occur with a presidential system, a system "built for no," over the instability that can possibly come with a parliamentary system, where we could see sharp changes in governments in power and large swings in public policy.

For more punditry on this topic, see the following:

http://www.minnpost.com/eric-black-ink/2012/10/us-or-parliamentary -system-one-nearly-gridlock-proof-and-it-ain-t-ours

http://www.minnpost.com/eric-black-ink/2013/10/second-guessing -shutdown-would-parliamentary-system-have-avoided-crisis

http://www.npr.org/blogs/itsallpolitics/2013/10/12/232270289/ would-the-u-s-be-better-off-with-a-parliament

Bureaucracy

Presidents or prime ministers or chancellors obviously don't govern entirely by themselves. They have the bureaucracy of the government behind them. In fact, the head of the executive branch is the head of a massive bureaucracy in most advanced industrial democracies. A **bureaucracy** is any organization that is organized hierarchically and has specialized workers. Madison took steps to create the first bureaucracy in the United States with the creation of the State Department in 1789. Examining the German government, Max Weber (1864–1920) came up with a model of bureaucracy based on four points: hierarchy, specialization, explicit rules, and reward based on merit. Weber was reacting to what he saw around him, and in contrast to Marx, argued for a government system and bureaucracy based on political culture by arguing for religious (Protestant) cultural influences on capitalism.

Table 7.2 Bureaucracy, Share of Employment in the Public Sector

Country	Share of Employment in Public Sector
Australia	20.4%
Austria	15.2%
Belgium	19.6%
Canada	19.9%
Denmark	31.4%
Finland	27.0%
France	24.9%
Germany	12.9%
Ireland	19.5%
Israel	18.5%
Italy	18.3%
Japan	12.9%
Luxembourg	22.1%
Netherlands	17.3%
New Zealand	13.4%
Norway	37.8%
Portugal	18.4%
South Korea	10.3%
Spain	17.9%
Sweden	26.0%
United Kingdom	21.5%
United States	15.8%

Source: Data from "Share of employment in the public sector by sex (%)." International Labour Organization. https://www.ilo.org, retrieved May 21, 2018.

Germany today has about 13 percent of its population employed by the government. This is actually lower than the 16 percent employed by the U.S. government.

Government bureaucracies are supposed to operate independently in what is known as **neutral competence**, this means that they are not beholden to the legislative or executive branches of government. Why do we need a bureaucracy? Governments are very large enterprises that take a lot of people working to make things run, especially if we want things to run smoothly. It would be impossible to coordinate a state visit, engage in counterterrorism, or even get a driver's license without the government bureaucracy. It is also important to have experts in charge of these aspects of government, that is, those with merit and expertise. Just as we wouldn't want a car mechanic (or political science professor) doing life-saving brain surgery on us, we probably don't want to rely on nonexperts to ensure our country's counterterrorism organizations are cooperating with those in Europe or developing energy policy that will help decrease global warming.

The United States is like other democracies in this regard. Democracies are generally believed to have well-developed and well-functioning bureaucracies that are free from corruption and made up of experts. At the federal level in the United States, we see the bureaucracy manifest in the different departments of the federal government. These departments collectively make up the president's cabinet. In a presidential system, the cabinet is independent of the legislature; however, in a parliamentary system, cabinet ministers (in the United States mainly called secretaries) are often themselves members of parliament. While technically their agencies ought to operate independently of legislative or executive interference, there still is a tighter connection in parliamentary countries. Thus, in the United States, unlike in parliamentary democracies, political authority over the bureaucracy is shared among several institutions (legislative, executive, and to a lesser extent, judicial). This is in contrast to a parliamentary system like the British system where the prime minister in theory rules supreme.

A second difference between the American bureaucracy and bureaucracies elsewhere is that since the United States is a federal system, its national-level bureaucracy shares functions and responsibilities with state and local bureaucracies. For example, while there is a national Department of Education, you also see state-level education departments and local-level education departments as well. In a unitary system, we don't see this. For example, in France, education, healthcare, and transportation are centralized nationally with little local-level control.

We see similar departments in every democracy, with some local variations. Almost every democracy, for example, has a department of defense and education. France has a Ministry of Culture and Communication that is in part tasked with maintaining the integrity of the French language. Many democracies that are consociational and more homogenous have ministries of culture; the United States does not. Culture comes into play in other ways as well with bureaucracy. American individualism has led to an adversarial culture, where personal rights are given central importance. In other words, we argue more with every decision made by the government, including the bureaucracy. For example, we have debates about how to fund education or what forms need to be filled out for a hunting license. In other countries, similar bureaucratic decisions go largely uncontested.

JUDICIARY

No institutional arrangement illustrates American exceptionalism as much as the role of the judicial branch in the United States. It differs greatly from the judicial systems of every other advanced industrial democracy, especially from the judiciaries of social democracies. The framers' loyalty to principles of legitimate government being limited to protect life, liberty, and property can be seen in the judiciary by (1) the power of the American judiciary as a political body relative to other branches of government and (2) the role of the judiciary to protect citizens' liberties in the criminal justice system.

One key distinction that drives the differences between the American and other advanced industrial democracies' judicial systems stems from the type of judicial tradition the United States follows. As with most other former British colonies, America has a **common law** legal tradition. The far more common democratic judicial tradition, particularly among social democracies, is the **civil law** tradition.

Civil Law Legal Tradition Systems

Roman Emperor Justinian pushed to have Roman law put into a single written code in the sixth century CE, referred to thereafter as Corpus Juris Civilis, or Body of Civil Law. Following the fall of the Roman Empire, most European countries lacked any single coherent legal system through the Middle Ages. The resulting patchwork of folkways and laws that popped up in these societies lacked any consistency or coherence other than the Catholic Church's Canon Law, which governed many areas of people's lives.[15] As a result, when European countries undertook their national revolutions, where modernized central governments began to extend their power to govern all geographical areas of a country with a singular set of laws and standards, they found little common foundation to build a national legal tradition.

It was vital for these national governments to develop a single set of laws and standards for the entire enterprise of nationalizing the country. The Justinian Corpus Juris Civilis became the foundation for many of these countries' legal codes because it was a coherent code of laws governing public law (administrative rules, criminal law) and private law (commercial and trade law, family law).[16] Further, the study of the Corpus Juris Civilis had begun in earnest in Italian universities in the twelfth century, so legal experts who could aid in the development of a country's legal system were often trained in the legal science of the Roman code.[17] Consequently, different countries borrowed heavily from the Corpus Juris Civilis but also tailored their own codes to fit national customs.[18] Perhaps the clearest example of this is the French Civil Code of 1804, often referred to as the Napoleonic Code, which still has large residual components in the French legal system today.

The key distinction between the civil law tradition and the common law tradition is the primacy of the **legal code** in the judicial system. The code is the supreme source of justice in a society and is meant to provide the common good for society.[19] The code is meant to be comprehensive in all areas of law, leaving no gaps between the law and human interactions in governing administration, crime and punishment, commercial relations, social and family life, and social norms of society.[20] Ideally, the national legal code provides citizens with a sort of handbook about citizen rights, responsibilities, and the law.[21] In this way, it would in principle be both simple enough to understand and broad enough to foresee all areas where law would need to be applied in a society.[22]

The role of the legal code means that legislative bodies that craft such codes hold substantial power because it is to be carried out and adjudicated as written. Democratic reformers in European societies in the 1700s through 1800s viewed the judiciary with suspicion because democratic reforms often had been frustrated by courts.[23] Consequently, the design of democratic governments left little power for the judiciary to check the law-making authority of legislatures.[24] With the legal code as the main source of legal power, little room was left for judicial interpretation other than situations where wording of the law does not meet a situation with complete clarity.[25]

This means the role of the judiciary and the actors within the judiciary end up being very different in most social democracies from the role seen in American and other common law tradition legal systems. The appetite to restrict judges' powers centuries ago meant that judges in civil law countries now do not end up playing the prestigious role presiding over the court that Americans are used to. Rather, judges often study a particular area of law—criminal law, family law, administrative law—and then begin their careers as judges immediately out of their law degree.[26] In this way, they are members of the bureaucracy in many other countries. In the American system, a judgeship is the culmination of a prestigious legal career, not a starting point. Judges in countries with a civil law tradition tend to be mostly civil servants who lack an ability to interpret law but are more like "expert clerks," whose job is to find the relevant provision of the legal code that covers the situation.[27] The civil law tradition is often referred to as **inquisitorial** because the judge often investigates the facts of the case in pretrial actions and plays a key role questioning witnesses collecting evidence.[28] The role of the judge is to apply the legal code rather than interpret the constitutional fairness of the legal code or the process.

The process of trials in the civil law tradition tend to be non-adversarial relative to the American system, where one side lays out a case against the other side in front of a neutral judge whose job it is to ensure a fair trial. As mentioned earlier, judges often play an active role in the investigation of a case prior to the court hearing. The prosecutor's job is to investigate and argue cases but also to provide an argument about the public interests involved in a case, not the one-sided pro-prosecution role that Americans would be familiar with.[29] In civil law tradition courts, cases also lack the courtroom argumentative drama of American courts because trials actually take place in multiple meetings over time and rely on written evidence more than oral arguments and court testimony.[30]

Just as the political culture of social democracies places more weight on the common good rather than individual liberties compared to the United States, so, too, does the civil law tradition seek to resolve cases based more on whether the legal code—the embodiment of the common good—was followed.[31] In criminal cases, defendants are expected to testify and answer questions, and even though they may refuse to do so, that is taken into consideration. Conversely, the clear presumption of innocence in the American system means that whether a defendant testifies or not, the court and the process treat them with a presumption of innocence. The presumption of innocence does not occur in the same way that it does in the U.S. system because a judge and court will not continue a case if it is clear the legal code was not violated.[32] This does not mean that civil law tradition systems assume a defendant is guilty or lacks any of the civil rights provided to American defendants. Rather, it is more that the American system puts at its core whether a defendant's life, liberty, or property should be taken away, and Americans would prefer to let a guilty person go free rather than wrongly take away an innocent defendant's life, liberty, and property. Fitting with American political culture, Americans believe their legal system needs to ensure a fair process even if the outcomes are not fair. In other democracies, outcomes need to be fair. In particular, the focus is whether the legal code was followed.

Common Law Legal Tradition Systems

The civil law tradition grew out of a useful legal code being adopted as the basis of law for countries with weak national laws and the weak application of law. Consequently, the codes that were adopted were done so *comprehensively* to produce national control. The legal system was defined at the moment of modern governance and national administration. The common law tradition started out differently. English kings recognized the need to administer the entire country far earlier and began to develop laws incrementally, with new laws built from previous legal findings. Rather than a single comprehensive code, common law is the continuous pragmatic development of a nation's legal system built from the precedent set by earlier legal decisions rather than by a fixed, established, comprehensive legal code.

When the Normans conquered England in 1066, they brought their significant administrative skills and applied them to the existing English social customs that served as the legal basis of the country.[33] This established a government that could administrate and apply standards to the whole country built from the existing English customs. Another key step occurred in 1215, when the king of England agreed to limit the monarchy's power over land-owning lords or barons. The **Magna Carta**—or Great Council—resulted, which was made up of lords who swore allegiance to the king in return for assurances that the king would follow set legal processes when dealing with any potential illegality by lords, and a set of the lord's peers would decide whether the lord had broken any custom or law (a precursor to the modern jury and Supreme Court function of the House of Lords in the U.K., a function it held until 2009).

Giving lords and their peers the ability to limit the king required them to establish whether legal procedures and the king's legal decrees were fair. The Great Council that emerged was the precursor to the House of Lords, the upper house in the United Kingdom, but also triggered the development of professional legal minds within the king's court to deal with legal problems in the country. As a result, some of the king's ministers were sent around the country to hear cases, and this developed a professionally trained group of legal experts who based decisions off of earlier decisions made by colleagues under similar conditions.[34] The legal system grew to develop a law *common* to the entire country but with an ability to slowly and organically build public and private laws as society changed.[35] The existence of a professional legal class also kept Roman legal codes from finding purchase as the basis of the legal system.[36]

The role of judges in these cases is to ensure that the balance of citizen rights and governmental criminal justice are upheld based on the **precedent,** or example, set by earlier cases' findings. The system is referred to as **adversarial** (rather than inquisitorial in the civil law tradition) because the court and judges act as neutral actors, while two opposing sides argue their case before a jury. The role of the judge is to ensure that the procedure fits with the precedent set in earlier cases.

While both the United Kingdom and the United States have common law-based judicial systems, the American common law tradition differs from the British common law tradition in important ways. First, Britain has no single constitution. So, precedent about the proper legal procedures and balance of citizen rights with the criminal justice interests of a government rely on precedent set in earlier cases. The United States has a Constitution that sets most of the core rights and liberties of citizens, but even then, the courts are left to interpret constitutionality of particular situations based on precedent established in earlier decisions. The First Amendment, for instance, provides for freedom of the press, but it does not firmly establish what that completely means in the Internet age. Can anyone lodge false stories about someone on Twitter and be protected as a member of the press? Clearly the framers did not see every application of freedom of the press, but the idea is that precedent built over time concerning newspapers and other media should provide judges with precedent to apply freedom of the press in this new era.

Another strong distinction between the American common law tradition and the British common law tradition relates to the power of the judicial branch. First, the actors in the judiciary—the judges, in particular—are there to ensure the fair legal process for those being accused of a crime or being sued in a civil trial. Second, American courts often settle disputes after problems have arisen in the marketplace and the marketplace of ideas, but this keeps regulation from constricting risk taking in society.

So Americans are often suing each other in civil trials because regulation did not keep problematic products or ideas from causing harm. Thus, in order to avoid rampant vengeance against people who have harmed others, the U.S. government provides courts as a neutral conflict resolution institution. Other democracies regulate their marketplace and the marketplace of ideas more than the United States through their bureaucracies, which leads to fewer lawsuits among private actors but also may be a disincentive to individual risk taking and not fit the American political culture. So, Americans dislike of people suing each other does not mean the alternative of greater regulation would be better.

Finally, American courts have tremendous **judicial review**, or oversight of legislative or executive actions by the judiciary—powers uncommon elsewhere. In civil law tradition, there is no judicial review because judges tend to be lower level officials, and the supremacy of the legal code means that the collective good embodied through the legal code should not be undone by judges. In Britain, there is no established constitution that clarifies constitutionality, so precedent provides the guideposts for legal decisions. The House of Lords used to have, and the United Kingdom's Supreme Court now has, the role of checking legislation passed by the lower House of Commons. This power is limited to legislative oversight, and the House of Commons retained **legislative sovereignty**, or the ultimate power to make law.

In the United States, courts check both the constitutionality of laws as passed, plus whether the president executes those laws constitutionally. This is an amazing power, as Lipset noted—nine justices can overturn the will of a majority of the American people and the democratic institutions that make and execute law. No other country concentrates judicial review of any such power with such a small group. Nevertheless, to avoid tyranny of the majority and protection of life, liberty, and property against government, the United States provides this constitutional body and the entire court profession of judges the power to protect the rights of the accused and those being sued—a key difference in the United States.

CONCLUSION

This chapter looked at the difference in the United States in terms of national governing institutions. Keeping in mind that the United States faced a different historical founding and has a different political culture that led to different constitutional choices than other democracies, we see that this has combined to create different governing institutions. This is not to say that the institutions in the United States are superior to institutions in other countries; it simply means that on many measures of institutional configuration, the United States is different than other advanced industrial democracies.

Perhaps the largest difference in the United States discussed in this chapter is the horizontal organization of power, discussed in terms of presidentialism. The United States is a presidential system, while most other democracies are parliamentary systems. One other key difference stems from the extraordinary power that American democracy gives to the judicial system, which can toss out congressional laws and presidential actions. In the American political culture that values the protection of life, liberty, and property, even democratic majorities and representative institutions have pushed policies deemed unconstitutional; thus, the judiciary is there to provide this important check on possible tyranny. Finally, could

Table 7.3 Summary Table of Select OECD Advanced Industrial Democracies' Institutions

Country	Vertical Concentration of Power	Executive System	Legislative Houses	Judicial Review	Separate Head of State
Australia	Federal	Parliamentary	Bicameral	Yes	Yes
Austria	Unitary	Parliamentary	Bicameral	Yes	Yes
Belgium	Federal	Parliamentary	Bicameral	Yes	Yes
Canada	Federal	Parliamentary	Bicameral	Yes	Yes
Denmark	Unitary	Parliamentary	Unicameral	Yes	Yes
Finland	Unitary	Parliamentary	Unicameral	Yes	Yes
France	Unitary	Parliamentary	Bicameral	Yes	No
Germany	Federal	Parliamentary	Bicameral	Yes	Yes
Ireland	Unitary	Parliamentary	Bicameral	Yes	Yes
Israel	Unitary	Parliamentary	Unicameral	No	Yes
Italy	Unitary	Parliamentary	Bicameral	Yes	No
Japan	Unitary	Parliamentary	Bicameral	Yes	Yes
Luxembourg	Unitary	Parliamentary	Unicameral	Yes	Yes
Netherlands	Unitary	Parliamentary	Bicameral	No	Yes
New Zealand	Unitary	Parliamentary	Unicameral	Yes	Yes
Norway	Unitary	Parliamentary	Unicameral	No	Yes
Portugal	Unitary	Semi-presidential	Unicameral	Yes	Yes
South Korea	Unitary	Presidential	Unicameral	Yes	No
Spain	Unitary	Parliamentary	Bicameral	Yes	Yes
Sweden	Unitary	Parliamentary	Unicameral	Yes	Yes
United Kingdom	Unitary	Parliamentary	Bicameral	Yes	Yes
United States	Federal	Presidential	Bicameral	Yes	No

the United States thrive under a different set of political institutions? Many people argue it could. If you have not already, at some period in your life you will have someone tell you why the United States should be a parliamentary system. If you are reading this for class, hopefully the instructor will raise the issue. If not, you will likely hear it from some know-it-all at a bar, cocktail hour, or Thanksgiving dinner.

What also needs to be considered beyond the nuts-and-bolts of how institutional change could work in the United States is whether American political culture would accept any other institutional system—especially parliamentary government—as we discuss in Box 7.5. American political culture prefers individualism and limited government that does not infringe on life, liberty, and property. In deciding who gets what and how, the framers of the U.S. Constitution designed a system that would have tight checks among the branches and a federal system with big policies decided within states. They feared that too centralized or not centralized enough government could lead to tyranny, and they did so from their very experiences of tyranny by the king of England and by American voters under the Articles of Confederation. It is no wonder why Madison felt he dealt with the "mischiefs of faction" by making tyranny of the majority difficult to bring about by making majorities particularly hard to form. Further, Madison again felt the Framers had reigned in tyranny by unleashing the power-seeking goals of federal branches against each other through checks and balances. Would a man who said in *Federalist 51*, "If men were angels, no government would be necessary" really think that a fused executive and legislature would be good? Would Americans think so now?

POINTS TO REMEMBER

- A head of state is a ceremonial position that carries with it little to no real decision-making power.

- A head of government is the state's chief political officer, responsible for presenting and developing policies, and has decision-making authority.

- The legislative branch of government is responsible for legislating or making laws.

- In a bicameral legislature, there are two legislative chambers, whereas in a unicameral legislature, there is one. The United States has symmetrical bicameralism, where both chambers have equal legislative powers. Most other democracies have asymmetrical bicameralism, where one chamber holds supreme power over legislation. This means there are fewer checks within the legislative branch in other democracies relative to the United States.

- The executive branch of government is the branch of government that "executes" the laws passed by the legislative branch of government. It is responsible for putting the laws into action.

- A governmental system in which the executive branch of government is independent from the legislative branch of government, and the two branches balance each other through a system known as "checks and balances," is called a presidential system.

- In the parliamentary system, the executive and legislative branches of government are fused. The executive and the cabinet typically dominate the creation of legislation. This fused system is much more common than a presidential system in democracies throughout the world.

- A mixed, or semipresidential system has elements of presidential and parliamentary systems.

- Whether or not a country is governed by a civil or common law code greatly influences the role of the judiciary in a system, including the presence and role of judicial review.

- In civil law tradition countries, judges have limited roles, and court processes are driven by the legal code. Common law legal systems are rarer and are adversarial, and decisions tend to be based on precedent.

KEY TERMS

Adversarial 151
Asymmetrical
    bicameralism 129
Bicameral 129
Bureaucracy 145
Cabinet 138
Checks and balances 128
Civil law 148
Coalition
    government 140
Cohabitate 142
Common law 148
Commonwealth
    countries 136
Confidence votes 140
Congressional
    gridlock 130

Consensus 133
Constituency 130
Delegate 131
Executive branch 137
General election 132
Head of government 135
Head of state 135
Inquisitorial 149
Judicial review 152
Legal code 148
Legislative branch 129
Legislative
    sovereignty 152
Magna Carta 150
Midterm loss 132
Midterms 131
Mixed system 141

Neutral competence 148
Parliamentary system 139
Party government 133
Party list systems 134
Pork barrel spending 131
Precedent 151
Presidential system 137
Primaries 131
Representation 130
Republic 129
Snap election 145
Symmetrical
    bicameralism 129
Trustee 130
Unicameral 129
Votes of no
    confidence 140

REVIEW QUESTIONS

1. Explain the difference between a head of state and a head of government. What are examples of each?

2. What does vertical organization of government refer to? What does horizontal organization of government refer to?

3. Explain the difference between presidential, parliamentary, and mixed systems of government. How does the United States compare to other democracies?

4. Why when you are looking at governing institutions comparatively does it not make sense to think of legislative and executive as separate institutions?

5. Why might the United States have ended up with a structure of government very different than the structures of government found in most European democracies?

6. Describe the key difference between civil and common law. In which way is the United States unique with regard to its judicial organization? What role does judicial review play in the United States, and why is it absent (or not as strong) in other countries?

7. Is it time to rethink U.S. national governing institutions? How might a parliamentary system work in the United States? Who would be the proponents? Who would be opponents?

8. Has the role of the American head of state changed in the era of President Trump? Why, or why not?

SUGGESTED READINGS

Lowell, A. L. *Governments and Parties in Continental Europe*. Boston, MA: Houghton Mifflin, 1896.

Madison, James. *Notes of Debates in the Federal Convention of 1787*. Columbus: Ohio University Press, 1985.

Powell, G. Bingham. *Elections as Instruments of Democracy: Majoritarian and Proportional Visions*. New Haven, CT: Yale University Press, 2000.

Tsebelis, George. "Veto Players and Law Production in Parliamentary Democracies: An Empirical Analysis." *American Political Science Review* 93, no. 3 (1999): 591–608.

United States Senate. http://www.senate.gov.

NOTES

1. This was an argument made by Madison in *Federalist 10*.

2. Madison, *Federalist 39*.

3. Eva H. Önnudóttir, "Styles of Representation and Voters' Evaluations of Democratic Performance: Parties and Party Voters," *Journal of Representative Democracy*, 52, Issue 2–3 (2016). DOI: https://doi.org/10.1080/00344893.2017.1288164.

4. Önnudóttir, "Styles of Representation and Voters' Evaluations of Democratic Performance."

5. Donald D. Searing, *Westminster's World: Understanding Political Roles* (Cambridge, MA: Harvard University Press, 1994).

6. Önnudóttir, "Styles of Representation and Voters' Evaluations of Democratic Performance."

7. Angus Campbell, "Survey and Decline, A Study of Electoral Change," in *Elections and the Public Order*, eds. Campbell et al. (New York: Wiley and Sons, 1966), 40–62.

8. Gary Jacobson and Jamie Carson, *The Politics of Congressional Elections, 9th Edition*, (Lanham, MD: Rowman and Littlefield, 2015).

9. For an in-depth discussion of differences in American views of representation versus other democracies, see Russell Dalton, *Citizen Politics: Public Opinion and Political Parties in Advanced Industrial Democracies* (Washington DC: CQ Press, 2013).

10. See Joel H. Silbey, "From 'Essential to the Existence of Our Institutions' to 'Rapacious Enemies of the Honest and Responsible Government:' The Rise and Fall of American Politics," in *The Parties Respond, Changes in American Parties and Campaigns*, 4th ed., ed. L. S. Maisel (New York, NY: Westview Press, 2002), 1790–2000; and John Aldrich, *Why Parties? The Origin and Transformation of Party Politics in America* (Chicago, IL: University of Chicago Press, 1995), for a broader discussion of this view of parties.

11. See Hans-Dieter Klingemann, Richard Hofferbert, and Ian Budge, *Parties, Policies, and Democracy* (Boulder, CO: Westview Press, 1994).

12. See Martin Wattenberg, *The Rise of Candidate-Centered Politics* (Cambridge, MA: Harvard University Press, 1991).

13. Daniel Rubin, "On the Firing Line: Charlton Heston Steps into a New Role," *Philadelphia Inquirer* (June 9, 1998), http://articles.philly.com/1998–06–09/entertainment/25728579_1_nra-president-national-rifle-association-gun-death.

14. Jonathan Karl, Richard Coolidge, and Sharisse Pham, "Elton John: George W. Bush Taught Me a Lesson," *Yahoo News* (July 25, 2012), http://news.yahoo.com/blogs/power-players-abc-news/elton-john-george-w-bush-taught-lesson-040430553.html.

15. H. W. Ehrmann, *Comparative Legal Cultures* (Englewood Cliffs, NJ: Prentice-Hall, 1976).

16. J. H. Merryman, *The Civil Law Tradition: An Introduction to the Legal Systems of Western Europe and Latin American*, 2nd ed. (Stanford, CA: Stanford University Press, 1985); Ehrmann, *Comparative Legal Cultures*.

17. Ehrmann, *Comparative Legal Cultures*.

18. A. T. von Mehren and J. R. Gordley, *The Civil Law Tradition* (Boston, MA: Little, Brown, 1977).

19. Merryman, *The Civil Law Tradition: An Introduction to the Legal Systems of Western Europe and Latin America*.

20. Von Mehren and Gordley, *The Civil Law Tradition*; Merryman, *The Civil Law Tradition: An Introduction to the Legal Systems of Western Europe and Latin America*.

21. Von Mehren and Gordley, *The Civil Law Tradition*.

22. Von Mehren and Gordley, *The Civil Law Tradition*.

23. Merryman, *The Civil Law Tradition: An Introduction to the Legal Systems of Western Europe and Latin America*.

24. Merryman, *The Civil Law Tradition: An Introduction to the Legal Systems of Western Europe and Latin America*.

25. Von Mehren and Gordley, *The Civil Law Tradition*.

26. Merryman, *The Civil Law Tradition: An Introduction to the Legal Systems of Western Europe and Latin America*.

27. Merryman, *The Civil Law Tradition: An Introduction to the Legal Systems of Western Europe and Latin America*; F. G. Kempin, Jr., *Historical Introduction to Anglo-American Law* (St. Paul, MN: West Publishing, 1973).

28. M. A. Glendon, M. W. Gordon, and C. Osakwe, *Comparative Legal Traditions* (St. Paul, MN: West Publishing, 1982).

29. Merryman, *The Civil Law Tradition: An Introduction to the Legal Systems of Western Europe and Latin America*; Glendon, Gordon, and Osakwe, *Comparative Legal Traditions*.

30. Merryman, *The Civil Law Tradition: An Introduction to the Legal Systems of Western Europe and Latin America*.

31. Von Mehren and Gordley, *The Civil Law Tradition*.

32. Merryman, *The Civil Law Tradition: An Introduction to the Legal Systems of Western Europe and Latin America*.

33. Kempin, Jr., *Historical Introduction to Anglo-American Law*.

34. Von Mehren and Gordley, *The Civil Law Tradition*.

35. Von Mehren and Gordley, *The Civil Law Tradition*.

36. Von Mehren and Gordley, *The Civil Law Tradition*.

CHAPTER EIGHT

INTEREST GROUPS

On January 21, 2017, the day after Donald Trump's inauguration, the largest single-day protest in U.S. history took place, the Women's March. The march in Washington, DC is estimated to have been as big as 1 million people. Up to 5 million people are thought to have participated throughout the United States and up to 7 million worldwide. Why did people march? Upset with what was seen as sexist and degrading policies and rhetoric toward women by Donald Trump as a candidate, organizers stated that the march was intended to show that "women's rights are human rights." The march grew into a movement, with organizers putting out 10 actions for 100 days for the first 100 days of the Trump administration. The second Women's March took place a year later to commemorate the work of the year and to continue to press for the rights of women and protest what was seen as infringement on women's rights by the Trump administration. These dramatic responses to Trump's election demonstrate a lot about interest group dynamics in democracies. People respond to something that upsets them, mobilize, take collective action, change tactics, and address political concerns.

Citizens in all democracies have interests and try to influence the political system—that is, they try to influence who gets what, when, and how—or change how those decisions are made. A country's political culture and institutions shape the form and function of this influence. Two important vehicles through which interests are conveyed in democracies are political parties (discussed in Chapter 9) and interest groups. **Intermediary institutions**, like parties and interest groups, make citizens' political behavior easier to achieve and understand by providing key information and political cues to voters, transmitting political values to guide political leaders, organizing the avenues of political behavior, and providing access to elected officials. Parties and interest groups differ greatly on many regards, but they share the above-mentioned functions, as well as two crucial democratic functions: they articulate and aggregate the public's opinions to political leaders.[1]

INTEREST GROUPS, SOCIAL MOVEMENTS, AND SOCIAL MOVEMENT ORGANIZATIONS

In advanced industrial democracies, interest groups, sometimes called social movements in comparative politics, are powerful and important interest articulation and mobilization vehicles. An **interest group** is defined as an organization of people with similar policy goals who enter the political process to try to achieve those aims. For example, those who passionately champion the survival and preservation of pandas may join groups that advocate for pandas like Save the Pandas or the World Wildlife Fund. Those passionate about gun rights may join the National Rifle Association in the United States. Interest groups bring together people who share common purpose and interest to act jointly and in a coordinated fashion. Interest groups and social movements differ from political parties in that they do not run their own slate of candidates for election. This chapter later shows, though, how the line between interest group and political party can be blurred and differs depending on a country's type of democracy.

Observers of American politics often strictly refer to interest groups, but *social movements* is a term usually used more broadly by comparativists and sociologists. Social movements are defined as large groups of individuals or organizations organized around a common social or political issue. Sidney Tarrow, a prominent American social movement scholar, defines social movements as "collective challenges [to elites, authorities, other groups, or cultural codes] by people with common purposes and solidarity in sustained interactions with elites, opponents and authorities."[2]

The conceptual differences between social movements and interest groups are blurry. Some scholars argue that there is no difference at all,[3] whereas others argue that social movements are political outsiders, and interest groups are political insiders.[4] In essence, this means that social movements act through noninstitutional means (outside political institutions), while interest groups work institutionally. This distinction is not always as clear in the real world as it is in a textbook. Many groups start off acting through noninstitutional avenues, and over time, adopt more institutional actions that they use alongside other tactics. For example, Greenpeace started as a protest group, engaging in sit-ins, blockades, and so on, but over time, it became more "mainstream," engaging in lobbying activities and campaign contributions, actions it uses alongside more protest-type activities. In fact, if you went to Capitol Hill or the parliament of any major capital city in democracies around the world on a day Greenpeace was lobbying, you would not be able to tell the Greenpeace lobbyist of today from any other suit-wearing politician. Although, like Clark Kent, they shed their suits when they take to the streets for protests.

Other scholars refer to the term **social movement organization (SMO)** to mean essentially the same thing as an interest group, defining SMOs as "a complex, or formal, organization which identifies its goals with the preferences of a social movement."[5] In short, a social movement, for example, the women's movement or the save-the-pandas movement, can be comprised of many different interest groups or social movement organizations.

Scholars typically have concluded that any real distinction between SMOs and interest groups has largely evaporated in advanced industrial democracies.[6] With the exception of radical SMOs, which opt out of the established system, most groups in advanced industrial democracies use similar action repertoires (from protest and unconventional activities to lobbying and conventional activities) and have been incorporated, either formally or informally, into the policy-making process. Thus, in this chapter, the term *interest group* refers to both interest groups and social movement organizations.

INTEREST GROUP LIFE CYCLE

Most interest groups have a **"life cycle"** (Figure 8.1): they are created, they grow, they achieve successes or failures, and eventually, they die, or dissolve, and cease to exist. Groups are more likely to evolve in a time and place friendly to their development. For example, temperance movements appeared in the United States in the early 1900s during a time when publics were receptive to hearing about the social ills attached to alcohol. In fact, the proliferation of interest groups in the 1900s was a direct result of the increase in ideas of individual rights, freedom of speech, and civil disobedience emerging out of Western societies in the late 19th century. Usually, some sort of polarizing difference between people needs to exist for interest groups to form. For example, during the Industrial Revolution, there were poverty and wealth gaps. Many of the same cleavages discussed in Chapter 9 as the basis for political party formation in other democracies also helped to spark interest groups.

At the start of a movement, in order for interest groups to mobilize, there needs to be an **initiating event**, or a disturbance that shifts a potential interest group into an actual interest group as pluralist scholar David Truman argues.[7] Sociologist Neil Smelser defines this as a particular, individual event that will begin a chain reaction leading to the creation of a social movement.[8] For example, Rosa Parks, a well-trained and active member of the early civil rights movement, energized the American civil rights movement by riding in the white-only section of a bus in Alabama. The South African shack dwellers' movement (discussed in terms of direct democracy in Chapter 2) grew out of a road blockade in response to the sudden selling off of a small piece of land promised for housing to a developer. These types of events are also called **volcanic models** to refer to the fact that interest groups are often created after a large number of people realize that there are others sharing the same values and desire for a particular social change; they come together, and a movement erupts. This does not mean the individuals working on the issue suddenly take notice, as for example, Rosa Parks was working on civil rights before the Montgomery Bus Boycott. It means that these events cause others to come together in critical mass to see a smaller movement erupt into a much larger one.

Once interest groups form, one of the main difficulties facing the nascent movement is spreading the word that it exists. This is why many groups expire after being in operation for only a short period of time. A second problem is overcoming the **free rider problem**, when people reap the benefits of group membership without joining. In other words, groups face a challenge convincing people to join with them instead of following the mentality "why should I trouble myself when others can do it, and I can just reap the benefits after their hard work?" College students with any experience with group work assignments know the free rider problem all too well, where at least one exasperating group member does none of the work on a project, but free rides off the others' hard work for a solid grade. The same thing happens in interest groups. If you love pandas, you can sit idly by while others advocate for protection of their habitat without ever having to write a letter, give money, or lobby a politician. In pluralist interest group countries (discussed in the following section), groups often provide selective incentives that only active members can enjoy as an incentive to not free ride. These benefits include **material incentives** (tangible awards that only members get—discounts or goods), **solidary incentives** (intangible social benefits from working with others), or **purposive benefits** (intangible benefits derived from genuine belief in the cause).[9]

For example, March for Our Lives, a gun control organization that formed from youth protest after the Stoneman Douglas school shooting in February 2018, garners support from those who genuinely believe in commonsense gun laws to stem the wave of school shootings; members reap purposive benefits. Very successful interest groups in the United States do a great job of providing all these benefits, like the National Rifle Association, which provides members who really believe in gun rights a powerful voice and community, as well material benefits such as gun safety and hunting classes, trade magazines, and discounts on firearm-related goods. Not all groups can afford the time and effort to ensure that all of these incentives are satisfied, along with concentrating on the central interest the group was formed to confront. Interest groups in neo-corporatist countries (discussed in the following section), on the other hand, often have laws that mandate interest group participation, which greatly helps to overcome free rider problems.

After interest groups form, they begin to **bureaucratize**. This means that they create levels of organization in order to function and try to influence policy making. At this point, several options are possible:

- The group can be successful at achieving its policy aims. For example, women's suffrage groups were successful in the 1900s in the United States when they achieved votes for women.

- They can fail and have their ideas rebutted. That is, the public is not responsive, and the groups no longer exist as a result.

- They can be coopted. For example, many of the ideas of green movements in Europe were coopted into green political parties. (This can also be seen as a success if the goal was institutional political activity. Thus, "going mainstream" can be sometimes cooptation, sometimes failure or sometimes success.)

- Or, the group can be repressed. The crackdown on radical, separatist groups like the Basque separatist group ETA in Spain and France can be seen as an example of repression. In every instance, the interest group eventually will go into decline if a perceived or actual need for the group no longer exists.

In this respect, interest groups in the United States are similar to groups in other countries. Interest groups in all countries follow this basic life cycle of activity.

PLURALIST VERSUS NEO-CORPORATIST INTEREST GROUP ARRANGEMENTS

Interest groups have been pressuring governments since the guilds in the Middle Ages. The way in which they interact with governments differs from the methods born from the dawn of the modern nation-state, and the particular techniques interest groups use vary based upon the interest group arrangement present in each country.

Pluralism

At a broad level, we can divide interest group arrangements in advanced industrial democracies into two types, pluralist and corporatist. One exceptional fact about the United States is that it is likely the most pluralist of advanced industrial democracies. **Pluralist interest group** arrangements are characterized by

Figure 8.1   Life Cycle of a Social Movement

large numbers of interest groups competing for policy influence. The government plays no formal role in their formation (but may allow special tax status and other financial incentives). By and large, interest groups in democracies with pluralist arrangements are privately funded organizations, and membership is voluntary. Pluralist interest group arrangements are above all characterized by their competition. In pluralist countries, there is competition between groups within sectors to arrive at policy outcomes. For example, in the reproductive policy area, prolife and prochoice groups compete to influence public policy related to abortion and reproductive policy.

Many scholars of pluralism in American policy championed a view that understanding American politics simply required understanding the nature of interest-group competition in American society. In this view, interest groups drive the public policy agenda, and the American government is a neutral and passive mediator for interest group participation. Pluralists largely assumed that interests would balance each other out like competitors in the marketplace or plants and wildlife in a healthy biological environment. Compared to the formal role that interest groups are provided in the corporatist model highlighted later, interest groups in pluralist democracies influence politics informally through different actions: lobbying policy makers, educating the public, and helping sympathetic politicians through electioneering. (Although, as we'll note later, interest groups' action repertoires can be broader still and encompasses nonconventional activities.)

Photo courtesy of the authors

▶ **Photo 8.1** Scenes from the Women's March Jan. 21, 2017.

Interest groups lobby elected officials to make policy favorable to the group. Americans hate the idea that special interests influence public policy because they equate it with a group getting their wishes rather than policy being made for the common good. Scholars also have found fault with the influence of lobbying on policy in the public interest, though some scholars find that interest group politics concentrates power in too few interests, while others have found that there are too many interests persuading policy makers into pursuing incoherent and wasteful policies.

Some argue powerful interests exert too much influence over governmental policies. If particular interests dominate public policy making, this violates the assumption that interests will balance each other out. One classic critique is what analysts call the **iron triangle**. The iron triangle refers to a "cozy" policy-making relationship found in the United States between congressional committees, an executive agency (bureaucracy), and an interest group. A congressional committee is likely made up of members whose reelection or political power benefits from a policy that benefits their district or state. The executive branch agency appreciates support for its reason for existence and its well-supported budget. The associated interest group satisfies its membership, provides key persuasive information to the congressional committee members when they weigh policies, and rewards the congressional committee members with electoral support. A classic example of an iron triangle is the relationship between the Department of Defense, Armed Services committees, and defense contractors. Some critical of Trump's White House have argued that iron triangle–like relationships exist between the head of the EPA, environmental regulation committees, and the coal industry. Iron triangles go against the idea that the state is a neutral and passive mediator in interest group competition and that there is balance among interest group voices, which are ideals that undergird positive views of the pluralist interest group arrangement.

Others argue that iron triangles only affect particular policy areas, and most policies actually bring a broader competitive web of interest groups into the debate. Those critics do not always find a sympathetic ear with the American public, who fear that the best idea may not win out, but the interest group with the loudest voice or deepest pockets may hold a disproportionate amount of sway over policy making, leading to policies that benefit the minority, rather than the public interest.

Ironically, the second type of critique of pluralism is that there are too many interests affecting policy rather than too few. **Hyperpluralism** is an argument that too many interest groups have become too powerful, leaving the government trying to satisfy far too many interests. According to this view, policy makers end up trying to please all interests, which leads the government to develop confusing, redundant, or contradictory policies. As Theodore Lowi (1931–2017) noted decades ago, under hyperpluralist regimes, *the "public" interest is lost to the satisfaction of a series of "special" interests.*[10]

Interest groups also try to mobilize public opinion in the United States. Some of the most storied moments in American political history came from citizens banding together to change the public's view on issues, to change who got what, when, and how. The civil rights movement, anti-Vietnam movement, environmental movement, and the women's movement among others changed public policy only after shifting the public's attitudes through grassroots action. Often groups are locked out of an ability to lobby political leaders, so the group is forced to indirectly lobby leaders by shifting the attitudes of the public the leaders represent. This mechanism has been so successful that even the most powerful interest groups use this method, not just through protest but by advertising in the media. For example, in 2017 and 2018, resistance groups in the United States held airport protests and marches to get the public more engaged in issues around immigration. This is a tactic the resistance movement (the anti-Trump movement) took in 2018 up to the midterm elections. Changing public perception is not unique to the United States; interest groups in all democracies engage in this type of activity. For example, in 2014, peace groups across Europe put placards up at bus stations arguing for humanitarian intervention in Syria in an effort to get European publics to put pressure on politicians to become more engaged in the crisis in that country.

Advocacy groups spend considerable money highlighting issues they find important. This practice occurs in both the United States and its democratic brethren. Groups may run advertising campaigns at any time, but these days a myriad of differently named interest groups (political action committees [PACs], super PACs, 527 groups, social welfare groups, corporations, and labor unions) fund advertisements during political campaigns. The groups cannot coordinate with any candidate, and this historically has meant that such groups run negative advertisements against a candidate they want to defeat. The limits on raising money for these groups, spending by these groups, when they can run ads, and how they can fund each other have been severely reduced following the 2010 *Citizens United* and other recent Supreme Court decisions. *Citizens United* said that the First Amendment not only protects the free speech rights of individuals but also of nonhuman entities. Counter to a century of congressional laws and Supreme Court decisions, the *Citizens United* ruling prohibits the government from restricting independent political expenditures by corporations, associations, or labor unions because advocacy advertisements from these groups share all the First Amendment rights against regulation of political expression. Americans dislike everything about such advertising: the role of money in elections, the equation of money to free speech, and increased negativity in campaigns. Nevertheless, interest groups—even those who advocated against eliminating regulations on such advertising—are highly motivated to take advantage of the laws and this environment to influence how the public views candidates. Earlier United States' laws made it illegal for corporations to give money from their treasuries and for unions to give from their membership dues. Thus, corporations and unions created PACs to raise money, donate to candidates, and advocate on issues.[11] Another key expenditure by PACs, however, is on **issue advocacy**, that is, advertising through newspapers, Internet, radio, or television, and calls or e-mails to potential voters.

Political action committees also donate directly to candidates' campaigns. On its face, this makes sense since particular politicians are often closely related to particular interests either due to personal interest, or more commonly, because of an overriding economic, social, or cultural interest that exists in the region they represent. This is not unique to the United States, and in fact, is an artifact of democratic governance everywhere. What is exceptional in the United States is the degree to which interest groups are able to influence candidate platforms and the electoral process, referred to as **electioneering**. Candidates in the United States spend considerable time and effort seeking financial help from interest groups to fund their political campaigns. While interest groups in other countries also give money to candidates, pressures to fund-raise are greater in the United States primarily because TV time for candidates is not free as it is in other countries.

Americans dislike this relationship and often hold that interests are buying votes. The evidence shows that PACs tend to give to ideologically favorable (to their cause) candidates and more importantly target their contributions to gain access to politicians who sit on committees that craft relevant legislation more than buy votes, which is likely more important than simply gaining support on a vote.[12] Other studies suggest that donations do affect votes.[13] Though the evidence bends toward donations going to ideologically favorable candidates and mostly gaining access to key politicians—which may be more upsetting than PACs chucking around money pell-mell to everyone trying to gain votes—the American public thinks that PACs donate to gain access and buy votes no matter what the evidence demonstrates. There are many constitutional and political reasons why reform of interest group money in politics through issue advocacy or through donations is unlikely. Not surprisingly, many of the political cultural and political institutional features of American politics relative to other democracies really play out in harmony to allow the "liberty" and "property" components of life, liberty, and property freedoms to come to the fore when it comes to interests and money in politics.

The combination of decentralized politics, a presidential institutional system, and lax campaign finance laws (compared to other countries) means that money through interest groups enters into the political system more in the United States than in other countries. When special interests take hold in democracies, it is easy to point to the downsides of pluralism. Proponents of pluralism, however, hold a normative assumption that pluralism promotes democracy because it allows many voices into the policy-making sphere. It has been heralded as a major and exceptional benefit of the American political system and is certainly a characteristic that distinguishes the United States from its democratic cousins. The pluralist system in the United States is built on the early founders' wish to promote the rights of citizens to organize while also preventing individual citizen liberty being overrun by a vocal minority. Thus, pluralism is thought to mediate tyranny, allowing citizens to collectively come together to voice concerns over *varied* interests. In fact, some countries, like the United Kingdom, have moved over time from more corporatist interest group systems (discussed next) to more pluralist systems for exactly these reasons.

Corporatism

Rather than interest groups playing an informal agenda-setting or outside lobbying role as the pluralist interest group model finds, corporatist interest group systems provide a formal role in conjunction with government officials in the public policy-making process. This is why corporatist or neo-corporatist interest group systems inhabit the opposing end of the interest group continuum from pluralist interest group arrangements. While we will use the terms interchangeably, as they are often used interchangeably in the political science literature, *corporatism* was originally used to refer to a system of government and an economy formulated as an alternative to socialism. While corporatism has origins in ancient Greece, it mainly refers to the latter half of the nineteenth century and efforts by the Catholic intelligentsia in Europe to offer an alternative to socialism that maintained a market economy and private property, yet emphasized social justice.[14] Corporatism, while sounding similar to corporation, does not refer to corporations but derives from the Latin word, *corpus*, meaning body. The idea was that a society should be organized into major interests (corporations) and representatives of these interests should settle problems and develop policies through negotiation. Corporatism had its dark side as well. **Fascist corporatism** was a system of totalitarian state control of society through interest groups seen in Hitler's Germany, Mussolini's Italy, and Salazar's Portugal.

Neo-corporatism was used to describe the resurgence of corporatist (not fascist corporatist) ideas in welfare states in the post–World War II era. In the postwar period in the war-torn countries of particularly Austria and Germany, many felt that national unity was necessary and that industry and labor had to work together to repair and rebuild the fractured society. It is not an accident that explaining neo-corporatism was a dominant focus of West European politics scholarship of the postwar period, particularly in the 1970s and 1980s. Neo-corporatism was defined in 1974 by Phillipe Schmitter, a leading scholar in the field, as "a type of interest group arrangement characterized by a small number of groups that had monopoly over certain policy areas."[15]

Thus, *neo-corporatism* was coined to refer to a situation where there was tight policy making between government, labor interests, and business interests. These three large interests are in constant negotiation to influence, in particular, fiscal policy. As interests in society have moved beyond only the financial, and postmaterialism has propelled other interest groups into the center stage, we see similar negotiation between government and interest groups over a host of policy areas. The Nordic countries typify a neo-corporatist interest group arrangement, but it exists in other social democratic countries like Germany and Austria, as well.

The structure of neo-corporatist interest group arrangements differs significantly from pluralist arrangements. Whereas in pluralist democracies we see many interest groups, neo-corporatist countries are characterized by their small number of interest groups. In neo-corporatist countries, the government controls the number of interest groups, providing licensure for groups and grants and/or subsidies. Groups usually operate as federations and have monopolistic representation over a policy issue. For example, while in the United States, a pluralist country, there are many different women's groups, in Germany, which is more neo-corporatist, women's groups operate in broad federations, and there are significantly fewer groups (see Box 8.1). Membership in groups is also often compulsory in neo-corporatist countries. This is particularly true for labor groups. Neo-corporatist governments have informal and formal influence of the group, in practice melding them into the legislative process. In neo-corporatist countries, groups act as policy experts, providing expertise in a formal policy-making relationship with the government. In essence, interest groups have a seat at the policy-making table. In pluralist countries, interest groups are *influencing* policy, whereas in neo-corporatist countries they are actually *formulating* policy. For example, in Sweden, the government is required by the constitution to send copies of bills to affected interest groups for review. The bill is then discussed by a commission that is made up of civil servants and representatives from interest groups influenced by the bill, before it is voted on by the parliament. Once voted on and passed, the administration, or implementation, of the new policy, is carried out by a board of those affected groups. The end result is that policies are enacted in a spirit of cooperation and compromise and have buy-in from the relevant interests upon enactment.

Advocates of neo-corporatism argue that this type of interest group arrangement allows for efficient policy making and better laws, making the argument that policy makers are able to seek and find more relevant information to arrive at better public policies, and that corporatist states have more flexible policy adjustment.[16] In addition, in neo-corporatist countries, there is a search for consensus and social harmony while conflict is minimized as the government enters in to a "pact" of sorts with society. Conversely, detractors argue that due to the federated structure of groups in neo-corporatist countries, small groups are at a disadvantage, and regional and local concerns are not heard. In addition, this allows for nonelected political participation, in essence bypassing the electoral process.

Table 8.1 Characteristics of Pluralist and Corporatist Arrangements

Characteristic	Pluralist	Corporatist
–Number of groups	Large numbers	Few, organized by sector and licensed by government
–Role of government	No formal role	Formal role in organization
–Source of funding	Private	Mix of private and public
–Membership	Voluntary	Can be compulsory
–Competition	Highly competitive between groups to arrive at policy outcomes	Not very competitive, positions negotiated with government and few groups per sector
–Role in policy making	*Influencers* of policy	*Makers* of policy

BOX 8.1

Women's Groups in the United States and Germany

Interest groups form because groups of citizens coalesce around interests that they share in common. One type of group we hear quite a bit about is a women's group. **Women's movements,** or groups, are groups with central goals pertaining to "women's gendered experiences, women's issues, and women's leadership and decision making."[17] They can be feminist, antifeminist, or nonfeminist. **Feminist women's movements** challenge "political, social and other power arrangements of domination and subordination on the basis of gender,"[18] while **antifeminist women's movements** "protect women's socially ascribed gender roles, like mother or wife in the private sphere."[19] "**Nonfeminist women's movements**, unlike antifeminists, accept women's entry into the public sphere, yet do not actively seek changes in gender relations."[20] A feminist women's movement would protest against sexism, an antifeminist women's movement would advocate for women to stay in the home, and a nonfeminist women's movement would work on "women's issues" such as day care, education, or family violence. All advanced industrial societies have feminist, antifeminist, and nonfeminist groups. In the United States, however, compared to a country like Germany, the concentration of such groups is different.

The first thing you notice when you look at a listing of women's groups in the United States and Germany is the stark difference in the sheer number of groups in each country. In Germany, a more neo-corporatist state, there are relatively few groups. Groups work in "federations." In fact, in Germany, there are fewer than a dozen nationally active women's groups. The group Deutsche Frauenring is a good example. This federated group has about sixty local branches, but it operates as a single organization. Because of its federated structure, it focuses on activities from protesting sexism in society to a capital campaign to invest in job training for women in West Africa. Groups moderate their message in neo-corporatist countries as well. While few groups in Germany could be strictly classified as feminist, there are also few antifeminist groups. Most would be considered nonfeminist because of the wide range of issues upon which they focus. While there are groups with federated structures in the United States, there are many, many more groups in the United States than in Germany. While in Germany, you would have one group that took on both sexism and fair trade/work empowerment issues of women in Africa, in the United States, you would see this done by many different groups. This is because the United States has a pluralist interest group arrangement. This means that in the United States you have much broader differentiation of groups and many groups which would fall into the feminist and antifeminist camps, while most women's groups would be considered nonfeminist in all advanced democracies, including the United States.

The type of interest group arrangement influences how groups act in the two different countries as well. In Germany, given its corporatist structure, research has shown that protest makes up less than 1 percent of activity among women's groups. That said, according to research by Poloni-Staudinger and Ortbals (2014),[21] women's groups are less likely to engage in consultation with the government over policies in Germany (a characteristic of a neo-corporatist state) than social groups in other sectors, indicating that women's groups continue to be less likely to be invited to the proverbial policy-making table. In the United States, women's groups are also not often seen consulting with government; yet, due to the sheer number of groups, we find some that often engage in protest as an activity choice, particularly in the current Trump era, and others that choose more conventional activities such as lobbying. In all countries, however, research points to the idea that women's groups are most likely to engage in "service" work, such as educational campaigns or social gatherings.[22]

WHY PLURALIST OR NEO-CORPORATIST?

Historical trajectory and political culture influence a country's preference for pluralist versus neo-corporatist interest group arrangements. Similarly to majoritarian versus consensus democracies, neo-corporatist states are consensus states. In order for neo-corporatism to work, the political culture needs to be one based on broad social values, which are also shared by the state, unions, and employers. A preference for negotiated rather than conflict-driven decisions exists in neo-corporatist societies. In short, the social democratic political culture of neo-corporatist states is more communal than that of liberal democratic countries with pluralist interest groups. Perhaps the single most distinctive feature of pluralist interest group systems is that they are characterized by conflict rather than consensus. This does not mean that individuals in pluralist countries welcome conflict; it simply means that they tend to be more individualistic in their political cultural orientations and prefer competition over ideas rather than communal solutions to policy problems. Neo-corporatism is seen most prominently in Catholic countries (due to the historical origins in Catholic thought) and in post-conflict countries, like Austria and Germany. It is also seen in countries where there is a long tradition of social democracy and highly developed social welfare systems (like Nordic countries).

ROLE OF INTEREST GROUPS IN THE UNITED STATES HISTORICALLY AND TODAY

In the United States, interest groups have historically been viewed negatively. In fact, the framers warned that such groups were a threat to democracy, and fear of interest group power helped to motivate the redrafting of the new United States Constitution after the Articles of Confederation. Madison argued that greater power needed to be granted to the national government to spread out interests so that no one faction could receive a majority and increase tyranny. Yet, in the Bill of Rights, the First Amendment—guaranteeing protections of expression (speech), religious belief, and assembly—protected the foundations that allowed interest groups to flourish and proliferate in the United States and vie for government influence. As a result, the United States Constitution actually "protects [interest groups], has multiple points of access for advocacy groups, and often requires that vigilant interest groups shepherd legislation through the intricate decentralized policy-making process."[23] When this is coupled with the fact that American political parties are less ideological and organizationally weaker than parties in other democracies, more space opens up for interest groups to provide articulation of citizen preferences and to compete for policy positions compared to other democracies.

There are definite upsides to a large number of interest groups in pluralist democracies like the United States. The frequency of American elections and the frequent lack of competitiveness of these contests mean that while voting for political parties may be the most conventional type of political participation, it is not always the most effective (see Chapters 10 and 11). This is where interest groups can step in. If a broad-based party in the United States does not champion your interest, you can always turn to an interest group. If, for example, neither the Republican nor Democratic parties champion panda protection, you can choose to join an environmental group to express and act upon your concerns. These groups, then, may provide an especially effective means of democratic participation for American citizens and may lead to greater citizenship skills and citizenship development[24] and an increase in social capital among citizens.[25] Political scientist Robert Putnam argues that when people work together in associations and/or interest groups, the social benefits from their efforts such as increased interpersonal trust and a stronger affinity for democracy trump the actions a citizen can achieve alone.[26] Interest groups provide an avenue by which we can build social capital among citizens and undergird democratic health. This idea reflects thinking by de Tocqueville from centuries before.

Associational life in the United States is very healthy. Nine out of ten Americans belong to at least one association, and in true pluralist form, there are over twenty-five thousand nonprofit membership organizations of national scope in the United States.[27] These groups cover anything from where not to build a local railway to quilting clubs to reproductive rights organizations. Putnam's alarm about Americans "bowling alone" rather than joining bowling leagues highlights the negative consequences of Americans not joining voluntary associations and even political interest groups.[28] Putnam's argument was that the civic republicanism of American political culture is falling victim to individualism. Nevertheless, even though Americans are very clearly joining groups, most of the associations Americans join do not deal directly with advocacy before government. Instead, they help govern society outside the realm of government. Indeed, an average of less than 10 percent of associational revenue is spent on political activity.[29] That said, when we consider that 10 percent of revenue of these twenty-five thousand-plus nonprofit associations is spent on political persuasion, the aggregate amount spent on political activity is significant. In addition, if we add in local and regional organizations, this number multiplies many times over. This number is also growing. One remarkable thing to happen after the 2016 election is the degree of organization among those in opposition to President Trump. Indivisible, an umbrella group for the resistance to the Trump administration, has registered more than 6,000 grassroots groups, and Erica Chenoweth has detailed over 8,700 protests in the United States, counting every day from the Women's March of January 21, 2017, through December 31, 2017, with about 74 percent of these protests being either directly against President Trump or his policy agenda. Estimates are that between 1.8 to 2.8 percent of the U.S. population participated; this is a dramatic increase in participation and does not count nonprotest activity that has also ticked up post-2016.[30]

In short, Americans' penchant for association, yet distrust of parties and government, has led to a situation where we both despise and embrace associational life in both its political and nonpolitical iterations. Thus, as seen in this American example, historical trajectory, political culture, and institutional configuration influence whether or not a country gravitates to a pluralist or corporatist interest group system (see Figure 8.2).

Figure 8.2 Continuum of Advanced Industrial Democracies: Neo-Corporatist to Pluralist

| Austria Sweden Germany | Netherlands Denmark Germany Switzerland | Luxembourg Iceland Belgium | Spain France UK Ireland Canada Portugal | US |

Neocorporatist - → Pluralist

TYPES OF GROUPS

All countries, regardless of their interest group structure, have various types of interest groups, and all interest groups want to achieve some sort of change. At a broad level, these groups are determined by who their target is and how much change they want (see Figure 8.3). In this regard, the United States is very much like other advanced industrial democracies. All democracies have alternative, redemptive, reformative, and revolutionary movements and groups.

Alternative groups seek rather limited societal change. They target a small group of people and a specific behavior and attempt to change the behavior of individual people in relation to that issue. Mothers Against Drunk Driving would be an example of an alternative group in the United States. There are similar groups in all advanced industrial democracies.

Redemptive groups form when a society is "repenting" for what it perceives as earlier mistakes. The "Jesus Freak" movement of the 1970s is a prime example seen as atonement for the hippie movement of the 1960s. "Jesus Freak" was the somewhat pejorative term given to the religious Jesus movement that arose in reaction to the "acid freak" and "hippie" movements of the 1960s. At the time, "freak" was a neutral term and described any counterculture member with a specific interest in a given subject. The civil rights movement in the United States could be seen as atonement for slavery. Roma (the politically correct term for the ethnic group most Americans refer to as gypsies) rights groups in Europe are seen as an atonement for years of discrimination against the Roma, particularly during the Holocaust.

Reformative groups try to cause limited change for the whole society. Trade unions who work on behalf of increasing wages for all workers would be an example. There are two types of reformative groups: progressive and reactionary. **Reactionary groups** try to keep things the way they are or try to go

Figure 8.3 Types of Social Movements

	How Much Change?	
	Limited	**Radical**
Specific Individuals	Alternative Social Movements	Redemptive Social Movements
	Example: Mothers Against Drunk Driving	Example: Civil Rights Movement
Everyone	Reformative Social Movements	Revolutionary Social Movements
	Example: Pro-Life/Anti-Abortion Movement	Example: Anarchist Movements

back to the way things were. For example, the Ku Klux Klan is a reactionary movement that tries to keep up the old idea of white superiority. National social (Nazi) groups in Germany would be a similar example. **Progressive groups** try to create change in a new direction. Environmental groups in the United States and Europe that work on increasing air quality standards would be an example of progressive groups. Indivisible, discussed above, would be an umbrella for progressive groups as well. Many progressive groups are called **new social movements**.

NEW SOCIAL MOVEMENTS

Until the post–World War II era, many of the interest groups in both corporatist *and* pluralist states focused on economic issues, either from the point of view of labor or business (capital). In fact, neo-corporatism specifically articulated a formal position for business and labor interests in the drafting of policies. In advanced industrial democracies in the 1960s and 1970s, issue concerns expanded beyond the traditional economic and labor arenas into a new area of politics concerned less with economics and more with quality of life. Scholars have referred to these groups as new social movements, and they include interest groups such as peace groups, environmental groups, civil rights groups, feminist rights groups, and gay rights groups, among others. Many social movement scholars attribute the rise of new social movements to a value change among publics of advanced industrial democracies. Scholars argue that the citizens who participate in new social movements are marked by a common concern over social issues, which they often prioritize over economic concerns.[31] The same forces that gave rise to the green parties of Western Europe also led citizens to agitate for interests beyond economic interests. As a result, we see that in terms of the types of groups we can expect to see in a democratic society, there is not much difference between the United States and other advanced industrial democracies. The way in which groups participate, however, is tightly tied to the institutional arrangement in which they find themselves.

HOW DO GROUPS PARTICIPATE IN POLITICS?

At a broad level, interest groups participate in the political system using insider or outsider tactics. **Insider tactics**, like voting, are those that occur inside existing political institutions. **Outsider tactics**, like protesting, occur outside of political institutions. Whether or not a group chooses to engage in insider or outsider tactics is in part a function of the ideology and focus of the group and in part a function of whether or not the group is embedded in a pluralist or neo-corporatist state. As a savvy student might suspect, neo-corporatist states promote insider strategies, whereas in pluralist states outsider strategies are more likely. Some groups vary their tactics depending on the issue or the impact they wish to make using a mix of both insider and outsider strategies. Thus, save the panda activists may dress up as pandas and march in protest or block forest logging, or they may lobby national governments or international organizations for policies and laws that promote panda habitat protection.

Institutions influence interest groups in other ways as well. At a broad level, when institutions are "closed" to interest groups, groups will pursue outsider strategies, such as protests, demonstrations, and letter writing. In extreme cases, groups will pursue violent political activity (see Box 8.2). Institutions are closed when a party is in power that is not hospitable to the group's goals, when cabinets are divided in power, and when electoral volatility—a measure of electoral change discussed more in Chapter 10—is low. When institutions are "open," groups pursue insider strategies, such as lobbying and consulting on policy making. Institutions are open for interest group action when a favorable party is in power, cabinets are unified, and electoral volatility is high.[32] Research also shows that much of what groups actually do is nonpolitical in nature. A women's rights group may promote breast self-exams, an environmental group hold a park cleanup, or a labor group a member picnic. This harkens back to the associational life that de Tocqueville and Putnam heralded. Democratic citizens join groups, and sometimes these groups act politically, and sometimes they do not. Many believe, however, like de Tocqueville, that even when groups are not acting politically, they are building a civic identity among their members. Due to the pluralist nature of the United States, the United States has many different groups to join, an exception to what we see in other democracies.

Because of the decentralized nature of government in the United States, interest groups must employ numerous mechanisms to influence politics. This is different from pressures in more centralized states, or parliamentary states. The separation of powers among the different branches of government and the different levels of government—for example, between the federal, state, and numerous local governments—in Americans' lives means that a large number of political elites must agree that an issue is sufficiently important before they consider changing the status quo.[33] This means that groups in the United States must act in *many* more arenas than groups in other advanced industrial democracies. An upside to this is that while groups may face a closed system at one level of government, they may find more hospitable waters at other levels of government. A similar situation exists among groups in the European Union. European groups that find institutions closed at a national level will often bump participation up to the European Union level in order to try to influence policies. In this way, the **"venue shopping"** done by groups in the United States between state, local, and national governmental institutions is similar to what we see being done in Europe between the nation-state and the European Union.[34]

This idea that institutions present open or closed opportunities for social groups is referred to as the **political opportunity structure approach** to interest group activity. An important thing to keep in mind is that political opportunities are not static but are dynamic and always changing. While a group may find itself confronted with a closed opportunity at one point in time, promoting nonconventional or extra-institutional activity, an open opportunity structure may later present itself, causing the group to shift to different, more institutional and conventional activities. Opportunity structures are not the only thing that influences group activity. **Resource mobilization** scholars believe that what is most important in determining interest group activities are group resources, such as money, staff, knowledge, and connections. Critical scholars point more to **group identity**, or the ideological orientation of the group, in influencing activity choices.

BOX 8.2

Violent Groups

When we think of interest groups in the United States and in other democracies, we probably think of special interests, of lobbying, of PACs, or money in politics. We probably don't think of bombs, abductions, and assassinations. Nevertheless, while we may not agree with it, violent political action is just as much a form of political participation as lobbying. Violent political participation is a type of extra-institutional participation. If we think of group activity along a continuum from most to least conventional, violent participation would be on the far end of unconventional activity past such activities as protests, demonstrations, and sit-ins. Violent political activity brings up ideas of terrorism, particularly when thinking about violence in the United States. When we think of terrorism, however, we often think of it as originating outside of the United States. This is a false perception. Every democracy has bred its own violent interest groups.

National-separatist groups, which agitate for "independence, autonomy or reunification of a splintered homeland,"[35] are the most common type of violent group in most democracies. Examples of separatist groups in democracies include the IRA (Irish Republican Army) in the United Kingdom, ETA (Euskadi Ta Askatasuna) in the Basque regions of Spain and France, and FLQ (Front de Libération du Québec) in Canada. While the United States differs from other democracies in that it does not have prominent separatist groups, it has many of its own domestic terrorist organizations (some have been named as such by the FBI; others have engaged in what the government calls "terrorist acts" but have not been named to the FBI terrorist list). Why does the United States not have national-separatist terrorism to the same degree as other democracies? It has to do with our founding and the fact that the United States grew through immigration and territorial expansion westward and not through conquest of independent kingdoms and cultures. For example, ETA in the Basque regions of Spain and France, grew out of a Basque nationalist movement in place since the unification of the

(Continued)

(Continued)

Basque country with Spain. This movement was heightened under the Franco dictatorship in Spain (1939–1975) due to the harsh action of the Spanish state against mainly student agitators for Basque independence. Officially established in 1959, ETA is responsible for over 800 deaths, of mainly police and politicians in Spain and France. ETA declared a ceasefire in 2011, yet there are rumblings of continued unhappiness and remobilization among the more militant members of the group.

Terrorist groups in the United States fall into three broad categories: radical environmental groups, far-right Christian and/or white supremacist groups (including anti-abortion groups), and radical left-wing groups. While American radical left-wing groups share much in common with groups from other democracies, most have disbanded or dissolved since the late 1980s, a trend mirrored in other democracies. For example, groups like the Red Brigades in Italy, the Red Army Faction (RAF, Bader-Meinhof Gang) in Germany, and Weather Underground in the United States all targeted symbols of business and capitalism in their attacks. All groups came into existence and mobilized in the late 1960s, reached their peaks in the 1970s, and declined through the 1980s and 1990s. Radical right groups are the most active in the United States today, an exceptional nature of violent United States politics. While not seen in as large of numbers in other countries, the ideology that underlies these groups is certainly present in other democracies. This led the British Home Affairs Committee to warn of growing far-right terrorism in the United Kingdom and across Europe, citing "persuasive evidence."[36] These groups take different incarnations, but most adhere to a radical and militant form of Christianity. Often mobilizing over abortion, they engage in bombings and targeted assassinations. Others seek separation from the government or follow a doctrine of white supremacy. Thus, while the concentration of violent political groups is different in the United States than in other democracies, the United States, like its democratic cousins, has violent interest groups within its borders.

CONCLUSION

Interest groups, sometimes referred to as social movement organizations, are a mechanism through which citizens' interests are combined and articulated in advanced industrial democracies. Present in all democracies and engaging in a variety of activities, from conventional to violent, the nature of the interaction between groups and the state is in part a function of political culture and in part a function of institutional arrangement. While the United States is exceptional in that it is the most pluralist of all countries, many of the functions carried out by interest groups in the United States are similar to functions carried out by groups in more neo-corporatist states. The increase in the number and types of interests involved in elections and the money spent by interest groups to influence campaigns has caused some to bemoan the growth of "moneyed" interests in the United States. While this is a concern in all democracies, it is heightened due to the pluralist nature of the United States' system and the weakening regulation of campaign finance laws, which were always already much weaker than other democracies. Nevertheless, interest groups provide an important vehicle through which people can participate in politics.

Americans may not like some aspects of interest group politics, like the power of lobbyists or the free flow of money in elections. Americans ironically possess simultaneously held beliefs that there are not enough interest groups considered on some public policies but way too many interests considered in other public policies. Given the American political culture of individualism, premium of individual liberty, and distrust of strong government, however, one is left to ask whether there could be any alternatives to the way pluralist interest group politics plays out in the United States. There is no way that Americans would want the government restricting political expression, and advocacy money now equals a form of expression in the eyes of the courts. Americans would also shudder at the thought that the private sector could not provide expert advice to policy makers, yet this is how lobbying is viewed legally. The American public would completely reject a massive hiring of policy advisors who could provide expert advice in lieu of the private sector. So the American public does not like some aspects of interest group politics, but they certainly fit Americans' political beliefs better than alternatives and certainly more than neo-corporatism would.

While the United States is starkly different from democracies with neo-corporatist interest group arrangements, and the level of money spent by interest groups to influence debate is much higher in the American system, it shares much in common related to interest groups with other democracies. In every democracy, interest groups follow a life-cycle model, which varies based on how much change they want to bring about and who their target is and possess broad action repertoires that vary based upon the openness of the institutional environment with which they are confronted.

POINTS TO REMEMBER

- Interest groups, or social movement organizations, are a way outside of political parties for people with similar interests to influence politics.

- Interest groups have life cycles. They emerge, coalesce, bureaucratize, mobilize, and eventually decline.

- Interest groups are subject to free rider problems, when a person can reap the benefits of group action without having to participate in this action himself or herself.

- At a broad level, we can divide interest group arrangements in advanced industrial democracies into two types, pluralist and corporatist. The United States is the most pluralist of all countries; some have referred to the United States as hyperpluralist and influenced by special interests and PACs. Most European countries are more neo-corporatist, with interest groups participating in policy making.

- Groups can be broadly categorized as alternative, redemption, reactionary, and revolutionary.

- *New social movements* is a term used to describe movements and groups that focus on noneconomic concerns and have increased in number with the growth of postmaterialist values.

- Groups can participate in politics institutionally or extra-institutionally; the form participation takes is often influenced by the institutional structure in a country, resources, or ideological orientation of the group.

KEY TERMS

REVIEW QUESTIONS

1. What is an interest group? What is a social movement organization? What debates have there been over the similarities and differences of these terms?

2. Describe the life cycle of an interest group.

3. Explain the difference between pluralist and corporatist interest group arrangements.

4. What sort of factors influence whether or not a country has a pluralist or corporatist interest group arrangement?

5. Discuss the pros and cons of pluralist versus corporatist interest group arrangements.

6. What are redemptive, revolutionary, alternative, and reformative interest groups? Describe and provide an example not used in this chapter.

7. How can groups participate in politics? What sort of factors mediate group action?

8. How do you participate in associational life? What skills/benefits have you acquired from membership in an interest/associational group?

SUGGESTED READINGS

Burstein, Paul. "Social Movements and Public Policy." In *How Social Movements Matter*, ed. Mario Giugni, Doug McAdam, and Charles Tilly, 3–21. Minneapolis: University of Minnesota Press, 1999.

McCarthy, John, and Mayer Zald. "Resource Mobilization and Social Movements: A Partial Theory." *American Journal of Sociology 82*, no. 6 (1977): 1212–1241.

Meyer, David, and Sidney Tarrow, Eds. *The Social Movement Society*. Lanham, MD: Rowman and Littlefield, 1988.

Pichardo, Nelson A. "New Social Movements: A Critical Review." *Annual Review of Sociology* 23 (1997): 411–430.

Poloni-Staudinger, Lori. "The Domestic Opportunity Structure and Supranational Activity: An Explanation of Environmental Group Activity at the European Union Level." *European Union Politics 9*, no. 4 (2008): 531–558.

Putnam, Robert. *Bowling Alone: The Collapse and Revival of American Community*. New York, NY: Simon and Schuster, 2000.

Ruffner, Frederick. *Encyclopedia of Associations*, 47th ed., vol. 1. Detroit, MI: Gale Research., 2009.

Snow, David, Sarah Soule, and Hanspeter Kriesi, Eds. *The Blackwell Companion to Social Movements*. Malden, MA: Blackwell, 2004.

Tarrow, Sidney. *Power in Movement: Collective Action, Social Movements and Politics*. New York, NY: Cambridge University Press, 1994, 2011.

Verba, Sidney, and Norman Nie. *Participation in America: Political Democracy and Social Equality*. New York, NY: Harper and Row, 1972.

Verba, Sidney, Kay Schlozman, and Henry Brady. *Voice and Equality: Civic Voluntarism in American Politics*. Cambridge, MA: Harvard University Press, 1995.

Wolf, Michael. "Special Interests and How They Help Shape United States Legislation: Interesting Possibilities or Potential Pitfalls?" In *Public Opinion and Interest Group Politics: South Africa's Missing Links*, ed. Heather Thuynsma, 12–41. South Africa: Africa Institute of South Africa, 2012.

NOTES

1. Gabriel Almond and James Coleman, *The Politics of the Developing Areas* (Princeton, NJ: Princeton University Press, 1960).

2. Sidney Tarrow, *Power in Movement: Collective Action, Social Movements and Politics* (New York, NY: Cambridge University Press, 1994).

3. Paul Burstein, "Social Movements and Public Policy," in *How Social Movements Matter*, ed. Mario Giugni, Doug McAdam, and Charles Tilly (Minneapolis: University of Minnesota Press, 1999), 19; Burstein claims that there is "no theoretical justification for distinguishing between social movement organizations and interest groups."

4. David Snow, Sarah Soule, and Hanspeter Kriesi, eds., *The Blackwell Companion to Social Movements* (Malden, MA: Blackwell, 2004), 7–8; in this view, social movements are much less formal, but both are "different kinds of collectivities."

5. John McCarthy and Mayer Zald, "Resource Mobilization and Social Movements: A Partial Theory," *American Journal of Sociology* 82, no. 6 (1977): 1212–1241; see pages 1217–1218.

6. David Meyer and Sidney Tarrow, eds., *The Social Movement Society* (Lanham, MD: Rowman and Littlefield, 1998).

7. David Truman, *The Governmental Process* (New York, NY: Alfred A. Knopf, 1951).

8. Smelser, Neil J. 1963. *Theory of Collective Behavior*. New York: Free Press.

9. Peter Clark and James Q. Wilson, "Incentive Systems: A Theory of Organizations," *Administrative Science Quarterly* 6 (1961): 129–166.

10. Theodore Lowi, *The End of Liberalism* (New York, NY: Norton, 1969).

11. Michael Wolf, "Special Interests and How They Help Shape United States Legislation: Interesting Possibilities or Potential Pitfalls?" in *Public Opinion and Interest Group Politics: South Africa's Missing Links*, ed. Heather Thuynsma (South Africa: Africa Institute of South Africa, 2012), 12–41.

12. On not buying votes, see John Wright, "PACs, Contributions, and Roll Calls: An Organizational Perspective," *American Political Science Review* 79 (1985): 400–414; on gaining access, see Richard Hall and Frank Wayman, "Buying Time: Moneyed Interests and the Mobilization of Bias in Congressional Committees," *American Political Science Review* 84 (1990), 797–820; or Joshua Kalla and David Brockman, "Congressional Officials Grant Access Due to Campaign Contributions: A Randomized Field Experiment" (working paper, 2014, https://onlinelibrary.wiley.com/doi/full/10.1111/ajps.12180.).

13. Doug Roscoe and Shannon Jenkins, "A Meta-Analysis of Campaign Contributions and Roll Call Voting," *Social Science Quarterly* 86 (2005): 1.

14. Paul Clarke and Joe Foweraker, *Encyclopedia of Democratic Thought* (London, UK; New York, NY: Routledge, 2001).

15. Phillip Schmitter, "Still the Century of Corporatism?," *Review of Politics* 26, no. 1 (1974): 85–131.

16. Kaare Strom and Stephen Swindle, "Political Parties, Institutions and Environmental Reform" (working paper 2.17, Political Relations and Institutions Research Group, International and Area Studies, Berkeley, CA, 1993), 7.

17. Karen Beckwith, "Lancashire Women against Pit Closures: Women's Standing in a Men's Movement," *Signs* 21, no. 4 (1996): 1034–1068.

18. Karen Beckwith, "Beyond Compare? Women's Movements in Comparative Perspective," *European Journal of Political Research* 37, no. 4 (2000): 437.

19. Sonia Alvarez, *Engendering Democracy in Brazil: Women's Movements in Transition Politics* (Princeton, NJ: Princeton University Press, 1990), 24.

20. Lori Poloni-Staudinger and Candice Ortbals, "The Domestic Determinants of Transnational Activity: An Examination of Women's Groups in the United Kingdom, France and Germany," *International Studies Quarterly* 59, no. 1 (2014), 68–78.

21. Poloni-Staudinger and Ortbals, "The Domestic Determinants of Transnational Activity: An Examination of Women's Groups in the United Kingdom, France, and Germany."

22. Poloni-Staudinger and Ortbals, "The Domestic Determinants of Transnational Activity."

23. Wolf, "Special Interests and How They Help Shape United States Legislation."

24. Sidney Verba and Norman Nie, *Participation in America: Political Democracy and Social Equality* (New York, NY: Harper and Row, 1972); Sidney Verba, Kay Schlozman, and Henry Brady, *Voice and Equality: Civic Voluntarism in American Politics* (Cambridge, MA: Harvard University Press, 1995).

25. Robert Putnam, *Bowling Alone: The Collapse and Revival of American Community* (New York, NY: Simon and Schuster, 2000).

26. Putnam, Robert D. 1993. *Making Democracy Work: Civic Traditions in Modern Italy*. Princeton, New Jersey, USA: Princeton University Press

27. Frederick Ruffner, *Encyclopedia of Associations*, 47th ed., vol. 1 (Detroit, MI: Gale Research, 2009), vii–ix.

28. Putnam, *Bowling Alone*.

29. Ruffner, *Encyclopedia of Associations*, vii.

30. See https://sites.google.com/view/crowdcountingconsortium/home.

31. Nelson A. Pichardo, "New Social Movements: A Critical Review," *Annual Review of Sociology* 23 (1997): 411–430.

32. See for example, Lori Poloni-Staudinger, "The Domestic Opportunity Structure and Supranational Activity: An Explanation of Environmental Group Activity at the European Union Level," *European Union Politics* 9, no. 4 (2008): 531–558.

33. Wolf, "Special Interests and How They Help Shape United States Legislation."

34. Poloni-Staudinger, "The Domestic Opportunity Structure and Supranational Activity."

35. Dennis Pluchinsky, "Ethnic Terrorism: Themes and Variations," in *The Politics of Terrorism: A Survey*, ed. A. T. H. Tan (London, UK: Routledge, 2006), 40–54.

36. Casciani, Domini, "Home Affairs Committee Warns of Far-Right Terror Threat," BBC News, February 6, 2012, http://www.bbc.co.uk/news/uk-16900108.

CHAPTER NINE

POLITICAL PARTIES

George Washington in his farewell address to the young nation of the United States warned of political parties, stating that they "gradually incline the minds of men to seek security and repose in the absolute power of an individual." While Washington acknowledged it was natural for people to coalesce into groups to push their demands on government, he warned that the effort of one party to defeat another would lead to despotism and in extreme cases war. More than two centuries later, political parties are still competing in the United States for votes, although some might argue that there was a grain of truth in Washington's warning.

Chapter 8 explained how interest groups help to articulate citizen preferences and how this is exceptional, or different, in the United States compared to other democracies. Even more so, the paradoxical role of political parties in American democracy serves as one of the most glaring distinctions between the United States and other advanced industrial democracies. Scholars often refer to parties (and interest groups) as intermediary or linkage institutions because they serve as intermediaries that link citizens with political leaders. This is an enormously important role in contemporary representative democracy because intermediary institutions make politics easier by providing key information and political cues to voters, transmitting political values to guide political leaders, organizing the avenues of political behavior, and providing access to elected officials.

While both interest groups and parties articulate and aggregate different political views to political leaders, interest groups often form around a single issue or a series of interrelated issues. Political parties, the focus of this chapter, tend to aggregate interests *far more than even broad-based interest groups*. For example in a politically left party, one party member may be very concerned with conservation issues while another party member cares more for organized labor. Decisions about curtailing a particular industry's jobs to stop negative consequences for particular animals' conservation would then pit one party member who champions workers' rights against another party member who favors environmental conservation. As a result, the party might wish to not articulate very clearly on the issue, in order to build and aggregate both pro-environment and pro-labor members. Thus, **political parties** organize people with at least roughly similar political aims and opinions to elect candidates to public office, differing from interest groups' focus primarily on influencing public policy.

PARTY HISTORY AND FORMATION

Social Cleavages: The European Party System Formation

One of the key distinctions among American parties and parties in other advanced industrial democracies comes from the history of the country and reasons that parties originally formed. Parties formed from different conditions in other democracies and often the bases of their formation created roles for parties that reach deeper into society and reflect more permanent and fundamental social and political divisions than do parties in the United States.

Party systems in most European democracies followed similar foundational patterns. Scholars Seymour Martin Lipset and Stein Rokkan tie the genesis and persistence of parties to what they refer to as significant social cleavages that emerged from large-scale historical changes.[1] In particular, the national revolutions that swept through these societies in the eighteenth century and the Industrial Revolution in the nineteenth century opened up significant social divisions that provided the popular base for different parties. Lipset and Rokkan's deep historical explanation has been criticized, but it is a powerful tool for understanding the different determinative and formative influences for political parties. Their theory helps to explain why—from their origin—American political parties differ from parties in other democracies.

The national revolutions occurred in these countries as national governments began to centralize governance with common laws, certification of trades, and the creation of standards, and governments began to reach out to govern the entire geographic area of their country with modernized bureaucratic control. Marriage and burial laws may not seem like drastic social changes, but to cultural communities living far from a country's capital, having laws that undermined cultural and religious traditions dictated by a distant government created a threat. An urban capital laying down standards for agricultural areas challenged ways of life. This created two large-scale divisions according to Lipset and Rokkan:

1. A **center-periphery cleavage** formed. The cosmopolitan, educated, and modern capitals pushed standards and laws to modernize society and to provide order and uniform governance and public safety. This conflicted with peripheral regions that often had agricultural values rather than urban values and very often had distinctive cultural, ethnic, and religious beliefs that they did not want swept away by national dictate. These ethnic, cultural, and linguistically separate groups bound together against the reach of the central government. Also, agricultural and fishing interests pushed back against land ownership and other regulations.

2. National control also often meant the secularization of standards and institutions. This challenged religious control of marriage, burial,

medicine, and schooling. Therefore, Catholic, Lutheran, and Calvinist churches pushed back against legal changes that would undermine religions' control of their believers' social order if not their lives. Sometimes the government adopted laws that favored one of these religions, which drove the others to coalesce to defend their ways of life in opposition. This led to the **church-state cleavage**.

Both of these divisions growing out of the national revolution led to groups building social institutions that would further connect members together in a common identity and mindset. They developed their own guilds, trades, social groups, sports clubs, media, and eventually political parties.

Another key social revolution that created cleavages in society and influenced party formation was the Industrial Revolution. In previous eras, social, economic, and political power in European societies came from the landed aristocratic class. These dukes, lords, or barons owned large plots of land and relied on the labor of peasants. The political power and economic riches from this system lasted for centuries. With the Industrial Revolution, a new class of rich inventors, industrialists, and investors arose in the urban centers of these countries. Not only did the emergence of this new class dislodge the hold the landed aristocrats had on politics, but the fruits of their new industries reshuffled the nature of relationships between agricultural production and the marketplace. Now burgeoning urban centers created the demand and set the price for agricultural products. New mechanized production from these industries made more of the new urban rich class even wealthier. The market power of these industrialists brought political power as well, especially when so much of the production and economic growth occurred in the capitals and other large cities of these countries. Thus, the Industrial Revolution created cleavages of its own:

1. First, this resulted in an **urban-rural cleavage** among those of means. Often these new captains of industry wanted market forces to drive the economy without government oversight, as one would expect from people who had earned such fantastic wealth in a relatively short period of time. The landed aristocratic class preferred that the governments of these countries protect the economic, social, and political status quo rather than allow such great changes to society. The new urban upper class embraced the changes in society that benefited them so much, and their embrace of liberal economics and limited government split off the political values of this group relative to the longer-established countryside wealthy.

2. Even more dynamic than the urban-rural split was the split that developed between the owner class and the working class in these new industrialized cities, what Lipset and Rokkan called the **owner-worker cleavage**. The Industrial Revolution brought with it very challenging

working and living conditions for the working classes. The socialist movement involved an enormously sized working class who lacked political or economic power. Their push for both led socialist leaders to demand greater political power—including the right to vote—in the attempt to gain control of government and regulate or own businesses in order to reduce the difficulties of the market on this class. Indeed, the glue that kept the working class together during the socialist movement was far more than economic arguments, rather the right to vote for these citizens created common purpose.

These two large-scale social revolutions developed the major parties of the European democracies and even East Central European parties.[2] The particular number and type of competitive parties that ended up emerging depended on whether the leaders of these movements were viewed as legitimate bargaining partners to other political leaders and whether or not divisions were cross-cutting. For instance, a religious ethnic group concentrated in a distant region of a country speaking a distinct language from the rest of the country might well have developed a single party that blended these cleavages. In other countries, these may have resulted in separate divisions and separate parties. Also, when voting rights were extended in European democracies, the specific voting laws could discourage some parties from competing on their own and instead encourage them to link up with other smaller parties sharing common interests. The effects of electoral laws on the number of parties will be discussed in more depth in Chapters 10 and 11. In short, European party systems mapped onto the existing social cleavages born out of the National and Industrial Revolutions and articulated these different interests in society.

Lipset and Rokkan noted that these parties built from the social cleavages continued to thrive into the 1960s and concluded that European party systems were in effect "frozen party systems" despite the fact that the social divisions forming them had been established sometimes a century or more previously. Thus, the social cleavages endured as parties, even though two world wars had ravaged the political, economic, and social systems of many of these countries.

Just as the ink was drying on Lipset and Rokkan's classic, other scholars questioned how frozen these party systems were. In particular, Ronald Inglehart posited that a third **"silent revolution"** had occurred in these advanced industrial democracies introducing a new social division that would lead to weakening of these cleavage-based parties and likely lead to the development of new parties.[3] Inglehart noted the post–World War II generations held different political values than earlier generations. Borrowing from Maslow's needs hierarchy, Inglehart noted that these younger generations did not experience **scarcity**—the economic difficulties and threat to survival from war—as their parents' and earlier generations had in World War I, the worldwide depression of the 1930s, and World War II during the late 1930s and early 1940s. Further, a new middle class had grown substantially that did not fit on either side of the owner vs. worker social cleavage that divided labor, social democratic, and socialist parties from the center-right conservative or church denomination-based parties. This is because these new middle-class workers worked for wages like the blue-collar working class did from earlier ages but did so in professional environments. Insurance sales, middle-level management, bank tellers, technical workers, and others, as a result, had political interests that neither fit the owner class nor the working class directly. Consequently, earlier generations whose party choice centered on debates about issues (wages, employment, social order) that tied to **materialist values**, differed from this younger generation who worried more about civil rights, social equality, and having more say in democracy—or what Inglehart called **postmaterialist values**. To these voters, established political parties got in the way of democracy and ignored vital issues of equality, peace, and environmentalism.

This so-called silent revolution weakened existing parties as it broke the transmission of party allegiance from generation to generation. Further, the new postmaterialist political values received their voice through new parties such as the Greens that began to compete broadly throughout Europe in the 1980s. These voters and new parties pushed for entirely new issue appeals and weakened established parties long used to championing materialist value issues, which led to dwindling numbers of people supporting the established cleavage-based parties and generational battles over party politics and political values generally. It's no wonder politics were so expressive, protest-based, and perhaps messy in the 1960s in the United States and in other democracies, where university campuses were turned into centers of protest for the children whose parents built their upper-middle-class status on the status quo of society, while the working class clamored for more social and political conservatism in the face of the changing social, political, and party dynamics.

Taken together, the social cleavage model of party development based on major social revolutions means that in European democracies in particular we see the formation of party systems that are like each other, even if some parties could not overcome the thresholds that kept political interests from forming into parties. Nevertheless, party observers often refer to similar "party families" that have emerged across these democracies.[4] This includes agricultural, ethnic, religious, or regional parties from the national revolution and center-periphery cleavage and the conservative or Christian Democratic parties representing the center or social order interests from the National Revolution. In turn, the liberal parties grew from the urban-rural split from the Industrial Revolution as well as the many socialist, social democratic, or labor parties that emerged to represent the working classes. Green parties and other new politics parties represent the last social cleavage between established materialist parties and the postmaterialist values citizens. Table 9.1 shows the transmission of political values from social revolutions to the differing party families that have emerged as a consequence.

Table 9.1   Revolutions, Cleavages, and Resulting Parties

	Cleavage	Groups Affected	Resulting Party
National Revolution	Center-Periphery/ Religious-Secular	Industrialists/Urban Middle Class	Liberal Party
	Center-Periphery	Linguistic/Cultural/ Regional Groups	Ethnicity Parties
	Religious-Secular	Religious Groups Religious Reform Groups	Christian Democrats Orthodox Party
Industrial Revolution	Worker-Owners	Workers	Socialist Party Social Democratic Party Labor Party
	Urban-Rural	Agriculture/Fishing/ Farmers Regional Groups	Agrarian Parties
Silent Revolution	Materialists-Postmaterialists	New Middle Class	Green Parties

Source: Derived from Seymour Martin Lipset and Stein Rokkan, *Party Systems and Voter Alignments: Cross-national Perspectives* (New York, NY: Free Press, 1967).

AMERICAN PARTY DEVELOPMENT—WHY AREN'T PARTIES AS STRONG?

The Founding and the Aversion to Parties

American political parties did not form as champions of a huge sector of society growing out of society-changing social revolutions. Scholars of American political parties differ in their interpretations of how political parties formed and how and why they change, but they all agree that parties do not furnish the primary linkage between citizens and government in the United States that they do elsewhere.[5] American parties began under a cloud of antiparty suspicion. James Madison laid out the logic for the new federal Constitution in *Federalist 10*, championing greater powers for the national government, as a means of combating the "mischiefs of faction." Madison tried to build a better mousetrap to keep parties from driving government, which is hardly the way other democracies viewed parties in their constitutional writing process as we will see below. Madison was not alone in his antipathy toward factions or parties. In his farewell address, George Washington pleaded with his country to not become entangled in foreign affairs and to not allow parties to form. In particular, Washington feared that the carefully crafted Constitution with an institutional architecture that required careful deliberation to function and enormous popular sentiment to change could be hijacked by short-sighted partisans driven by human nature and "sharpened by the spirit of revenge" that comes with party dissention. Such actions would ultimately break down the institutional protections for "tranquil enjoyment of the rights of person and property" and could even end up with a single person holding far too much power. Table 9.2 shows just how concerned key founders of American democracy were about political parties.

Madison's and Washington's fears about parties, though functionally ignored, have culturally remained among Americans. Americans have never liked political parties and have remained suspicious of them. Even at their high point in American history in the urban party machine era (1890–1920) and spoils system in the federal government, critics and progressives noted that they were less genuine institutions of popular democracy than they were functionally effective at best and perhaps even injurious to American democracy at worst. Compare that view of parties to the post–World War II era in other democracies. In particular, Dr. Konrad Adenauer, who some say is the George Washington of Germany, is credited with building German democracy by building the Christian Democratic Party as a viable democratic institution that engaged Germans at the grassroots, ensured against the type of extremism that led to the Third Reich, and helped to develop a civic political culture among the German citizenry.[6] Parties may function in American democracy, but they have not been seen as entirely beneficial to democracy.

THE NATURE OF AMERICAN PARTIES

Despite the founders' concerns, political parties did form in the United States with some irony for Madison and Washington. First, just after Madison penned *Federalist 10*, he and the Federalists agreed with key Anti-Federalists to include the Bill of Rights upon the ratification of the Constitution. What is key is that the First Amendment assured the freedom of association that ensured that parties, interest groups, and a free media could easily form. Further, newspapers were key components of parties in the early republic, and party scholars discuss early party leaders as collections of elected officials, elite clubs, and newspapermen.[7] Also contrary to our view of Madison, his banding together of the Federalists to write the *Federalist Papers*, as well as his political career, suggests that he viewed parties as productive as well as potentially dangerous. The American public also did not listen to the father of the country on either the warnings about foreign entanglements or political parties. Washington had to have seen the development of parties right underneath his nose between

Table 9.2 Founders' Views and Warnings about Factions and Parties

James Madison in *The Federalist Number 10*

"Complaints are everywhere heard from our most considerate and virtuous citizens, equally the friends of public and private faith, and of public and personal liberty, that our governments are too unstable, that the public good is disregarded in the conflicts of rival parties, and that measures are too often decided, not according to the rules of justice and the rights of the minor party, but by the superior force of an interested and overbearing majority. . . . By a faction, I understand a number of citizens, whether amounting to a majority or a minority of the whole, who are united and actuated by some common impulse of passion, or of interest, adversed to the rights of other citizens, or to the permanent and aggregate interests of the community. . . . It is in vain to say that enlightened statesmen will be able to adjust these clashing interests, and render them all subservient to the public good. Enlightened statesmen will not always be at the helm. Nor, in many cases, can such an adjustment be made at all without taking into view indirect and remote considerations, which will rarely prevail over the immediate interest which one party may find in disregarding the rights of another or the good of the whole."

George Washington's Farewell Address

"All obstructions to the execution of the laws, all combinations and associations, under whatever plausible character, with the real design to direct, control, counteract, or awe the regular deliberation and action of the constituted authorities, are destructive of this fundamental principle, and of fatal tendency. They serve to organize faction, to give it an artificial and extraordinary force; to put, in the place of the delegated will of the nation the will of a party, often a small but artful and enterprising minority of the community; and, according to the alternate triumphs of different parties, to make the public administration the mirror of the ill-concerted and incongruous projects of faction, rather than the organ of consistent and wholesome plans digested by common counsels and modified by mutual interests."

Vice President John Adams and former Secretary of State Thomas Jefferson in the run-up to the 1796 election. By the 1800 election, when Jefferson defeated Adams, the level of vitriol reached such a level that it makes today's campaigns look like they are run by Miss Manners. In that election, Adams's side argued that if Jefferson were elected the country would see the guillotine and French Jacobin terror, and Jefferson's side, not to be outdone, said that Adams would bring the United States back to the tyranny of the British monarchy.

The parties that did develop in the United States did not involve deep-seated social divisions. Some scholars argue that American parties should be viewed as malleable creations of politicians in order to regulate access to office, to coordinate policy in government, and to mobilize the public.[8] Parties were formed and have changed not because of large-scale and long-standing social divisions but because ambitious American politicians find new uses for them. Consequently, parties formed early on not as some broad representation of social concerns but as mechanisms to broker deals among legislative leaders and to produce Electoral College majorities.[9]

The more conventional view of American party formation and history comes from the **critical realignment** party history model. Accordingly, American parties are built on diverse group coalitions that loyally support a party for a generation before out-of-power party leaders seize a new issue that destroys the old majority party coalition and creates a new coalition that usually either brings the previously minority party or a new party into majority control.[10] American parties have long streaks of stability, punctuated by dramatic "critical" elections centered on large outstanding social issues—like slavery, industrialism, and the Depression—that fundamentally change the party coalitions and the terms of political debate for decades.[11] What is distinctive about this view of party development is that the cleavages are not "frozen" around large-scale social divisions with real commitment. Rather, party leaders maintain attention on the issue that brought them their majority status and avoid or straddle new issues that are bound to come up after years of avoidance by the major party.[12] Also, the seeds of each coalitions' demise are sewn into the particular conditions of the coalition coming together because the coalition brings together such diverse groups that it is likely to burst with new social problems coming to the fore as history moves forward and with new generations coming into the electorate with their own issue concerns.[13] Therefore, American party history and the parties themselves are built on shifting coalitions that have limited life cycles historically rather than being party systems built on rather permanent social cleavages, like the party systems described by Lipset and Rokkan in European democracies.

WHERE ARE THE AMERICAN CLEAVAGES?

The distinctive cleavages that have led to enduring party systems elsewhere do exist in American politics, but they have not developed into the frozen divisions that established long-standing party divisions elsewhere. Further, the United States has a more diverse population than many other democratic societies, which makes the nature of the cleavages that do emerge more cross-cutting, and coalitions are more likely to form as a result. Shifting political concerns bring different social identities forward for voters that earlier may have been submerged by other interests. For instance, political scientist V. O. Key (1908–1963) showed how northeastern Catholics began to shift their loyalties from the Republican Party to the Democratic Party after the Democrats fielded a Catholic presidential candidate in 1928.[14] Earlier, these voters' regional affiliation had kept them loyal to the Republican Party at the same levels as Protestants based on the northeastern industrial interests that Republicans had championed. Those regional interests—an important part of those voters' identity previously—had taken a backseat in 1928 and thereafter to their religious identity.

There are other reasons the cleavages that formed the basis of parties else-where had less traction in the United States. Certainly, class has been a long-term distinction throughout American history. Madison noted this in *Federalist 10*: "But the most common and durable source of factions has been the various and unequal distribution of property." This has been present throughout American party his-tory, whether the mobilization of class by Jacksonian Democrats, the Populists in the late nineteenth century, or the Depression-era championing of the working class with programs of the New Deal Democratic Party. Classic American litera-ture such as *The Great Gatsby* and *The Grapes of Wrath* highlight class-based social problems. Even today, class division remains important even though social issues complicate its effects on party identification and voting.[15]

Despite its long-term division, this party divide has been slight in degree rela-tive to other class-based parties born of the socialist movement. Class has never entirely dominated American society to the level that it defined a party's basis for being. This goes back to American exceptionalism and the fact that the United States did not experience the socialist movement. Americans' broad agreement on social contract and Lockean liberty kept class from defining the American ideo-logical belief and party systems. Further, as emphasized in Chapter 3, another impulse of the socialist movement dealt with the provision of the right to vote. In the United States, voting rights were defined by states, and many states did not restrict voting based on class. The relatively early vote for the lower classes as well as individualism reduced the potential of class as a fundamental long-standing cleavage in society for parties in the United States.

Religious divisions, too, have had their influence in American politics as in other democracies. Americans have numerous religions and tend to be more reli-gious than citizens in other democracies. Despite the depth and breadth of reli-gion in American life, no consistent religious party has formed. Likely this is due to the First Amendment, which prohibited the establishment of any official reli-gion. It also has provided broad religious liberties to citizens, so the government does not forbid many religious practices that would lead a left-out religious group to drive to form an officially religious party. To be sure, there are many who have chosen their party out of frustration about the government not allowing open religious practice (prayer in school) or based on liberal social policies (gay mar-riage or the life issue). These latter positions do reflect more key Republican posi-tions, but this divide is rather recent. As recently as thirty years ago, the partisan breakdown in the public and in Congress between Republicans and Democrats who were pro-choice or pro-life was not great.[16] Further, the divide is based more on religiosity as measured by frequency of church attendance than a divide based on religious denomination as had been the case in previous generations. Hence, while religion is important in the United States, there is no single long-term con-sistent religion-based cleavage that defines the party system.

Another key cleavage in democracies has been the center versus periphery cleavage where the national capital attempted to gain sovereign governing con-trol over the expanse of the country. This has been a theme in American politics, though our federal governing policies have been far more limited than governance in other democracies. True, American parties began with the Democratic-Republicans attempting to organize disparate regional interests across numerous disconnected states against those like Alexander Hamilton, who wanted greater national control of American politics.[17] This divide—those favoring national unity in governing political agenda through empowering the federal government versus those who prefer decentralized state control over their interests—has remained a theme in American politics, but the two parties have swung back and forth on this issue too much to have this considered a consistent cleavage that defines the parties.

Whatever divisions exist within the United States, they have not translated as solidly or directly into party divisions. Scholars note that the United States has a particular historical "duality" in its party system.[18] The Democrats and Republicans are two of the consistently longest serving parties in the world; they have had tremendous staying power. The contemporary American party system does have deeper divisions than earlier periods of party competition in the United States, but the divisions do not follow any single overwhelming cleavage. Even if the cleavages have weakened in other democracies, and single-party systems now see competitive parties, the residual effects of those initial sources of party dominance still play a greater role in governance in other countries than the interrupted and inconsistent divisions of the American party system.

ROLE OF PARTIES IN GOVERNMENT

American parties play a much more reduced role officially and unofficially in governance relative to parties in other advanced industrial democracies. Given that Madison explicitly pointed to the dangers of factions as his argument for the American Constitution and federal system, it is not surprising that parties do not appear anywhere in the Constitution of the United States, even if freedom of association appears in the First Amendment in the Bill of Rights. In many other democracies, parties appear directly in their constitutions. For some countries that democratized after previously failed democracy, the constitutional position of parties attempts to provide solid democratic institutions, avoidance of extremism, a firm connection between electoral politics and governing processes, and means of citizen engagement.[19] Democracy does not exist without parties to help formulate preferences of citizens, and even though political parties are not institutions on par with the executive, legislative, or judicial branches of government, parties have a quasi-institutional role in many democracies. Table 9.3 demonstrates how some selected countries place this fundamental governing role squarely in their constitution. As the Norwegian example shows, some democracies place parties in their constitutions simply because the parties have an official mechanical role to play in constructing the executive and legislative branches. Many others place parties in the constitution as key democratic institutions. It is highly unlikely that Americans would like—or even accept—an official constitutional role for parties.

Table 9.3	Placement of Parties in Selected Democracies' Constitutions
Italy	**Title IV: Political Rights** **Article 49** All citizens have the right to freely associate in parties to contribute through democratic processes to determine national policies. **Article 98** The law can set limitations to the right to become members of political parties in the case of magistrates, career military in active service, functionaries and agents of the police, diplomatic, and consular representatives abroad.
Spain	**Section 6** Political parties are the expression of political pluralism, they contribute to the formation and expression of the will of the people and are an essential instrument for political participation. Their creation and the exercise of their activities are free insofar as they respect the Constitution and the law. Their internal structure and their functioning must be democratic.
Germany	**Article 21** (1) Political parties shall participate in the formation of the political will of the people. They may be freely established. Their internal organization must conform to democratic principles. They must publicly account for their assets and for the sources and use of their funds. (2) Parties that, by reason of their aims or the behavior of their adherents, seek to undermine or abolish the free democratic basic order or to endanger the existence of the Federal Republic of Germany shall be unconstitutional. The Federal Constitutional Court shall rule on the question of unconstitutionality. (3) Details shall be regulated by federal laws.
South Korea	**Article 8** (1) The establishment of political parties shall be free, and the plural party system shall be guaranteed. (2) Political parties shall be democratic in their objectives, organization, and activities, and shall have the necessary organizational arrangements for the people to participate in the formation of the political will. (3) Political parties shall enjoy the protection of the State and may be provided with operational funds by the State under the conditions as prescribed by Act 4.

	(4) If the purposes or activities of a political party are contrary to the fundamental democratic order, the Government may bring an action against it in the Constitutional Court for its dissolution, and the political party shall be dissolved in accordance with the decision of the Constitutional Court.
Norway	**Article 59** The election of representatives of constituencies is based on proportional representation, and the seats are distributed among the political parties in accordance with the following rules. The total number of votes cast for each party within each separate constituency is divided by 1, 4, 3, 5, 7 and so on until the number of votes cast is divided as many times as the number of seats that the party in question may be expected to obtain. The party which in accordance with the foregoing obtains the largest quotient is allotted the first seat, while the second seat is allotted to the party with the second largest quotient, and so on until all the seats are distributed. List alliances are not permitted. The seats at large are distributed among the parties taking part in such distribution on the basis of the relation between the total number of votes cast for the individual parties in the entire Realm in order to achieve the highest possible degree of proportionality among the parties. The total number of seats in the Storting [the Norwegian parliament] to be held by each party is determined by applying the rules concerning the distribution of constituency seats correspondingly to the entire Realm and to the parties taking part in the distribution of the seats at large. The parties are then allotted so many seats at large that these, together with the constituency seats already allotted, correspond to the number of seats in the Storting to which the party in question is entitled in accordance with the foregoing. If a party has already through the distribution of constituency seats obtained a greater number of seats than it is entitled to in accordance with the foregoing, a new distribution of the seats at large shall be carried out exclusively among the other parties, in such a way that no account is taken of the number of votes cast for and constituency seats obtained by the said party.

AMERICAN TWO-PARTY SYSTEM VERSUS OTHER PARTY SYSTEMS

As discussed above, except for the most involved partisan and the unique (some might say bizarre) set of Americans who as political scientists study political parties, Americans tend to look dimly at political parties, even if they generally understand their functional place in American politics. What really makes Americans shrug, however, is the fact that we only have two parties. In a diverse society that celebrates its multiethnic historical immigration patterns, multicultural society, and regional flavors, how can the United States have only two parties when far smaller and more homogenous countries have multiple parties? For instance, the Netherlands is a major, rich, European country with a population over 17 million. Its population is largely homogenous, with about 80 percent of the population calling themselves Dutch.[20] Meanwhile, California has over double the Dutch population, with more than 39 million people, with Californians breaking down their self-identified ethnicity in 2015 as 72 percent white, 39 percent Hispanic, 15 percent Asian, and 6.5 percent African American.[21] Other states larger than the Netherlands include Texas (over 28 million), Florida (close to 21 million), and New York (close to 20 million). Each of these states also has very diverse ethnic breakdowns within its borders, and it would be hard to imagine much similarity between these states based on their regional positions, culture, food, and lifestyles. Nevertheless, the Dutch have eight to ten parties that regularly compete and have realistic chances to end up in some governing role. California, Texas, Florida, and New York have the same two competitive parties each, and among them, and in presidential elections in the past two decades, California, Texas, and New York have had one and only one—and the same party each time—dominate every election, leaving only Florida to be a true two-party presidential election state. How come the Netherlands gets a full menu of parties when America's largest and most diverse states usually get only one party and maybe up to two competitive parties?

In short, the number and type of political parties in a country has to match the political culture of the country. As Chapters 6 and 7 highlighted, a country's institutions must fit with its political culture and values to provide the proper mix of governing stability and representation of diverse interests. Electoral institutions are not designed in a vacuum without consideration of fitting a society's need for representation of diverse interests (as discussed for consociational democracies) and stability (for more homogenous majoritarian countries). Encouraging many parties in consociational systems brings an opportunity for democracy to operate and strong cultural, religious, and ethnic differences to coexist. So electoral institutions provide incentives for many parties to compete, the specific type of these is discussed in depth in Chapter 10. In the United States, the federal system with real sovereign policy control being held at the national versus state levels means that some of the strain that diversity can bring to democracy has an outlet in localized policy control that differs from state to state and hopefully satisfies regional political cultural preferences. Further, the checks and balances within the federal government provide postelectoral checks on elected officials that partisan electoral politics and coalition formation processes would provide in other democracies. Electoral laws must suit these institutions for democracies to work, and the U.S. electoral laws differ from most other democracies.

The key electoral institutional influence on the United States having two parties is that American electoral offices have single-member districts, and elections are decided by plurality. (We see this discussed as single-member plurality in Chapter 10.) So one person wins the election by simply having one more vote than any other candidate. Maurice Duverger noted that under plurality single-member district electoral systems, only two competitive parties likely emerge for both mechanical and psychological reasons. The mechanical explanation is that only one party's candidate can win, and all other competitors end up as losers, no matter how close they come. As will be demonstrated in Chapter 10, most other electoral systems provide more proportional results from elections. That is, most countries provide more assurance that parties will win a proportion of seats in a legislature that roughly matches the proportion of votes they received. While this seldom tends to be the exact percentage, these systems would not have a House of Representatives race in North Carolina in the 2012 election where one candidate received 49.9 percent of the vote and lost. His opponent won by less than 0.2 percent of the vote and ended up the only winner.[22] To Duverger, this mechanical effect of one party winning, even if it wins by the narrowest of margins, produces a psychological effect that third parties—or any minor parties—end up undersupported because people do not want to support a loser.[23]

This is very human. We have all decided on our second choice in life rather than our dreams when the alternative of reaching for our dreams may mean our worst option comes true. You have probably heard stories of people who "settled" for Mr. (or Ms. or Mx.) "Now" rather than waiting for Mr. (or Ms. or Mx.) "Right." What if Mr. Right never came along and they would be alone? You've likely also heard of people who stay in dead-end jobs rather than risking failure, quitting, and following their dream job to be a circus performer or a travel writer, or a professor. Why if people choose cars, apartments, places to eat, jobs, and perhaps even significant others based on settling for what is possible now rather than what *may be* in the future, would we not expect people to choose a second favorite option among political parties rather than see their dreams leave them with the worst option? This likely means many Americans who might support another party's political values, such as libertarianism, environmental politics, or religious-based parties, end up supporting one of the two major parties so that they do not end up "left behind" and governed by their worst favored party.

Ironically, **Duverger's Law** is titled this because it holds so soundly that it mirrors the scientific proof of hard sciences. The logic is clear and generally works, though as we will see in Chapter 10, the British bucked this "law" in 2010 and had three competitive parties despite having the same electoral system. In 2015, the U.K. election once again did not produce a parliament with two parties. Ten parties are represented in the British Parliament; although parties like the Green Party only have one seat. This created a situation where no one party had a majority of the seats. Thus, the Conservative Party has formed a minority government and has signed a "confidence and supply" agreement with the Democratic Unionist Party. This means the Democratic Unionist Party members will either support or abstain on votes of confidence (calls for the party in power to step down and new elections held, see Chapter 10) or supply (budget).

Other political factors back up the reasons for the American two-party system, though they do not carry the same weight as the American exceptionalism, political cultural, and Duverger's Law of institutional explanations, though many third-party adherents hold to these as the main explanations for the lack of third-party competition. Colleagues, friends, and third-party adherents we have run across have developed intriguing explanations of the two major parties scheming against other parties. We imagine the marijuana rights party would likely not be very competitive even if the following two-party "conspiracies" did not exist because of the cultural and institutional effects emphasized above. Nevertheless, it is true that states typically provide automatic placement for Democrats and Republicans on electoral ballots while minor parties tend to have to present extensive signatures on petitions to get on a ballot, which takes time away from electioneering; the major parties do not lose. Often third parties have gained traction based on success in presidential elections, but particular rules make it difficult to compete here as well. First, the presidential public campaign finance system requires that parties receive 5 percent of the vote in a previous presidential election to receive funds for a subsequent presidential election, and the amount of money varies by how successful the party was. So, if a minor party bursts on the scene with compelling timely issues and a viable candidate to challenge the major parties, it will receive no public funding, because it would not have done sufficiently well in an election four years before. Second, perhaps this strong new party and candidate would break through if they defeated the major parties' candidates in a debate, then fund-raising and public opinion could swing their way. However, the bipartisan Commission on Presidential Debates has strict rules that any third-party candidate must have at least 15 percent public support in major polls to be able to debate with the major party candidates. Money and debate success would help third parties, as witnessed in the 1992 presidential election where a rich, self-funding businessman, Ross Perot, ended up receiving 19 percent of the vote for president, which was slightly more than half of what the sitting president received. So third-party supporters can point to that situation to explain why their party cannot break through, but Perot's subsequent performance in 1996, where he received 8.4 percent of the vote, likely demonstrates the psychological effects Duverger highlighted about the single-member plurality electoral system more than it does about major party obstruction.

The United States is not the only "two-party" system, and we have had more party competition than other democracies have had in their history. For instance, party scholars distinguish party systems into three categories. **Dominant-party systems** are systems where a single party dominates elections and governance. These are not like old authoritarian systems from the Communist era in the Soviet Union nor are they like single-party systems that dominated the Middle East with the Ba'ath Party in Iraq or Syria, or even the contemporary Chinese Communist Party single-party dominance. Rather, these are countries with strong democracy, but where one party tended continually to win elections and govern effectively enough to expand their electoral base.[24] Nordic democracies, Italy, Israel, India,

South Africa, and other democracies fit this model for long periods, even if party competition has subsequently picked up over time in most of these examples. It seems inconsistent with democracy, but these dominant-party systems remained democratic because electoral competition and democratic governance remained, even if one party continually succeeded in both areas. Consequently, democracy does not always have to equate with the number or amount of competition of among parties, even if it seems as if **two-party systems** like the United States would provide more democratic voice to citizens than dominant party systems. We can also imagine that **multiple-party systems** that have numerous parties regularly competing in elections actually provide citizens with more choice than either dominant- or two-party systems.

Simply categorizing parties by the number of parties that participate—as done in the dominant-party, two-party, and multiple-party categorization—does not fully explain the dynamics of party power in democracies. For instance, some countries may have multiple parties, but some remain functionally uncompetitive in affecting public policy because they fail to win enough votes to place them in governing roles. Merely winning marginal percentages of votes continually does not make a country's party system necessarily more "multiparty" than a vigorously competitive two-party system. Consequently, scholars have developed ways to gauge the relative number *and* size of the parties that compete measured by the share of the vote each party receives.[25] This is referred to as the **effective number of parties** (Table 9.4) and represents how many parties have any real competitive strength in each democracy. Thus, the measure counts parties and weights the count by their relative vote share. If all parties have equal vote share, then, the effective number of political parties is equal to the actual number of political parties in the system.

By comparing the effective number of parties in the United States to other democracies, it becomes clear that whether one defines different democracies' party competition as dominant-, two-party, or multiparty systems, there are not many competitive parties in the American system compared to other democracies. The very small effective number of parties for American presidential elections (2.11) and House elections (2.15) shows that there is little real spread of party competition in the United States compared to other democracies. Moreover, other two-party systems—like the United Kingdom (Britain)—have more parties competing and receiving some level of votes (3.49) compared to the United States. The only country with a fewer effective number of parties is South Africa, which is probably the strongest example of a dominant-party system in any democracy today with the African National Congress dominating elections since the end of apartheid in the early 1990s. Consequently, it is not just the type of election rules that restrict the number of parties that compete in the United States, but more importantly, the narrow ideological band of liberalism that American parties compete within that keeps the number of parties so low. Whatever the explanations for the American two-party system, the limited number of parties is striking relative to other democracies. Even if Americans have hundreds of parties, there is really no competition

Table 9.4 Average Effective Number of Parties in Select Advanced Industrial Democracies' Elections 2000–2013

Country	Effective Number of Parties
Australia	3.70
Austria	4.15
Belgium	9.39
Canada	3.66
Denmark	5.37
Finland	6.14
France	5.41
Germany	5.02
Ireland	4.81
Israel	7.96
Italy	5.29
Japan	3.91
Netherlands	6.38
New Zealand	3.27
Norway	5.25
Portugal	3.45
Scotland	4.14
South Africa	2.12
South Korea	3.34
Spain	3.85
Sweden	4.84
Switzerland	5.81
United Kingdom (Britain)	3.49
United States House of Representatives	2.15
United States President (Electoral College)	2.11

Note: Figures calculated by authors with data from Gallagher, Michael, 2018. Election indices dataset at http://www.tcd.ie/Political_Science/people/michael_gallagher/ElSystems/index.php, accessed May 17, 2018.

beyond the two major parties. As noted previously, even in countries with similar election laws that favor two parties, such as in Britain, Canada, and to some extent France, there are more parties competing than in the United States. Other democracies, with election laws that favor multiple parties, *have extraordinarily many more* competitive parties than the United States. Thus, in the United States, we see catch-all parties in the Democrats on the left and Republicans on the right. This means they aggregate a spectrum of voters with varying ideology within the left and the right. Other countries have many more parties to represent different ideological spaces (see Chapter 4). This also means that extreme views, on the left and right, in the United States are not necessarily represented by parties like they are in other democracies. Box 9.1 explains this further with the exploration of **far-right parties**.

BOX 9.1

Far-Right Political Parties

Throughout Europe and the United States, a topic of concern to those interested in democratic governments is the rise of far-right political parties. Once "blocked off" from political participation, these parties are gaining a foothold in countries from Italy to France. While not fascist in the 20th century definition of the term, these parties have nationalistic leanings with some fascist tendencies. (Note, **fascism** is defined as a form of radical authoritarian nationalism that came to prominence in early 20th-century Europe.) The first fascist movements emerged in Italy during World War I, before spreading to other European countries. Fascism led to the rise of leaders such as Mussolini in Italy, Hitler in Germany, and Tojo in Japan. Today's far, right parties are not fascist and should not be confused with fascist parties. They do compete in democratic elections, have gained substantial percentages in some countries, and are generally united in their **xenophobic** (anti-immigrant) stances. Conventional wisdom in academic circles held that fascism of the twentieth century in Europe emerged out of "trauma," namely the global economic crisis of 1929 and harsh reparations levied against Germany under the Treaty of Versailles—the treaty that ended World War I. Today, we see the financial crisis of 2008 from which many have not recovered, growing wealth inequity between rich and poor, and increased migratory pressure throughout advanced industrial democracies.

The Le Pen name in France is synonymous with far-right politics. Jean-Marie Le Pen established the National Front political party, the far-right party in France, in 1972. He led the party until 2011 at which point he passed the baton to his daughter Marine Le Pen. In 2017, the National Front made it to the runoff vote in the presidential election (France operates in a system where the top two vote getters run off in a final election). In the final election that saw Emmanuel Macron elected, Le Pen walked away with 33.9 percent of the vote. Marine Le Pen argues against what she calls the "two totalitarians"—Islam and globalization—that are trying to subjugate France. She refers to the French economy as "besieged" (it is the sixth largest in world) and herself as a "candidate of the people." The National

(Continued)

(Continued)

Front is against France's participation in the EU and calls for strong curtails on immigration. Marine Le Pen has also aligned herself with Russian President Vladimir Putin, referring to him as "the defender of Christian Europe."

Many were shocked when Norbert Hofer, leader of the Freedom Party in Austria, won the most votes in the first round of the Austrian presidential election (they have a system similar to France). Hofer ran on a platform of "putting Austria first" and "restoring Austria" that sounded very similar to the "Make American Great Again" slogan used by American President Donald Trump. Central to Hofer's and the Freedom Party's platform was an anti-immigrant agenda and the dissolution of trade agreements. Hofer lost in second, round voting but walked away with 48 percent of the vote in a country that has a recent history with far-right politics and Nazism.

This same concern has been echoed in Germany around the AfD and Frauke Petry. While Germany has outlawed the Nazi party, the AfD (Alternative for Germany) has skirted within the law and is considered a far-right party. Petry, the AfD leader, has compared multiculturalism to a compost heap, has said border patrol should "use firearms when necessary" when dealing with refugees, and has a manifesto that says "Islam is not part of Germany." Petry also called for a ban on minarets and burqas. The AfD has been successful in peeling votes from CDU (the traditional party of the right), but in the last election (2017), received only 11.5 percent of the vote.

The Netherlands has seen the rise of Geert Wilders and the Party for Freedom (PVV). Wilders, like the other far-right party leaders, ran on an anti-Islamic, anti-immigrant platform. He was charged and on trial for inciting hatred against Dutch Moroccans at the time of his campaign. The PVV argues to leave the EU, close borders, and similarly to the AfD in Germany, close all mosques. Wilders and his party gained 13 percent of the vote in the last election (2017), putting the PVV in second place. No other party would form a coalition with the PVV, however, so they remained out of government.

What all these parties and leaders have in common is an anti-immigrant, antiglobalization stance. There are hints of protectionism and restoring the country to "greatness" in the platforms of all of these parties. They are also led by charismatic individuals. While there are certainly variations by country, support of far-right parties in many democracies hovers around 30 percent. This support is accompanied with a "crisis" among the left, a left that has split into traditional left (focused on worker's rights) and left-libertarian left. In Europe, parliamentary institutions help to moderate far-right influences as traditional parties would prefer to enter into grand coalitions (see Chapters 10 and 11) than a coalition with a far-right party. In the United States, our catchall two-party system means that far-right ideology is subsumed under the Republican party.

AN AMERICANIZATION OF PARTIES ELSEWHERE OR MORE PARTY GOVERNMENT IN THE UNITED STATES?

So far this chapter has laid out the distinctive components of American parties compared to other democracies' party systems. Despite the exceptional nature of the U.S. party system, some trends point to increasing similarities among democratic party systems. The first similarity relates to the shifting of many European parties away from the ideological positions born from their social cleavage beginnings. As noted above, the changing labor force, social mobility, and new political values that were punctuated by the development of Green parties and other postmaterialist values-based parties also changed the existing social cleavage-based parties. As the percentage of white-collared workers increasingly replaced blue-collared workers, and as religious denominational support tapered off in European societies, citizens began to be "**cross-pressured**" by their exposure to different political and social values. The established left, center-right, and liberal parties were not situated well to appeal to these cross-pressured voters, whose parents may have been working class, but they were professionals, or whose parents were conservative and religious, but their cosmopolitan lifestyles led them toward social change more than the traditional status quo. Consequently, the parties had to moderate their cleavage-based appeals. Ironically, just at the same time that Lipset and Rokkan developed the social cleavage model in the mid-1960s, Otto Kirchheimer (1905–1965) referred to the cross-pressuring of these publics and the response by cleavage-based parties to become **catchall parties**, which meant that these parties were making broad electoral appeals. Kirchheimer even warned that parties in other advanced industrial democracies were becoming much more like American nonideological parties.[26]

By the 1990s, this trend was entirely evident as center-right conservative and Christian Democratic parties began to embrace environmental policies, and Socialist, Social Democratic, and Labour parties were embracing more probusiness, "third-way"—neither left nor right—policies that rejected solely pro-left positions. Consequently, just as American parties have been viewed as vote-maximizing rather than ideological institutions, these parties softened the purity of their ideological appeals. Further, European parties began to adopt American-style campaign tactics that focused more on personal traits of party leaders, televised advertising, and even the hiring of American campaign consultants.[27]

Nevertheless, other democratic countries' party systems still represent a broader ideological spectrum than the American two-party system. Both the Republican and Democrat parties can be classified as liberal parties that stand well to the right of the center-right and mass parties of the left in other democracies. Just because other parties have loosened their ideological bases for electoral appeal does not mean they have abandoned their ideological commitment to social democracy, the social safety net, and larger government involvement in society compared to the United States.

Another growing similarity between the United States and other democracies has been the rise of partisan independents in recent decades. As citizens in most democracies have become more educated, and with the explosion of differing media and sources of information that has come onto the scene in these democracies, citizens do not have to rely as much on party cues to guide their voting and political decisions.[28] Further, many citizens have become frustrated with political parties as representative institutions and feel as though they can make sense of politics and meaningfully participate without the intermediation—if not interference—of political parties.[29] Following this approach, sometimes citizens may better express themselves through joining social movements, protest politics, or other forms of activism discussed in Chapter 8 than voting through a partisan-based electoral process that might not satisfy their particularized political values. Perhaps other democracies' citizens have adopted the skepticism toward parties that Americans have had all along, even though parties provide a much more fundamental role in representing citizens and driving the political agenda in those democracies. Table 9.5 demonstrates that Americans are not the only democratic citizens who lack confidence in political parties as institutions. Americans have the least amount of people saying they have "a great deal" or "quite a lot" of confidence in parties, but not by an extraordinary amount, and all of these regional democracies have a majority of citizens who do not "have very much" or "none at all" when describing their confidence in parties in the 2005–2008 World Values Surveys.

Table 9.5   Confidence in Political Parties in Advanced Industrial Democracies

	How much confidence do you have in political parties?				
	A Great Deal	Quite a Lot	Not Very Much	None at All	N
United States	1.9%	13.5%	69.2%	15.5%	1,209
Scandinavia	1.1%	29.2%	59.6%	10.0%	2,995
Northern Europe	1.2%	19.7%	55.3%	23.9%	5,111
Southern Europe	1.7%	21.3%	55.4%	21.6%	2,150
Commonwealth	1.5%	17.1%	63.9%	17.5%	4,310
Japan/S. Korea	1.3%	20.0%	54.6%	24.2%	2,206

Note: Data are from World Values Survey, 2005–2008 Wave. Respondents were asked the following question: "Here are a number of organizations. For each one, please indicate how much confidence you have in them: is it a great deal of confidence, quite a lot of confidence, not very much confidence, or none at all?" Political parties was then shown as one of the organizations to which respondents reacted; N refers to total number of respondents and is common notation in statistical charts. Percentages may not equal 100 percent due to rounding.

The lack of confidence in other democracies' parties does not mean, however, that parties changed their fundamental role in other democracies. Further, the American case of growing numbers of partisan independents differs from the other cases in key ways. As will be highlighted later, there is a growing division—some say polarization—among American parties, even if the ideological spread does not match the ideological party competitive space elsewhere. As part of this change in the past two decades, the rising number of Americans calling themselves independents has been offset by the rise in engaged strong party identifiers on both sides. So rather than being a moderately engaged and weaker identifying partisan public as Americans were throughout most of the twentieth century, contemporary voters tend to be more engaged and ideological partisans than in earlier generations, which diminishes the effect of increasing independents in the electorate. Further, many of these independents in the United States tend to "lean" toward one party and have in fact demonstrated stronger partisan issue stands and voting patterns than weak party identifiers.[30] Some scholars hold that the American public remains moderate and does not appreciate the rising partisan polarization of American political leaders.[31] Indeed, many Americans dislike the polarized partisan debate and bare-knuckled politics of contemporary U.S. politics, but a large percentage of the public does appreciate increasing substantive party divisions and actually embraces the aggressive if not uncivil style that parties take toward one another.[32]

While the patterns of partisan independence do not square directly between the United States and other democracies, American partisan divisions in governing have increased significantly in recent decades. In fact, the two major parties have become more ideologically uniform as southern conservatives who used to uniformly support the Democratic Party began to support the more conservative Republican Party as younger generations replaced older more Democratic generations. This was in response to those on the left in the Democratic Party helping ideologically moderate Republicans pass the Civil Rights and Voting Rights Acts in the mid-1960s, which weakened the political power of southern white conservative Democrats, as well as the faster-growing southern economy, and the Republican Party's outreach to southern conservatives on the role of the federal government, abortion and the life issues, racial political divides, and strong national defense.[33] This left the Democratic Party without many conservatives, and the move to attract southern conservatives ended up putting off northern moderates within the Republican Party, who slowly began to support and ultimately became loyal to the Democratic Party by the 2000s.[34]

These historical developments have produced two parties with far more internal ideological unity than has existed in the past. Further, Congress adopted rules changes that gave party leaders more institutional control, especially in the House of Representatives. Political scientists have even gone as far as to say the increased partisan context of American politics has created **conditional party government**.[35] Indeed, the amount of party unity in the U.S. Congress is unprecedented as is the partisan tone of presidential executive orders and decisions made by judges on federal courts based on the partisanship of the president who nominated them.[36] Even while this is a remarkable period in American politics in the approximation that parties drive the political agenda and behavior of political leaders to a level that could even be comparable to **party government** in other democracies, American parties still do not reach the governing power that parties do in other democracies.

First, they lack the institutional means to have a single party dominate the agenda, except for the rare situations of unified party control of the presidency and both houses of Congress, which has been the exception rather than the rule in the past few decades and seldom with a large enough majority to overcome party defections and quirks in the American system that require supermajorities in the U.S. Senate. Typically, divided government means that a party cannot implement its policies because the other party checks it, resulting in policy needing to be an unclear consensus, watered-down policy, or an unaddressed public policy problem.

Second, the breadth of party ideology in other democracies means that shifts in party control equate to significant shifts in policy. The general liberal pragmatism of the two American parties would not provide extensive policy change that would equate to a significant party shift in other advanced industrial democracies. Third, the conditions that have led to such conditional party government are temporary and depend on those conditions continuing. They are not institutionalized in the U.S. Constitution or in American political culture. Therefore, the norm in other democracies is both recent and potentially temporary in the United States.

As a result, American parties have developed some similarities to other democracies' party systems with conditional party government and unprecedented party unity, and other democracies have made broader "catchall" party appeals through more Americanized campaigns in recent years. The shifts in these directions appear dramatic when considering how established the American two parties have been in a pragmatic, Lockean liberal party system that has both parties promoting limited government involvement in the economy or society and how established other party systems have been as institutions reflecting deep social divides with significant governing power. Thus, the changing dynamics are important to gauge because understanding them in a comparative context demonstrates how noteworthy the changes have been but in turn also illustrate how different American parties remain.

CONCLUSION

Like interest groups discussed in Chapter 8, political parties are important interest articulation vehicles in advanced industrial democracies. The nature of the party system in part has to do with the cleavages in society shaped by historical development and political culture. Lipset and Rokkan saw these cleavages as "frozen" and emerging from the National and Industrial Revolutions. Later scholars, like

Inglehart, argued that cleavages were thawing, and a new divide between materialists and postmaterialsts was emerging in the post–World War II era. This new divide is thought to have given rise to left-libertarian parties, like green parties. The same cleavages that gave rise to political parties in Europe did not exist in the United States, resulting in a different-looking party system. The party system in the United States is much less differentiated with two catchall parties—Democrats and Republicans—than the party systems in other democracies, and from its beginnings has been viewed with skepticism. The next chapter will explore the degree to which electoral laws and institutions help to shape the effective number of parties in democracies. Thus, while the role of parties is similar in the United States as it is in other countries, the emergence of political parties in the United States as compared to European democracies is an exceptional aspect of American democracy.

POINTS TO REMEMBER

- Lipset and Rokkan trace the formation of modern parties to societal cleavages, which formed during the National and Industrial Revolutions.

- Inglehart argued that the "frozen" cleavages discussed by Lipset and Rokkan were thawing, and a new cleavage between postmaterialists and materialist was emerging in society, giving way to new political parties.

- Early founders like Madison and Washington were skeptical of political parties in the United States, a sentiment remaining in American political culture today.

- American party history and the parties themselves are built on shifting coalitions that have limited life cycles historically rather than being party systems built on rather permanent social cleavages.

- American parties play a much more reduced role officially and unofficially in governance relative to other advanced industrial democracies.

- Electoral laws and political culture influence the degree to which systems are dominant-party, two-party, or multiparty systems, although the effective number of parties takes into account the competitiveness of parties in the system.

- Other democracies' parties have become more catchall and have adopted a more American style of campaigns. American parties have become more polarized. This does not mean that American parties are becoming like others and vice-versa, however. Other party systems still have a much broader ideological range of debate compared to the liberal American parties.

KEY TERMS

Catchall parties 205

Center-periphery
cleavage 186

Church-state
cleavage 187

Conditional party
government 207

Critical
realignment 193

Cross-pressured 205

Dominant-party
systems 200

Duverger's Law 199

Effective number of
parties 201

Far-right parties 203

Fascism 203

Materialist values 189

Multiple-party
systems 201

Owner-worker
cleavage 187

Party government 208

Political parties 185

Postmaterialist values 189

Scarcity 188

Silent revolution 188

Two-party systems 201

Urban-rural cleavage 187

Xenophobic 203

REVIEW QUESTIONS

1. Discuss how Lipset and Rokkan explain political party formation. What cleavages are salient, and how did this affect political parties? What does it mean for cleavages to be frozen?

2. Explain what Inglehart meant by "the silent revolution." How did this influence the political party landscape?

3. How does democratization influence party formation?

4. Describe Madisonian and Washingtonian opinions of political parties.

5. What is the critical realignment party history model? How is it of relevance to explaining U.S. parties?

6. Compare the role of American parties in government to parties in other democracies. How does this relate to ideas about party government?

7. What is Duverger's Law? How does this relate to the two-party system in the United States?

8. What does the effective number of political parties measure? How does the United States compare to other democracies?

9. What do you make about the rise of far-right parties across democracies? When combined with what we learned in Chapter 2 about frustration with democracy, what do you think this means for the future of democracy?

10. In what way are far-right parties in Europe similar or dissimilar to what you may have read about the far-right in the United States?

SUGGESTED READINGS

Almond, Gabriel, and James Coleman. *The Politics of the Developing Areas*. Princeton, NJ: Princeton University Press, 1960.

Abramowitz, Alan. *The Disappearing Center: Engaged Citizens, Polarization, and American Democracy*. New Haven, CT: Yale University Press, 2011.

Carmines, Edward, and James Stimson. *Issue Evolution: Race and the Transformation of American Politics*. Princeton, NJ: Princeton University Press, 1989.

Dalton, Russell. *The Apartisan American: Dealignment and Changing Electoral Politics*. Washington, DC: CQ Press, 2012.

Fiorina, Morris, and Samuel Abrams. *Disconnect: The Breakdown of Representation in American Politics*. Norman: University of Oklahoma Press, 2009.

Gallagher, Michael, Michael Laver, and Peter Mair. *Representative Government in Modern Europe: Institutions, Parties, and Governments*, 4th ed. Boston, MA: McGraw Hill, 2005.

Hershey, Marjorie. *Party Politics in America*, 15th ed. New York, NY: Pearson, 2012.

Inglehart, Ronald. *The Silent Revolution: Changing Values and Political Styles Among Western Publics*. Princeton, NJ: Princeton University Press, 1977.

Kirchheimer, Otto. "The Transformation of the West European Party System." In *Political Parties and Political Development*, ed. Joseph LaPalombara and Myron Weiner, 177–200. Princeton, NJ: Princeton University Press, 1966.

Klingemann, Hans-Dieter, Richard Hofferbert, and Ian Budge. *Parties, Policies, and Democracy*. Boulder, CO: Westview Press, 1994.

Laasko, Markku, and Rein Taagepera. "'Effective' Number of Parties: A Measure with Application to Europe." *Comparative Political Studies* 12, no. 1 (1979): 3–27.

Lipset, Seymour Martin, and Stein Rokkan. *Party Systems and Voter Alignments: Cross-National Perspectives*. New York, NY: Free Press, 1967.

Putnam, Robert, Susan Pharr, and Russell Dalton. "What's Troubling the Trilateral Democracies?" In *Disaffected Democracies: What's Troubling the Trilateral Democracies?*, ed. Susan Pharr and Robert Putnam, 3–30. Princeton, NJ: Princeton University Press, 2000.

Wolf, Michael, J., Cherie Strachan, and Daniel Shea. "Forget the Good of the Game." *American Behavioral Scientist* 56, no. 12 (2012): 1677–1695.

Wolf, Michael, J., Cherie Strachan, and Daniel Shea. "Incivility and Standing Firm: A Second Layer of Partisan Division." *PS: Political Science and Politics* 43, no. 3 (2012): 428–434.

NOTES

1. Seymour Martin Lipset and Stein Rokkan, *Party Systems and Voter Alignments: Cross-national Perspectives* (New York, NY: Free Press, 1967).

2. James Toole, "The Historical Foundations of Party Politics in Post-Communist East Central Europe," *Europe-Asia Studies* 59, no. 4 (2007): 541–566.

3. Ronald Inglehart, *The Silent Revolution: Changing Values and Political Styles among Western Publics* (Princeton, NJ: Princeton University Press, 1977).

4. Michael Gallagher, Michael Laver, and Peter Mair, *Representative Government in Modern Europe: Institutions, Parties, and Governments*, 4th ed (Boston, MA: McGraw Hill, 2005).

5. See John Aldrich, *Why Parties*, 2nd ed. (Chicago, IL: University of Chicago Press, 2011) for a fuller discussion of the differing approaches to American political party scholarship.

6. See Kendall Baker, Russell Dalton, and Kai Hildebrandt, *Germany Transformed: Political Culture and the New Politics* (Cambridge, MA: Harvard University Press, 1981) for an in-depth look at the development of German civic culture through its parties.

7. See Joel Silbey, "American Political Parties: History, Voters, Critical Elections, and Party Systems," in *Oxford Handbook of American Political Parties and Interest Groups*, eds. Sandy Maisel, Jeffrey M. Berry, and George C. Edwards (Oxford, UK: Oxford University Press, 2010).

8. See Aldrich, *Why Parties*.

9. Aldrich, *Why Parties*; Silbey, "American Political Parties."

10. This tradition has its foundations on the seminal works of V. O. Key, "A Theory of Critical Elections," *The Journal of Politics* 17, no. 1 (1955); Walter Dean Burnham, *Critical Elections and the Mainsprings of American Politics* (New York, NY: W. W. Norton, 1968); and James L. Sundquist, *Dynamics of the Party System: Alignment and Realignment of Political Parties in the United States* (Washington, DC: The Brookings Institution, 1983). For an overview of this history, see Silbey, "American Political Parties."

11. See Burnham, *Critical Elections and the Mainsprings of American Politics*, and Sundquist, *Dynamics of the Party System*, for specific conditions.

12. See Sundquist, *Dynamics of the Party System*, for historical examples of issue straddling.

13. Edward G. Carmines, "The Logic of Party Alignments," *Journal of Theoretical Politics* 3, 1 (1991): 65–80.

14. V.O. Key *Southern Politics in State and Nation*, University of Tennessee Press,1984(original 1949).

15. Alan Abramowitz, *The Disappearing Center: Engaged Citizens, Polarization, and American Democracy* (New Haven, CT: Yale University Press, 2011).

16. Jeffrey Stonecash and Howard Reiter, *Counter Realignment: Political Change in the Northeastern United States* (Cambridge, UK: Cambridge University Press, 2011).

17. Silbey, "American Political Parties."

18. Keith Poole and Howard Rosenthal, *Ideology and Congress* (St. Louis, MO: Transaction, 2007).

19. For an explanation of why the Allied democracies of the United States, France, and United Kingdom preferred that the German Basic Law adopt a direct discussion of political parties, see Russell Dalton, *Politics in Germany*, 2nd ed. (New York, NY: Harper Collins, 1993).

20. United States Central Intelligence Agency. *The World Factbook*. https://www.cia .gov/library/publications/the-world-factbook/geos/nl.html, accessed November 16, 2013.

21. Numbers do not equal 100 due to people claiming more than one race; also, Hispanics may be of any race and are also included in other applicable categories. From https://www.census.gov/quickfacts/table/RHI705210/06#qf-headnote-a.

22. Craig Jarvis, "The Counting Continues in Aiken, Cisco Race". *Charlotte Observer*, May 7, 2014, https://www.charlotteobserver.com/news/politics-government/ article9119684.html.

23. Maurice Duverger, "Factors in a Two-Party and Multiparty System," in *Party Politics and Pressure Groups: A Comparative Introduction* (New York, NY: Thomas Y. Crowell, 1972), 23–32.

24. See J. T. Pempel, *Uncommon Democracies: One Party Dominant Regimes* (Ithaca, NY: Cornell University Press, 1990).

25. Markku Laasko and Rein Taagepera, "'Effective' Number of Parties: A Measure with Application to Europe," *Comparative Political Studies* 12, no. 1 (1979): 3–27.

26. See Otto Kirchheimer, "The Transformation of the West European Party System," in *Political Parties and Political Development*, eds. Joseph LaPalombara and Myron Weiner (Princeton, NJ: Princeton University Press, 1966), 177–200.

27. Paolo Mancini and David Swanson, *Politics, Media, and Modern Democracy: An Introductory Study of Innovations in Electoral Campaiging and Their Consequences* (Santa Barbara, CA, Praeger, 1996); David Farrell, "Political Consultancy Overseas: The Internationalization of Campaign Consultancy," *PS: Political Science and Politics*, 31 (1998): 171–178.

28. Russell Dalton, *The Apartisan American: Dealignment and Changing Electoral Politics* (Washington, DC: CQ Press, 2012); Michael Wolf, "An Attentive Public? The Response of Different Voter Groups to Campaign Cues in Advanced Industrial Democracies" (Dissertation, Indiana University, 2002).

29. Robert Putnam, Susan Pharr, and Russell Dalton. "What's Troubling the Trilateral Democracies?" in *Disaffected Democracies: What's Troubling the Trilateral Democracies?* eds. Susan Pharr and Robert Putnam (Princeton, NJ: Princeton University Press, 2000), 3–30.

30. See Alan Abramowitz, *The Disappearing Center: Engaged Citizens, Polarization, and American Democracy* (New Haven, CT: Yale University Press, 2011).

31. Morris Fiorina and Samuel Abrams, *Disconnect: The Breakdown of Representation in American Politics* (Norman: University of Oklahoma Press, 2009).

32. Michael Wolf, J. Cherie Strachan, and Daniel Shea, "Forget the Good of the Game," *American Behavioral Scientist* 56, no. 12 (2012): 1677–1695; Michael Wolf, J. Cherie Strachan, and Daniel Shea, "Incivility and Standing Firm: A Second Layer of Partisan Division," *PS: Political Science and Politics* 43, no. 3 (2012): 428–434.

33. Edward Carmines and James Stimson, *Issue Evolution: Race and the Transformation of American Politics* (Princeton, NJ: Princeton University Press, 1989); Earl Black and Merle Black, *The Rise of the Southern Republicans* (Cambridge, MA: Belknap, 2002); D. Sunshine Hilygus and Todd Shields, *The Persuadable Voter: Wedge Issues in Presidential Campaigns* (Princeton, NJ: Princeton University Press, 2009); Byron Shafer and Richard Johnston, *The End of Southern Exceptionalism: Class, Race, and Partisan Change in the Postwar South* (Cambridge, MA: Harvard University Press, 2009).

34. Howard Reiter and Jeffrey Stonecash, *Counter Realignment: Political Change in the Northeastern United States* (Cambridge, UK: Cambridge University Press, 2011).

35. David Rohde, *Parties and Leaders in the Postreform House* (Chicago, IL: University of Chicago Press, 1991).

36. Marjorie Hershey, *Party Politics in America*, 15th ed. (New York, NY: Pearson, 2012).

CHAPTER TEN

ELECTIONS AND ELECTORAL INSTITUTIONS

On November 8, 2016, 58 percent of eligible United States' voters went to the polls to elect, among other offices, the next president of the United States. This election was historic. It was the first time a woman was running as a major party candidate for president. As results came in, many pollsters and Hilary Clinton supporters were stunned. Donald Trump secured over the 270 Electoral College votes necessary to win the presidency. When the election was over, he walked away with 306 electors to Clinton's 232. This is despite the fact that Clinton secured 48.5 percent of the vote to Trump's 46.4 percent, a difference of nearly 3 million votes. This isn't the first time a U.S. presidential candidate lost the election while winning the popular vote. In what has happened only four times before in U.S. history (elections in 1824, 1876, 1888, and 2000), the loser of the popular election walked away with the presidency. The fact that two of these times have happened since 2000 has some Americans calling for the abolition of the Electoral College.

Normally Americans know who their next president is by the 11 o' clock news. In 2000, Americans went to bed, woke up the next day, and the election was still undecided. Election results hinged on Florida, ballot inconsistencies, and a small margin of victory that triggered a recount of the votes. Lawsuits also prompted recounts in select Florida counties, and Americans saw these lawsuits go all the way the U.S. Supreme Court, which in a landmark decision (*Bush v. Gore*) ended the recounting of ballots and led to Republican George W. Bush winning Florida. With Florida, Bush won the election with 271 Electoral College votes (compared to Democrat Al Gore's 266 Electoral College votes; to add to the drama and to Gore's displeasure, one of Gore's pledged voters did not end up voting for him in order to lodge an unrelated protest). Most dramatically, just like in 2016, Al Gore, actually walked away with a higher percentage of the popular vote compared to the winner, George W. Bush (48.4 percent to 47.9 percent, respectively). Many citizens in democracies around the world (and we daresay some Americans themselves) were puzzled about how the American system could produce a winner of an election that won a lower percentage of the popular vote. The 2000 and 2016 elections brought to light the complicated and somewhat bizarre electoral institutions in the United States, particularly the Electoral College and the exceptional nature of U.S. elections as compared to democracies elsewhere in the world.

Chapter 9 highlighted how a democracy's electoral institutions influence the effective number of political parties present in that society. Democratic electoral systems affect politics in many other ways as well. The American electoral system differs significantly from other democracies with very real consequences. The United States shares some electoral system features with its democratic cousins, like the fact that the American plurality system will lead to a single party winning if it receives one more vote than another party. That said, many democracies operate a proportional representation system quite foreign to the American voter. Differences in electoral systems bring with them strong distinctions among democracies. Consequently, electoral institutions provide a powerful influence on the nature of democracy practiced within a country and together with that country's political culture go a long way in influencing citizens' electoral behavior. This chapter examines the different types of electoral systems and the consequences of these systems across democracies.

CANDIDATE SELECTION

Prior to discussing how electoral institutions affect voting, a discussion of how candidates are selected to represent parties is required. This is an area where the United States, with its **primary system** (discussed in Chapter 7), really stands out as different. Primary elections occur among members of the same party to choose the candidate who will stand for office. Members of the Democratic Party compete against each other to see who will face the Republican candidate in the **general election**, or main election. The same goes for Republicans. The primary system is in place for the presidential, congressional, and many other elections. Depending on the state, since states control laws over elections, usually only registered members of a particular party can vote in that party's primary election (called **closed primaries**), but in **open primary elections**, any registered voter can vote in any primary election.

Almost every other democracy has the party leadership apparatus choose candidates in an internal process. Usually candidates are chosen through nominating conventions organized by the parties, which means party loyalists tend to emerge on parties' slates of candidates. Primaries are used by some green parties in Italy and the Socialists in France, but it is nearly unheard of to see an American-style primary system in other democracies. In this way, the exceptional candidate selection used in the United States is more "democratic" than that used in other countries.

ELECTORAL INSTITUTIONS

Chapters 6 and 7 demonstrated that democracies must craft constitutions and governing institutions to reflect the heterogeneity of their societies. Largely homogenous societies tend to have majoritarian institutions while heterogeneous democracies must provide consensus from institutions. The design of electoral institutions—the electoral system—provides the most powerful factor in producing majoritarian or consociational democracies because when faced with designing electoral systems, countries have a trade-off between the goal of producing **stability** or producing more **representation**. Both are admirable aspects of democracy, but they generally run contrary to each other. Electoral institutions that bring stability bring lower representation and vice versa.

Stability refers to a single-party government that will be strong enough to control policy, have stable leadership, and will serve for an established period.[1] Representation reflects how closely the electoral vote outcome matches the elected representation in government. In other words, do elections lead to more voices in society being represented in government? Those countries that are more majoritarian in their democratic configurations have systems that are very stable. This stability, however, sometimes comes at the expense of representation. Consociational systems, on the other hand, are very representative, meaning they are designed to have more voices involved in policy making, yet what they gain in representation they lose in terms of stability.

The particular mechanical features of electoral systems that affect stability and representation are district magnitude, ballot structure, and electoral formula. The crucial mechanism to bring about more representation is to not allow one single party to "win" an election. For more parties to win, there have to be more elected positions possible to win. This is what **district magnitude** distinguishes: the number of representatives elected from a constituency, or voting district. As you increase district magnitude, you increase the number of representatives, so more parties have the chance to win, and more representation is afforded. Just like the beginning of a game of musical chairs, there are more chairs and more winners and fewer losers. When there is only one chair, however, there can be only one winner. So a district magnitude equal to one means that there is only one winner to represent the entire constituency. This ensures stability but decreases representation and characterizes majoritarian systems. Higher district magnitude leads to proportional representation and characterizes consociational systems.

The **ballot structure** refers to the way parties/candidates are listed on a ballot and the sequence and number of elections in which voters can participate. Highly stable democracies tend to allow fewer ballot choices and elections at fixed terms, years apart. To introduce more representation into stable systems, governments may have two sequential elections so that the first phase includes numerous parties and whittles down the number of parties who may compete in a second vote, where the winner must receive a majority. Alternatively, the ballot may provide more than a single choice. Details of different ballot structures are presented below, but the most important point is that a ballot can be structured to allow voters in heavily stable systems with very low district magnitudes to make broader, more representative electoral choices at least at one stage of an election even if voting ultimately produces a stable government.

In high district magnitude electoral systems, numerous parties may receive votes, making it difficult to determine who should govern. In such systems, an **electoral formula**—a formula used for translating the number of votes a party receives into the number of seats the party gets in government—can mathematically magnify the number of seats in government for parties who earned more votes, which brings more governing stability to a system by minimizing the number of governing seats parties get when they don't receive many votes. In all cases, democracies attempt to produce the best balancing act for their society between representation and stability. The following sections look at how electoral formulas work to make representative systems more stable and how ballot structures can make stable systems more representative.

PLURALITY, MAJORITY, AND PROPORTIONAL REPRESENTATION SYSTEMS

At a broad level, electoral institutions can be divided into plurality, majority, and proportional representation systems depending on the district magnitude, ballot structure, and electoral formula present in each system. Newly forming democracies and those democracies looking for more representation or stability often shift electoral laws to produce a plurality, majority, or more proportional systems. Plurality and majority electoral institutions produce more stable governments with clear election winners and losers. They tend to be found in majoritarian democracies. For those consociational societies, representation of many sectors of society remains key to democracy, so the electoral institutions favor proportionality—or having the percentage of vote reflected in the number of seats a party has in its legislature. Consequently, these electoral institutions may seem mechanical at some level, but they are tightly connected to producing the type of democracy a society values.

Plurality Systems: Single-Member Plurality Elections

The United States stacks up similarly to particular countries as far as district magnitude, ballot structure, and electoral formula, yet it differs dramatically from others. Like the United States, other **single-member plurality (SMP)** systems divide the country into numerous voting districts. For example, in the United Kingdom, there are 650 voting districts. In the United States, for House of Representatives, there are 435 voting districts. Candidates run for elected office in these districts, and *each district is represented by one elected official*—a district magnitude of one. This is the single most distinguishing feature of a single-member plurality system and key to differentiating it from proportional systems discussed later.[2] SMP systems are found in majoritarian countries and are seen as very stable systems. These are also often referred to as **first past the post (FPTP)** elections because, like horses passing the finishing post in a horse race, it does not matter whether you win by a nose or a furlong, the first horse past the post wins. In elections, the candidate with the most votes wins. These are frequently classified as **plurality** systems because they differ from majority systems as it is just the candidate with the *most* votes, or a plurality, who wins, not necessarily meaning the candidate will have over 50 percent of the votes.

There is one caveat to SMP systems. Multimember plurality systems (MMP) are common in the Asian democracies. Sharing the majoritarian, or winner-take-all aspects of the SMP systems, they differ in that voters elect multiple representatives per district, thus district magnitude is greater than one, adding a bit more representation to the system as elections can have multiple winners (top vote getters) per district.

As was discussed in Chapter 9, Duverger's Law states that in single member plurality countries we are likely to see two major parties emerge. This is the case in the United States, with the Republicans and Democrats and in the United Kingdom with the Labour and Conservative parties (although the UK does have a strong third party and locally active nationalist parties). **Disproportionality** occurs when the relative number of governing seats a party receives is not nearly in proportion to the percentage of votes the party earned. Disproportionality is the norm in single-member plurality because parties can win the single governing seat with a relatively small plurality of the vote while other parties get nothing even if they received nearly as many votes as the wining party. The more parties involved in an SMP system, the more disproportionate the election will become. For example, in the United Kingdom, in 2005, the Labour Party secured a majority of the seats in parliament with the backing of less than 36 percent of British voters. Bill Clinton was elected president of the United States in 1992 with 43 percent of the vote (37.5 percent went to George Bush and 18.9 percent went to Ross Perot). In fact, in the United States and the United Kingdom, the majority of legislators are elected with less than 50 percent of the votes in their district.[3] The disproportionality associated with SMP systems has led to calls for reform in countries with these systems, namely Canada, India, New Zealand, and the United States. Only in New Zealand has single member plurality been abandoned.

Like other democracies, the United States has chosen disproportionality in elections in order to have a more stable system. The United States, however, is a special case in how it chooses its head of government. The president of the United States is selected through the Electoral College. In other SMP systems, because they are also parliamentary systems, the head of government is selected from the majority party in the legislature. The **Electoral College** elects the president and vice president in the United States based on the results of the popular election in each state. The number of a state's electors equals the number of its members of Congress (House and Senate). The presidential candidate who gets the most votes in a state takes all the electors from that state. Exceptions to these rules are found in Maine and Nebraska, where electors are broken up by congressional district, with the winner of each district taking that elector and two additional electors in these states going with the winner of the statewide vote tally. Candidates must have an **absolute majority** of electors (which means 50 percent plus one)—270 Electoral College votes—to win the presidency, or the U.S. House chooses the president, and the U.S. Senate chooses the vice president.

Majority Systems: Two-Round Voting

In the United States, citizens are used to voting in one electoral round. While Americans have a primary process to determine the candidate running for each party, the general election (the main election that awards the seat) for legislative or executive office takes place in one round of voting. Other countries have **two-round ballot** structures or operate based upon what is known as the alternative vote. As emphasized previously, ballot structures where you have two-round voting are designed to bring more representation to a stability-designed system.

Two-round systems are more common for executive voting as opposed to legislative voting. Several democracies have two-round voting, including Austria, Finland, Portugal, and France. Louisiana uses a variant of this as well. When French voters go to the polls to vote for president, they choose the candidate listed on the ballot they prefer. The top two vote getters run off in a second election a couple of weeks later, where the person with the majority of the votes wins. A two-round system ensures stability because the winner receives an absolute majority of votes cast (50 percent plus one). Thus, as discussed in Chapter 9 in the discussion of right-wing parties, Marine le Pen and Emmanuel Macron were the top two vote getters out of the last French election and then ran off against each other in the final round of voting. These systems also exist (although very rarely) in some statewide or local elections in the United States, where they are called "run-off elections," and typically occur where one party has tended to historically dominate elections (for example with Democrats in California).

Both two-round and alternative voting systems (discussed later) are referred to as **majority systems** because they strive to elect candidates with more than 50 percent of the vote. Data indicates, however, that electoral trends in majority systems are not unlike trends in SMP systems, meaning that in most instances, the result of the election would be the same if one-round plurality, rather than majority rules, were in place.[4] Thus, while it may seem democratic and appeal to us to have candidates elected with more than 50 percent of the vote, majority systems are criticized for being cumbersome, and in the case of two-round systems, requiring undue burden on voters to show up more than once at the polls. This is thought to depress voter turnout. Although, turnout in two-round systems is still higher than turnout in the majority of U.S. elections. Benefits of the majority systems are similar to benefits of SMP systems. They maintain a relationship between representatives and constituents as they have single-member districts, they are easy to understand, and have resulted in stable governments. On the downside, these systems, like SMP systems, disadvantage smaller parties.

Proportional Representation

If SMP and majority systems disadvantage smaller parties in the pursuit of stability, representation of these parties is the major selling point of **proportional representation (PR)** systems.[5] Proportional representation occurs when the district magnitude is greater than one and is especially present when the district magnitude is high because more people can be elected per constituency. PR is conceptually fairly straightforward: parties receive seats in the legislature in relative proportion to the vote they received from the public. Take the 2018 U.S. House of Representative election and assume for a minute it was decided based upon proportional representation (Tables 10.1a and 10.1b), with the entire United States being one constituency. We would see that the Democrats would actually have held the most seats, and smaller parties (Libertarian, Independent, and Green) would also gain seats in the proportionally elected legislature. (7 seats seen as "other" in table 10.1a). Democrats would have had the most seats in this hypothetical legislature, and they would not have had to join forces with smaller parties in order to get over 50 percent, or 218 seats. Thus they could have operated without coalition.

The actual results of the 2018 election, however, can be found on Table 10.1b.

The above example is hypothetical, and no system is this purely proportional, but the example illustrates the difference a PR system can make to election results. In PR systems, a distinguishing feature is that voters *vote for parties*

Table 10.1a	Hypothetical 2018 U.S. House of Representatives Results Based on Proportional Representation	
	Percentage of Votes	Corresponding Number of Seats (out of 435)
Republicans	44.9	195
Democrats	53.3	232
Other	1.7	7

Data from Cook Political Report, Compiled by David Wasserman & Ally Flinn. Accessed 3 December 2018 at https://docs.google.com/spreadsheets/d/1WxDaxD5az6kdOjJncmGph37z0BP NhV1fNAH_g7IkpC0/htmlview?sle=true#gid=0.

Table 10.1b	Actual 2018 U.S. House of Representatives Results	
	Percentage of Votes	Corresponding Number of Seats
Republicans	44.9	199
Democrats	53.3	235

Note: As of December 2018 one seat was not yet certified (North Carolina, CD-9). As of press, the Republican was slightly ahead in the race yet allegations of voter fraud have called the results into question.

Data from Cook Political Report, Compiled by David Wasserman & Ally Flinn. Accessed 3 December 2018 at https://docs.google.com/spreadsheets/d/1WxDaxD5az6kdOjJncmGph37z0BP NhV1fNAH_g7IkpC0/htmlview?sle=true#gid=0.

and not candidates. At a basic level, PR systems are frequently **list PR systems**, meaning that parties place as many candidates on their party lists as the district magnitude—or the number of seats available in the constituency. As a result, if a party wins 40 percent of the votes, the top 40 percent of candidates on the party list enter the legislature. A politician's position on his or her party's list becomes very important and provides a way for parties to get underrepresented groups, like women and racial/ethnic minorities, into government. In some cases, parties are mandated by law to arrange their PR lists in a gender-balanced or racially balanced way (see Box 10.1 for a gender example). Most quotas related to ethnicity are reserved-seat quotas (see Box 10.1 for an explanation of reserved-seat quotas). A few democracies have reserved-seat ethnic quotas including Belgium, which reserves seats for Flemish representatives, Croatia which reserves seats for Serbian, and New Zealand which reserves seats for Maori.

List PR systems developed with the advent of mass enfranchisement as parties needed easy ways to translate their message to voters, voters to votes, and votes to seats.[6] The stronger the cleavages in countries—particularly ethnic and religious cleavages—the stronger the move for list PR systems because it provides representative voice for disparate groups in government. Thus, we see PR systems in consociational democracies. A downside to the PR approach is that it does not allow for strong district representation, because district magnitude is greater than one, so politicians have more allegiance to party than the region they are representing. PR systems are more likely to encourage a trustee style of representation, though, which has benefits for satisfaction with democracy. The United States shares none of the attributes of PR electoral systems.

Variability in PR systems stems from differences in the mathematical electoral formula that translates the votes parties receive into the seats the parties receive. These formulas are named after the people who invented them—for example, Hare, D'Hondt, and Sainte-Laguë—and differ in the level of stability versus representation they try to add to vote results in already very representative PR systems. The formula in effect calculates the number of seats that each party will gain in the legislature. These may seem like algorithmic exercises, but founders like Thomas Jefferson proposed such formulas. The formula is not only about math; it is an extremely important mechanism of producing a superior representative democracy for a country by optimally translating election results into legislative representatives.

Single Transferrable Vote

A way to produce more stability in PR systems and more representation in SMP systems comes from the use of the **single transferrable vote (STV)** also called **alternative vote system**, **preferential voting**, **ranked choice voting**, or **instant run-off voting**. This is a ballot structure devised by an MIT professor in the late 1800s.[7] It is most commonly used in Australia and Ireland. Until recent changes in Maine, it had only been used in the United States in the State of Alabama in the early 1900s. In this system, voters rank order all candidates on a ballot, from first to last choice. If the voter's number one candidate does not have enough votes to be elected, the voter's vote can be "transferred" to the voter's second choice. Because computation can be difficult, special counting software is most often used. This may also be why STV is generally only used in small states. When votes are tabulated, candidates must reach a quota to be elected. Once that quota is met, the "extra" votes are transferred to the other candidates based upon the preference of the voters. New Zealand has an excellent online tutorial explaining STV. Readers of this book are strongly encouraged to check it out at http://www.stv.govt.nz/stv/how.htm.

Under alternative voting, a candidate must receive more than 50 percent of the vote to win, hence it is a majority system. When counting votes, the candidate with the lowest number of first preference votes is dropped, and these votes (the second-choice votes of electors who preferred this candidate) are reallocated to the other candidates. This process continues until a candidate emerges with more than 50 percent of the votes. In Australia, the candidate with the largest number of first-preference votes has usually gone on to be elected, but it is not *always* the case.

This system is both proportional and promotes politician ties to a constituency. Under STV, voters vote for candidates, not parties; but unlike SMP, voters have a better chance of seeing their preferred candidate elected, and voters choose from among many different candidate. While this system is most commonly used in Australia, New Zealand, and Ireland, it is also used by some U.S. municipalities like Cambridge, Massachusetts, and San Francisco, California. It was only used in the United States at the state level in Alabama and a few other Southern states in the early 1900s until 2016 when voters in Maine elected to adopt ranked choice voting through referendum. In Maine, a voter ranks gubernatorial candidates from one to six. If no candidate gets an absolute majority of first-choice votes, the last-placed candidate is dropped. Ballots for the dropped candidate move to the next-ranked person on each ballot. The process repeats until one person has a majority. The system has been taken to court by Maine Republicans who are leery of the system. Maine's Supreme Court upheld that the word "majority" was a problem, as it violates a state constitutional rule that only candidates with the *most* votes, not a *majority* of the votes win elections.[8] The system was put to the test in the June 2018 primary, with much consternation from its foes. Initial reports were that the system worked without incident, and proponents suggest it will decrease vitriol and spread to other locations.

Everywhere STV is used are current or former Commonwealth states, leading scholars like Lijphart to argue that there is a direct political culture link between Anglo-Saxon political culture and use of STV, making it the Anglo-Saxon PR system. Non–Anglo-Saxon PR countries pick a list system likely because of political cultural differences.[9]

BOX 10.1

The Use of Quotas to Increase Numbers of Women in Parliaments

In many democracies, governments have mandated quotas as a way to increase representation of underrepresented groups in the legislature. One common quota in advanced industrial democracies is the **gender quota**. Gender quotas are defined as the mandate that women must constitute a certain number or percentage of the members of a body, whether it is a candidate list, a parliamentary assembly, a committee, or a government.[10]

There are three dominant types of gender quota policies that countries use.[11] The first type of quota is the gender **reserved seats quota**, which establishes seats for which only women are eligible to compete. Reserved seats are found in the developing countries of Rwanda, Uganda, and Palestinian Authority. The second type of quota is the **party quota**. Party quotas are pledges by parties to aim for a particular proportion of women among their candidates to political office. For example, the Zapatero administration in Spain pledged equal representation of men and women in the cabinet during his time in office, achieving equality in the cabinet. Emmanuel Macron in France and Justin Trudeau in Canada similarly proposed gender-balanced cabinets. Finally, there are **legislative quotas**, the most common type of gender quota. Legislative quotas are mandatory provisions that apply to all political groupings that require a certain proportion of female candidates to address party selection.[12] France provides a good example. The French legislature mandated **parity**, or equality, between men and women in government. Parity most dramatically impacts the local and regional levels where parties are strictly mandated (in towns with more than 3,500 residents) to alternate women's and men's names on party lists, with the threat of decreased state funding if they do not.[13] Thus, when parties enter the government and bring in members off party lists, the same number of men and women enter government.

More than 100 countries in the world now have adopted some form of gender quota in politics, and they have been documented by scholars as a way to increase women's representation in government.[14] Countries with high levels of women in government are more likely to be those with instituted quotas in closed list proportional representation systems. In fact, in the top twenty-five countries for women's legislative representation, only Cuba does not have some sort of quota system. Clearly, quotas increase the numbers of women in legislatures, but do these numbers matter? In other words, does descriptive representation of women in legislatures translate into substantive country-level changes in gender equality? The data on this is mixed, and the answer is "sometimes."

In some countries, like Rwanda and Cuba, with high levels of women in parliaments and quota systems, we see that equality in government doesn't necessarily equate to equality in society. However, in other countries, like the Scandinavian countries, we are more likely to see equality as an embraced value in and out of government.

Additionally, while gender quotas positively impact **descriptive representation**, or the number of women in parliaments roughly matching the percentage of women in society, they may not affect **substantive representation**, where women drive an agenda and support legislation based on gendered interests. As far as women in executive branch positions around the world, their **portfolio assignments** may not be affected by gender. There is still a division of labor in governments, even governments with gender quotas, with women excluded from certain "masculine" policy responsibilities, also known as "portfolios," like defense, interior, or economics. It may also be the case that women prefer "women's portfolios."[15] No matter the reason, while gender quotas increase the number of women in parliaments, women usually still serve in portfolios considered "feminine," like education, health, social services, or culture.[16] The key is that list PR systems provide the opportunity to manage such quotas, whereas plurality systems like the United States lack the mechanical tools to produce gender balance.

Mixed-Member Systems

We have mentioned previously that one of the criticisms of PR systems is that they do not tie legislators to a legislative district, so PR has high levels of representation but lower levels of stability. To remedy this deficit, some democracies have mixed electoral systems. Prior to the fall of the Iron Curtain in the 1990s, Germany was the only example of such a system, but many postcommunist states, as well as Japan through reforms, have adopted **mixed-member electoral systems**, which basically combine elements of SMP and PR systems. Voters vote for a representative from their district, and they subsequently also vote for a party that will get seats in the legislature based upon proportional representation. In Germany, half of the lower house of the legislature, known as the Bundestag, is elected based upon an SMP formula, and half is elected based upon a PR list system. Voters have two votes, with half the ballot listing a candidate for the district and the other half listing parties in the country (see Figure 10.1).

The German system has two caveats: parties must win a **threshold**—a minimum percentage a party must achieve to gain any seats in the legislature—of at least 5 percent of the vote or three seats to take part in the PR allocation of votes.[17]

This threshold was put in place to produce more stability and to prevent the rise of fringe parties. Thus, while the National Socialist Party (NPD), otherwise known as the Nazi party, runs for election, it never makes the threshold and thus never has representation in the Bundestag. (See Chapters 2 and 9 for a discussion of the AfD, the "mainstream" far right party in Germany.)

Figure 10.1 German Ballot

Note: Here is an example of a German ballot. The top reads "you have 2 votes." The Erststimme (first vote) is for a district representative; the Zweitstimme (second vote) is for a party.

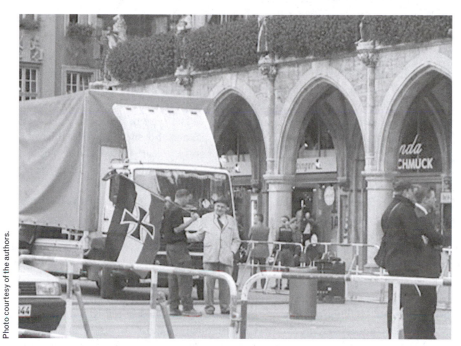

Photo courtesy of the authors.

▶ **Photo 10.1** Leader of the NPD in Munich getting ready for an election rally.

Table 10.2	Summary of Electoral Systems		

Type of Electoral System	Stability	Representation	Level of Disproportionality
Single Member Plurality	High	Low	High
Multi Member Plurality	High	Medium	Medium
Majority, Two Round	Medium	Medium	Medium
Majority, Alternative Vote	Medium	Medium	Medium
Proportional Representation	Low	High	Low
Single Transferable Vote	Medium	High	Low
Mixed-Member System	High	High	Low

Table 10.2 summarizes the different types of party systems discussed previously based upon their degree of stability, representation, and disproportionality.

CONSEQUENCES OF ELECTORAL SYSTEMS

One consequence of electoral systems hinted at in the introduction to this chapter is the influence of electoral systems on the effective number of political parties in a country. While it is not a hard and fast rule, SMP countries tend to have fewer political parties, and PR systems tend to have more political parties. Again, the mechanical nature of electoral systems helps to produce the type of democracy a society needs. Majoritarian democracies favor fewer parties and end up with stable governments because one party clearly wins and another clearly loses. Consociational democracies choose electoral systems that lead to multiple parties that represent these countries' diverse societies. The American system has many majoritarian features from its SMP institution but also has strange checks built in like the Electoral College and separate presidential and congressional voting.

A consequence of more political parties is that parties need to form a **coalition** to govern, where parties band together to obtain more seats in parliament with the hope of gathering a majority of the seats or at least more seats than any other possible coalition could muster so that the government could survive a vote of no confidence. Because the United States has both a presidential system and an SMP electoral system, coalitions never need to form. The United Kingdom has an SMP system, but its parliamentary structure meant that in the rare situation after the 2010 election where no party held a majority of seats, the Conservative Party had to enter into a coalition with the Liberal Democrats. After the 2017 U.K. election, the Conservative Party once again did not have an absolution majority, and Prime Minister Theresa May entered into a **confidence and supply** agreement with the Democratic Unionist Party (DUP), whereby the DUP agree to back the Conservatives in key votes—such as a budget and a confidence motion—but have not agreed to support them on other votes.

Usually ideologically similar parties form a coalition. For example, in the 1990s and early 2000s, the Social Democrat Party in Germany operated in coalition with the Green Party, allowing the coalition to command more than 50 percent of the seats in the Bundestag, or German parliament. The **junior coalition partner**, or the party with fewer seats, is usually given key cabinet ministries in exchange for its support. The leader of the major partner (the party with more seats) becomes the head of government. In coalition systems, smaller parties can be "kingmakers" and wield influence beyond their vote level. Nothing dictates the coalition partner a major party must pick. Parties that command more seats and received more votes in the election can sometimes be overlooked for parties that received less popular support. Sometimes coalition talks between a major and minor party don't work out, and two major parties enter into a **grand coalition** together, though because of their size, ideological differences, and long-term competitiveness, these types of governments are not usually long lived. For example, in Germany, the major party of the right, the Christian Democrats, entered into a grand coalition (Grosse Koalition) in recent years with the major party of the left, the Social Democrats. "GroKo" even became the German word of the year for 2013. Even if they might like it, could Americans even imagine the Republicans entering into coalition with the Democrats? This is certainly a difference from the United States.

Electoral systems also have consequences for interest articulation in democracies. The more proportional the system, the more interests are represented in the legislature. Far right parties have been able to gain a foothold in Europe in part because they stand a chance of gaining at least some seats in a PR system. In a system like the United States,' the interests of the far right have to be subsumed under the Republican Party, resulting in a negotiation between old guard Republicans and newer right-wing members. This is a tension that the United States has seen play out during the Trump administration. This affects interest group politics as well. It is no surprise that those countries with SMP systems are also more likely to have pluralist interest group systems with many different types of interest groups, as these interests are likely not represented or emphasized in the type of catchall parties single member plurality systems promote.

Systems with higher levels of proportionality tend to have higher levels of effective numbers of political parties as well. This can have real consequences in terms of representation. As David Farrell points out, disproportionality decreases, and representation by women (and other underrepresented groups) increases as effective number of political parties increases.[18] PR systems are "fairer to smaller parties and to supporters of smaller parties; provide better social representation; [and] certain PR systems provide voters with greater electoral choice."[19]

With all these benefits associated with PR systems, why would the United States, or any other country for that matter, opt for an SMP system? A large reason touched on above has to do with the fact that SMP systems are more stable. The more parties in the parliament and more members in a governing coalition means there is a greater likelihood for disagreement among parties and perhaps votes of no confidence and government coalitions falling. The average government duration for Italy, a system that is quite proportional and operates with many coalition partners, is 1.14 years (if a government actually served one full term it would be 7 years), while the United States and the United Kingdom, SMP systems, have average government durations of 4.45 and 5.52 years, respectively.[20]

In addition, the same forces that allow proportionality and representation can allow extremist small parties to take hold in PR systems. Thresholds, like the 5 percent one in Germany, can abate the influence of extremist parties. In addition, in SMP systems, it is not that extremist thought does not exist, it is just usually articulated through interest groups rather than parties. Furthermore, extremist thought is not always negative; it may be critical to advancing the causes of the underrepresented groups at key points in history.[21]

Another criticism of PR systems is that they are difficult for voters (and students reading and authors writing this book) to understand. Winner-take-all systems are conceptually simpler than a system like STV or understanding how the quota systems influence results. This criticism holds a little less water when juxtaposed against trying to explain the U.S. Electoral College system. Prior to the 2000 election, when George W. Bush won the Electoral College vote but lost the popular vote to Al Gore, most Americans had little idea how the Electoral College worked or could affect the outcome of elections. The complicated interpretation of the system took more than a month to figure out and bounced through Florida's state government, state court systems, and all the way to its ultimate split interpretation by the U.S. Supreme Court. Americans put thoughts of the Electoral College out of their heads until 2016 when once again a candidate, this time Hilary Clinton, lost the Electoral College but won the popular vote. Once again, there are renewed calls for getting rid of the Electoral College. Even President Trump himself, a beneficiary of the Electoral College system, has said he thinks it should go.[22]

While PR systems certainly are more representative and less disproportional, they do have their drawbacks. What is important to remember about electoral systems—which can be dry topics to understand—is that they are chosen as a function of a country's historical background, social cleavage structure, and political culture. Choosing SMP over PR, or even the wrong electoral formula within PR systems, can mean democratic governance does not properly represent the wishes of a society through elections.

CONCLUSION

When constructing electoral systems, democracies must balance a desire for stability, the ability for a government to control policy and serve for a fixed period, against a desire for representation, where the broad set of voices in society end up in government. District magnitude, ballot structure, and electoral formula all play a role in influencing the degree to which a country has more electoral stability or a more representational electoral system. The exact balance struck by a democracy's electoral institutions and context reflects that country's political cultural beliefs as enshrined in its constitution and other institutions. Single-member plurality systems like the United States tend to be stable, while offering less representation of alternative views. The political institutions offset this imbalance and actually mean that American electoral institutions and electoral context blend a lack of stability and a lack of representation.

Other countries privilege representation over stability, opting for PR systems. Some go even further by instituting quotas, particularly gender quotas. Often, we see blending of systems like in mixed plurality or STV, which attempt to find a balance between stability and representation. A downside to this is that they can become mathematically confusing to voters and would be difficult to implement in large population settings.

KEY TERMS

REVIEW QUESTIONS

1. We've stated that electoral system design is a trade-off between stability and representation. Which of these does the U.S. system emphasize? Why? What evidence do you have for your answer?

2. Explain how district magnitude, ballot structure, and electoral formula influence the stability and representation of a political system.

3. Explain the difference between plurality (majority) and proportional representation systems.

4. What type of electoral formula is present in the United States? How is this similar and different from formulas in other countries?

5. Why do you think the United States chose the type of electoral system it has? Do you think it is the best system for the United States? Why, or why not? What arguments would you make if you were advocating for a different electoral system?

6. Do you think the Electoral College is still needed? Should it be abolished? Should it be modified?

7. Should the United States move to a proportional system? What problems would it solve? What problems could it create?

SUGGESTED READINGS

Campbell, David. *Why We Vote: How Schools and Communities Shape Our Civic Life*. Princeton, NJ: Princeton University Press, 2006.

Dalton, Russell, and Christopher Anderson. *Citizens, Context, and Choice*. Oxford, UK: Oxford University Press, 2011.

Dalton, Russell. *Citizen Politics: Public Opinion and Political Parties in Advanced Industrial Democracies*. Washington, DC: CQ Press, 2013.

Fair Vote, "How proportional representation elections work," http://www.fairvote .org/how_proportional_representation_elections_work.

Farrell, David. *Electoral Systems: A Comparative Introduction*. New York, NY: Palgrave McMillian Press, 2011.

Grofman, Bernard, and Arend Lijphart (Eds.). *Electoral Laws and Their Political Consequences*. New York, NY: Agathon Press, 1986.

Krook, Mona Lena, Joni Lovenduski, and Judith Squires. "Gender Quotas and Models of Political Citizenship." *British Journal of Political Science* 39, no. 4 (2009): 781–803.

Lijphart, Arend. *Electoral Systems and Party Systems: A Study of Twenty-Seven Democracies, 1945–1990*. Oxford, UK: Oxford University Press, 1994.

Seelye, Katherine. "As Australia and the Oscars Go, So Goes Maine?" *New York Times* (June 11, 2018). https://www.nytimes.com/2018/06/11/us/maine-ranked-choice -voting.html.

NOTES

1. David Farrell, *Electoral Systems: A Comparative Introduction* (New York: Palgrave McMillian Press, 2011).

2. Farrell, *Electoral Systems: A Comparative Introduction*.

3. Farrell, *Electoral Systems: A Comparative Introduction*.

4. Farrell, *Electoral Systems A Comparative Introduction*.

5. Arend Lijphart, *Patterns of Democracy* (New Haven, CT: Yale University Press, 1999).

6. David Farrell, *Electoral Systems: A Comparative Introduction*.

7. Farrell, *Electoral Systems: A Comparative Introduction*.

8. Jack Santucci, "Maine's Citizens Passed Ranked Choice Voting: Why Did Republicans Shoot It Down?" https://www.washingtonpost.com/news/monkey -cage/wp/2017/05/31/maines-citizens-passed-ranked-choice-voting-why-did -republicans-shoot-it-down/?utm_term=.c75c83b52673.

9. Arend Lijphart, *Electoral Systems and Party Systems: A Study of Twenty-Seven Democracies, 1945–1990* (Oxford, UK: Oxford University Press, 1994). See also Vernon Bogdanor, *What Is Proportional Representation?* (New York, NY: Wiley and Sons, 1984).

10. Drude Dahlerup, "Increasing Women's Political Representation: New Trends in Gender Quotas," http://www.idea.int/publications/wip2/upload/4._Increasing_Women%27s_Political_Representation.pdf.

11. Mona Lena Krook, Joni Lovenduski, and Judith Squires, "Gender Quotas and Models of Political Citizenship," *British Journal of Political Science* 39, no. 4 (2009): 781–803.

12. Krook, Lovenduski, and Squires, "Gender Quotas."

13. J. Praud and S. Dauphin, *Parity Democracy: Women's Political Representation in Fifth Republic France* (UBC Press: Vancouver, 2011).

14. See for example Drude Dahlerup, "Increasing Women's Political Representation: New Trends in Gender Quotas"; Krook, Lovenduski, and Squires, "Gender Quotas and Models of Political Citizenship."

15. Mona Lena Krook and Diana O'Brien, "All the President's Men? The Appointment of Female Cabinet Ministers Worldwide," paper presented at the Midwest Political Science Association National Conference, Chicago, IL (2011), 10; see also Candice Ortbals and Lori Poloni-Staudinger, "Women Policymakers Framing Their Leadership and Lives in Relation to Terrorism: The Basque Case," *Journal of Women, Politics and Policy* 37, no.2 (2016):121–144.

16. Candice Ortbals and Lori Poloni-Staudinger, "Women Policymakers Framing Their Leadership and Lives in Relation to Terrorism: The Basque Case."

17. The three-seat threshold was instituted after the reunification of West and East Germany as the East German parties would never receive 5 percent of the total vote. It was a way to integrate the East into the democratic process in the postunification era.

18. David Farrell, *Electoral Systems: A Comparative Introduction*.

19. Farrell, *Electoral Systems: A Comparative Introduction*, 211.

20. Farrell, *Electoral Systems: A Comparative Introduction*, 216. One term for the United States would be four years and the United Kingdom five years. Numbers greater than this indicate reelections.

21. Joel Olson, *Abolition of White Democracy* (Minneapolis: University of Minnesota Press, 2004).

22. See for example https://www.politico.com/story/2018/04/26/trump-electoral-college-popular-vote-555148 and https://www.washingtonpost.com/opinions/does-trump-even-understand-the-electoral-college/2018/05/02/34b96728-4d69-11e8-84a0-458a1aa9ac0a_story.html?utm_term=.bf847d2f9703.

CHAPTER ELEVEN

ELECTORAL BEHAVIOR

We all know Belgium for its chocolate, its waffles, and maybe after the 2018 World Cup, its soccer; but did you also know that Belgium is known for its electoral crisis? That's correct. Belgium's electoral politics is synonymous with electoral crisis. Belgium earned the dubious distinction for the country that has spent the longest time without a government, a title they won from Iraq in 2010. What went wrong causing Belgium to be without a government for nearly one and one-half years (541 days to be exact)? On June 13, 2010, Belgium held an election, and no party gained a majority in the parliament. Negotiations proved fruitless, and coalitions were unable to be formed. How could this happen? The answer lies in part in the political culture of Belgium, its consensus-based institutional structure, and the voting behavior of its public.

There are deep divisions between the Dutch-speaking (Flemish) and French-speaking (Walloon) halves of the population; each side has its own political parties, and there are no real national parties. In 2010, like previous years, the Flemish held tightly to their parties and the French to theirs. Conservatives were more likely to be elected in the Flemish region of Belgium, and Socialists in the French region. Some even suggested Belgium may split into two countries over this stalemate and the degree of division in their electoral system. At the crisis's height, 57 percent of Belgium citizens indicated the failure to form a government was their biggest worry. That said, polls showed at the same time that a new election would produce a similar result.

Finally, after 541 days, in December 2011, a government was formed with an unusual six-party coalition that did not include the largest Flemish party. Prime Minister Eli diRuppo became Belgium's first Socialist and French-speaking head of government in more than three decades, as well as the country's first openly gay prime minister. He lasted until October 2014 when new elections were held. During his tenure, electoral reforms were put in place that were supposed to help ward off future stalemates. They (sort of) worked. Negotiations after the 2014 election took five months and eventually a center-right coalition government of four parties came into existence. This government excluded Socialists for the first time in twenty-six years and installed Charles Michaels, the youngest prime minister in Belgium's history. The government is predominantly Flemish, with only one French party participating, raising concerns about disaffection among French voters. The next election is slated for May-June 2019.

This chapter examines **electoral behavior**, or how electoral institutions, discussed in Chapter 10, coupled with political culture and a country's electoral environment, influence whether and how citizens vote for their electoral preferences. The end of the chapter looks at the consequences of electoral institutions, electoral environment, and voter characteristics for public policy, change in leadership, and evaluations of democracy.

CONTEXT OF ELECTIONS AND CAMPAIGNS

Given that American electoral institutions differ from other democracies' electoral institutions, it is not surprising that the practices of democracy—the context of elections and campaigns—differ as well. Understanding voting behavior cannot simply come from the details of American electoral institutions described in Chapter 10 or the individual-level characteristics of voters.[1] Political institutions and broader political cultural beliefs create an environment, or **electoral context**, that includes electoral laws, rules, strategies, and acceptable practices that affect how voters think about and participate in elections. Just like American political culture, some of the American electoral context is not easily perceived because Americans are used to their own electoral context. American students may not be able to understand how Belgium could go 541 days without a government. Similarly, students in Belgium may be perplexed by American electoral behavior that has citizens turning out to the polls on a Tuesday, sees low participation, and aggregates interests into two main parties.

When comparing the American electoral context to other democracies' electoral contexts, it becomes clear that it is peculiar and helps to explain why Americans participate the way they do. No one would design America's current electoral institutions and context. The system was not designed comprehensively nor designed to handle contemporary political demands and technology. It is a product of American political culture's individualism and skepticism of centralized power and political parties. States have sovereignty over elections, so there is no single set of American electoral institutions or procedures. When new technologies or electioneering methods or problems arose, each state took up incremental reforms that simply altered existing institutions designed for a different era.

Consequently, American democracy has institutions from the 1700s, mobilization practices from the 1800s, reforms and strategies from the 1900s, and innovations and media of the 2000s. The outcomes of electoral institutions and context are not neutral. They affect the number of competitive parties, campaign experiences, flow of campaign information, and incentives for citizens to vote or not—and whom to vote for if they do. The electoral institutions and context lead to substantially different voting behavior of Americans compared to citizens in other democracies in two principal areas: (1) whether citizens participate in elections and (2) what party/candidate they end up deciding to support.

VOTING BEHAVIOR: ELECTORAL PARTICIPATION

Strong social norms and political preferences should drive citizens to vote, so it is often easier to begin trying to explain voter participation with the question: why would people *not* vote? One of the explanations for why someone might not vote came from Anthony Downs's 1957 classic *An Economic Theory of Democracy*.[2] Downs argued that based on simple cost-benefit calculations, it actually may be rational for citizens to not vote if they could not detect a difference among the contestants and/or their vote would not matter in the outcome of the election. There is something to Downs's model. We see higher turnout across democracies when elections are more hotly contested.

Additional research shows that, on average, characteristics such as higher socioeconomic status (SES; e.g., income, education, occupational status) leads people to vote more frequently compared to those with lower socioeconomic status across the board in democracies.[3] Higher SES voters may have more time to engage in politics, a greater understanding of politics, and civic skills, so as a result, they likely have more **political efficacy**, a feeling that they can influence the political system, and it will be receptive to them. Socioeconomic status does not tell the whole story in voter turnout. Americans became steadily more educated, richer, and had greater media access in the twentieth century than ever before, yet their turnout dropped or rose unevenly. Strong party identification, firm ideological beliefs, concern for particular important issues under debate, or a sense of civic duty are other individual-level influences that increase participation.[4] Importantly, electoral institutions, political culture, and electoral context channel and condition these individual-level characteristics and lead to different levels of participation among democracies.[5]

Among advanced industrial democracies, the United States historically has relatively low voter participation, as Table 11.1 indicates. One common explanation for this is that Americans do not care enough about their democracy or value their democratic rights and responsibilities sufficiently. Another version says that Americans are just lazy. Each may have a kernel of truth, but Americans do not tend to show up as "lazy" on cross-national time-use surveys, and Chapter 3 showed that Americans hold similar levels of political interest as other democracies. In reality, contextual factors such as electoral rules and procedures, political party mobilization, campaign information flow, and clarity of choice/consequences of voting outcomes detailed in the following sections explain better why American voters turn out at lower rates than voters in other democracies. In addition, many of the countries that show up at the top of the voter turnout list have compulsory voting, something that would clash with American ideas of individual liberty.

Table 11.1 Electoral Turnout in Select Democracies

Australia *	94.96
Belgium *	92.28
Luxembourg *	89.96
Austria	88.98
Italy	88.15
New Zealand	87.90
Denmark	86.15
Sweden	85.42
Netherlands	85.19
Germany	83.07
Norway	79.91
Greece	77.82
Finland	74.45
United Kingdom	74.00
Spain	73.55
France	72.91
Portugal	72.50
Ireland	72.10
Canada	71.59
Japan	69.63
South Korea	68.44
United States	64.38
Switzerland	54.95

Source: Data drawn from Institute for Democracy and Electoral Assistance (IDEA), http:// www .idea.int.

Data represent average turnout in legislative elections since World War II or country's transition to democracy. *=compulsory voting

Electoral Rules and Procedures: Ballot Length and Voting Frequency

Americans elect dozens of governing positions. Other democracies tend to vote for parties and rely on parties to appoint governing officials. In the United States, voters elect a president, two senators, a representative to the U.S. House, a governor, and a handful of other state executives (secretary of state, attorney general, treasurer, and sometimes superintendent of schools), a state house representative (or two as in Arizona), state senator (except Nebraska), sometimes judges, county-level executives (prosecutors, sheriffs) and lawmakers, school boards, sometimes township officials, city or town council representatives, and sometimes mayors. Only the most engaged voter has detailed knowledge about many of these offices and candidates, much less the candidates' names.

The many offices Americans vote for are staggered with presidential elections every four years, congressional elections every two years, and state and local elections often fall on years in between. Americans regularly have elections three out of four years for both primary and general elections. This amounts to voting six times in four years, and that does not include special elections referendum, recall, or initiative votes that occur in many states.

In many unitary systems, citizens vote only for national-level offices and may even simply cast a single party vote every few years. In supply and demand terms, the focused importance of less frequent voting and fewer offices makes the concentration of voter interest greater for most democracies compared to the United States, where citizens may vote with great frequency for an enormous range of offices. Conversely, in Norway, citizens vote in only a handful of elections every four to five years. Not surprisingly, Switzerland, which also votes frequently and for many things, also has lower voter turnout. Thus, ballot length (the number of positions that are elected) and the frequency of elections explain lower American participation.

Instead of average voter turnout for a single election or type of election, political scientist Ivor Crewe looked at numerous measures to judge roughly the "amount of voting to which citizens of different countries were entitled" and concluded, "No country can approach the United States in the frequency and variety of elections, and thus in the amount of electoral participation to which its citizens have a right. . . . The average American is entitled to do far more electing—probably by a factor of three or four—than the citizen of any other democracy."[6] This cautions against a single statistic completely representing American voting participation.

Electoral Rules and Procedures: Voter Registration Requirements

American election laws do not provide the incentives to participate that other democracies' laws do. First, other democracies' governments automatically register their citizens to vote. South Africa and the United States are unique in placing responsibility on voters to register themselves in time to vote. In fact, some democracies not only register voters but also have laws making voting compulsory, though the punishments for nonvoting are not severe (see the starred countries in table 11.1).[7] The government compelling Americans to vote or even gathering the information needed to automatically register voters would likely be met with suspicion.

The fact that U.S. states require citizens to register themselves (and re-register whenever they move to a new address) fits with American political cultural notions of individualism. In other democracies, political cultural notions of the collective good trumps individualism and places responsibility for voter registration squarely on the government. The downside of the American government not registering voters is lower turnout. A classic study of turnout in democracies found that American registration laws decrease voter turnout in the United States by 14 percent relative to other democracies.[8] Further, American states with easier voter registration processes have higher turnout rates compared to those with stricter registration requirements.

Electoral Rules and Procedures: Tuesday Voting

Most democracies hold elections on weekends or national holidays when citizens have more time to make it to the polls. American elections are held during the busy workweek and mostly during the workday. Ironically, the American federal law making elections on *the first Tuesday after the first Monday in November* was an attempt to *increase* voter turnout.[9] In the 1800s, holding an election in early November would assure that harvests were in, and farmers had time to travel to the polling place. Weekend voting would have meant travel time to the polling place could make people miss church, so Tuesday relieved that conflict. Another religious/voting conflict was avoided by making voting day the first Tuesday *after* the first Monday in November, so never November 1st—the holy day of obligation for Catholics of All Saints Day. What once encouraged turnout now depresses it.

Electoral Rules and Procedures: Length of Campaign

The agricultural calendar also explains why American election phases are so long, particularly in presidential elections. States typically chose dates for party nominations to be anywhere from January through late winter or spring so that nominees were chosen prior to the late spring plant. Campaign activity then largely would end during the agriculturally busy summer except for a national party convention in one single week. Finally, the hot phase of campaigns did not start until after Labor Day—the end of summer—and picked up steam as the crops came in.

When parties began to require that presidential nominations from each state be tied to primary elections or caucuses in the 1970s, it meant that presidential elections followed existing state primary election calendars. Prior to the 1970s, presidential nominees were not known until the national party convention in the summer, so other than a few potential candidates jogging around the country to compete in the then-non-binding primary contests, presidential campaigns did not start in earnest until Labor Day. Now presidential campaign contests begin to be intense nine to ten months before the general election, and contenders and the media start revving up years before that. No candidates take the summer off for presidential and other major elections, so fund-raising, media events, and campaigning fill up the summer months, and the American public typically goes through at least six months of a general election. By mid-June 2012—four-and-a-half months before the election—a majority of Americans said that the presidential campaign was already "too long and dull," and majorities thought the race ahead was going to be "exhausting" or "annoying."[10] The same pattern emerged in 2016, a race that should have garnered a lot of interest between a reality TV star and the first major party woman candidate. By June 2016, 60 percent of Americans said that they were "exhausted" by campaign coverage.[11] The scheduling that made sense for an agricultural country of the 1800s now frustrates citizens, likely lulls them into missing voter registration deadlines, or leads some to say phooey to politics generally. Other democracies have short, concentrated four- to six-week-long elections, whose brevity piques rather than grinds down voter interests, attentiveness, and participation.

Electoral Rules and Procedures: Campaign Finance

American candidates must raise money to fund their campaigns and can do so independently of their political party. Americans hate this way of funding campaigns, but the effects of it are broad. Other democracies fund campaigns through public financing, or require that political parties be the only funding source. Even democracies that allow outside campaign financing regulate the flow, sources, and amount of campaign donations much more closely than the United States. The reason for this comes from the American preoccupation with individual liberty. In this case, the American concern that a government would regulate anyone's freedom of expression leaves the government without much power to regulate the flow of money to candidates or limit the amount of money in campaigns generally. In social democracies importance is placed on the sense of the common good rather than an individual's freedom of expression, meaning that regulating private donations promotes equality.

American campaign financing decentralizes the control over the political message away from parties and toward individual candidates. It also likely chases away potential candidates faced with the daunting challenge of taking on an established candidate with massive campaign finance war chests.

Electoral Rules and Procedures: Electoral College Strategy

The Electoral College made sense in an early republic that shifted power from states to a new federal government. Elections had been and remain the responsibility of states. Most citizens were unable to read, so getting information about potential presidents was not easy. Further, voters likely only knew potential presidents who were from their own state. Consequently, the Electoral College was thought to be a mechanism to have presidential preferences expressed by a body in each state that would have more information than the public to make such a choice.[12]

As is common in the American electoral context, the purpose of the original institutional design from centuries ago no longer holds, but the residual institution affects how politicians strategize and how citizens vote. Because a candidate wins all of the Electoral College votes of every state (except Nebraska and Maine) simply by winning one more vote than an opponent, presidential campaigns concentrate their efforts solely on competitive states. In the past two decades, four of the five largest American states have not been competitive in presidential elections—California, New York, and Illinois vote Democratic, and Texas votes Republican. Only Florida remains competitive. That means there is no real campaign activity occurring in those four states with about one-third of America's population. In the 2008 presidential election, the presidential and vice presidential candidates made 57 percent of their visits to only six states.[13] In 2016, two-thirds of the campaign took place in six states.[14] It also means that the nature of issues important to showdown states might be focused upon more by presidential candidates. This incentive to concentrate voter mobilization in particular **swing states** and ignore voters in other states affects voter turnout and voter choice. Party dominance occurs in other democracies, particularly where there are single member districts, and party mobilization differs as well. Many democracies treat the entire country as a district, pitch policies with a national focus, and compete for every vote across the country.

There are also distinctive political cultural distinctions within the United States that further the differences among states' rates of participation. Daniel Elazar's classic study about differing political cultures across regions of the United States correctly predicts that some regions participate more than others—the Northeast, Upper Midwest, and Northwest, for instance, relative to the middle band of the country and more than the American South and Southwest generally.[15] The cultural differences are reinforced by these regions' states pursuing different restrictions on registration and early voting.

POLITICAL PARTY MOBILIZATION: WEAK PARTY ORGANIZATION IN THE UNITED STATES

As emphasized in Chapter 9, parties drive the political dynamics and political behavior of voters in other democracies. Governing institutions encourage party mobilization, and strong organizations assure that parties do not lose their main role mobilizing voters. Much of the rise in the nineteenth century, fall in the twentieth century, and then renaissance of voter turnout in the United States in the twenty-first century (due to harnessing the use of technology for "get out the vote" efforts), comes from voter mobilization by parties.

Parties were far more organized and directly involved in American life in the 1800s than they are today. This led to high levels of voter mobilization but also led to unsavory, if not illegal, actions taken by parties through party machines in local and state government or patronage where federal government positions were handed out to party supporters based on loyalty rather than competence. To stop these questionable practices, most states and the federal government reformed election laws and hiring practices during the progressive reforms of the late 1800s and early 1900s. These reforms included adopting primary elections, where party nominees were elected rather than chosen based on loyalty to party leaders, resulting in more candidate-centered elections. The **Australian ballot**, or secret ballot, kept parties from handing out preprinted party ballots to voters, and laws disallowing party appointments to bureaucratic positions also weakened American parties' ability to mobilize voters.

Political Party Mobilization: Primary Elections for Candidate Nomination

Having party nominations decided by public vote rather than by the party apparatus weakened party machines and provided rank-and-file partisans with significant power over who represents their party. But there are downsides to the American primary system. First, the primary system pits party members against each other in an open process, which weakens parties. Candidates may try to "dig up dirt" on their primary opponents, which can damage their party's candidate in the general election. Other democracies have party leaders who would never weaken their control over party nomination.

Having to compete in primary elections also leads to strange candidate strategies in the United States. Candidates must make ideologically extreme appeals to win hard-core partisans' support in the primary, then shift to make moderate appeals to attract centrist voters in the general election. This duplicitous position taking upsets American voters who are already suspicious of politicians and parties, but it is much more a product of the strange incentives of competing in a primary and general election than the shady actions of politicians.

Political Party Mobilization: Candidate-Centered Elections

Political parties dominate the governing agenda and citizens' voting behavior in most other advanced industrial democracies. Strict party discipline in the nominations process and party-controlled career advancement lead to adherence to party positions in most democratic systems. This contrasts with the "candidate-centered" nature of American elections, where individual candidates can run as the party's candidate but independently of their party's policy positions.[16] While this type of nominating process stimulates campaign activity in the United States, it does not lead to unified party messaging. The result is that candidates can craft their own campaign independent of the party, tailoring their messages to the interests of their state or district, which leads to a patchwork of styles and messages that voters experience in the United States compared to the generally uniform, disciplined party message presented to electorates in other democracies.

CAMPAIGN INFORMATION FLOW

From the description of its electoral context above, it is clear that the American electoral environment is full of numerous influential actors relative to other democracies. This makes sense given the premium American political culture places on individualism, protection of citizen political liberty over government regulation, and decentralized federalism. More actors also muddy the information flowing during campaigns compared to democracies where parties dominate campaign messages. Advertisements from candidate-centered campaigns, parties, and interest groups fill the airwaves, making policy positions and the responsibility for policy outcomes harder for Americans to figure out. It is ironic that more information may lead to less understanding of political campaigns and depress turnout. Additionally, much of the messaging from interest groups in elections tends to be negative, which mobilizes some voters but demobilizes others.[17]

Much of the American media are in the business of making a profit. This means that so-called "horse-race" coverage of elections—highlighting poll results, campaign slip-ups, and more tabloid-type information that sells—trumps detailed analysis of policy positions. Many democracies invest heavily in public media, with television and radio stations that are not based on earning a profit. As a result, these media outlets can concentrate more on the less sexy topics of politics, such as policy positions and substantive political information, rather than who said what controversial thing and what that means for who will win. This fits the idea that social democracies pursue broader definitions of the public good while Americans do not much want the government engaged in making or regulating political expression. Americans do have public television and public radio that provide in-depth content, but they have a small market share, only receiving a small percentage of their budgets from the government, and even that minimal funding (about $3.60 per American taxpayer) is controversial.

CLARITY OF ELECTORAL CHOICE: LIBERALISM AND LIMITED GOVERNMENT

Since the American government involves itself less in citizens' lives than elsewhere, plenty of political space is left free from government in American civil society. This could mean that citizens may not be that fired up about elections when the outcomes do not affect them as greatly. This runs counter to the model of the dutiful citizen. Yet, the stakes of electoral outcomes may simply be less immediate for Americans relative to the information costs and time demands that full participation in elections would require.

This also does not mean people are not engaged in decisions over who gets what, when, and how in society. People may be extremely involved in making decisions in their community. They may give to or run charities that address problems that would be addressed by governments in social democracies. They may sit on neighborhood association boards or parent-teacher organizations that govern schools. These affect their lives and may do so in more direct ways than say voting for a senator or president, especially if elections are not very competitive. Other democracies' national governments affect their citizens' daily lives more directly, so it is no wonder why those citizens may be more motivated to vote.

Clarity of Electoral Choice: Ideological Similarity of Parties

Democracies with diverse and strong ideological party competition provide clear cues as to the ideological orientation of the party.[18] American parties may be much more polarized than in the past, but they still lack the ideological clarity of democracies elsewhere. American exceptionalism, as described in Chapter 3, has meant there was no feudalism or socialist movement in the United States, and the United States has no center-right conservative party. As a result, in the United States, there are two liberal parties—in the sense of limited government involvement in the economy and society, not that there are two parties on the left ideologically as American parties tend to be to the right of competitive parties in other democracies. Were the parties as different in their positions as many other democracies' parties are, voters might be far more motivated to show up to vote and may even consider voting for another party. When parties provide voters more clarity on policies and responsibility can be pinned directly on parties, voters participate more and have firmer policy bases for their vote.[19]

Clarity of Electoral Choice: One-Party Dominance

American party competition is high in presidential elections and in the breakdown in the number of each party in Congress, but that does not mean the parties are competitive in each district or state. One-party dominance has been the norm in most areas of America.[20] The United States is not unique in this regard; many democracies have had long eras where one and only one party had any shot at winning elections and controlling government, and those parties worked hard to govern in ways to satisfy the majority of the public, so they were not undemocratic.[21] The same may be true of areas of one-party dominance in the United States. **Gerrymandering**, or the process of drawing district lines in such a way as to create noncompetitive seats, has exacerbated one-party dominance in American politics. Congressional districts are drawn by state legislatures, most seats are "safe seats" and uncompetitive, and some have argued this is an undemocratic practice. Recent court rulings in states like Wisconsin and Maryland give some hope that gerrymandering may be judicially challenged and winnable in the United States. In both instances, courts ruled against the gerrymandering occurring within the states, though the Supreme Court failed to avoided deciding the constitutionality in a 2018 case on procedural grounds. Scholarship on participation shows that party competition drives up voter participation, and competition leads parties to sharpen their policy messages. So the lack of competitive parties and gerrymandering in general drives participation down compared to other democracies where party competition is typically high and gerrymandering not a concern. While gerrymandering upsets Americans, many political scientists suggest that it may have only a modest effect because Americans have chosen to live in concentrated Republican or Democratic areas.[22] There may be a few seats gained or lost at the margins based on gerrymandering, but the bigger story is the vast number of areas where people are generally Democrats and other areas where people are generally Republicans.

EVALUATING THE CONSEQUENCES OF THE ELECTORAL CONTEXT ON VOTER PARTICIPATION

Scholars who evaluate electoral institutions, number of offices, clarity of choices, frequency of elections, and party mobilization tend to be less critical of the American citizenry's low turnout.[23] They conclude that American electoral institutions and context depress voter turnout. One classic study found that Americans' political participatory attitudes rank as high or higher than other democracies, but voter turnout lags based on electoral contextual factors. In fact, other countries' turnout would increase by around 5 percent if their citizenries had the same political cultural attitudes as Americans.[24] Like the United States, Switzerland also often ranks relatively low on voter turnout, and that is because both systems are characterized by a multitude of elections at different levels of government with significant frequency.

Li, Pomante II, and Schraufnagel attempted to quantify voter turnout in the United States, with a "Cost of Voting Index (COVI)." This index comparatively examined the costs associated with voting (i.e., ease of registration, mail in ballots, etc.) across all fifty states. The authors found that the cost of voting is highest in Mississippi and lowest in Oregon. Oregon is the only state to have adopted automatic voter registration, easing the burden on voters to register. Mississippi, on the other hand, has limited polling locations and increased voter ID requirements.[25]

These explanations aside, there is no doubt that Americans (even in Oregon) turn out less than other democratic citizens. Genuine systematic institutional and contextual reasons tell why this participatory deficit exists but do not mean that the American public should be given a pass. Do these complex moving parts excuse low voter turnout, or are Americans failing to engage their democratic rights and responsibilities sufficiently and leaving American political life less vibrant than it should be?

ELECTORAL BEHAVIOR: DETERMINANTS OF VOTE CHOICE

The nature of the American electoral system also leads to different models of decision making related to whom American voters support in elections compared to other democracies. The ideal democrat would decide what party or candidate to support based on complex cost-benefit analyses of policy positions and parties' electoral promises. The ideal is infrequent for most voters in most democracies, however, because voters are not blank slates heading into election campaigns. Long-term political predispositions affect voting behavior as much or more than short-term campaign events or policy positions. The level to which such predispositions get dislodged by electoral policy debates and events differs by country. Different voting models explain the decision-making processes for different democracies.

Political scientists have developed numerous models to explain how voters decide whom to support in elections. Three of these will be looked at in depth here: sociological models of voting, social-psychological models of voting, and instrumental models of voting. All explain voting to some extent in each democracy, but the balance differs among democracies.

European political parties formed around strong social-structural cleavages as highlighted in Chapter 9, so the **sociological model** explains both why citizens join parties and vote based on social group identity. These societies divided along ethnic, regional, religious, or linguistic lines, so the party systems and voting reflected these divisions until the latter quarter of the twentieth century. Sociological factors still drive voting for many citizens in many democracies. For example, in the Basque regions of France and Spain, Basque parties control local councils in many localities. Often, the real contest for a local council is between the Basque parties of the left or right, rather than between the national left and right parties. This ethnic cleavage that led to the development of the parties also structures vote choice. In the example of Belgium that opened this chapter, we also see cleavages based upon a sociological factor, linguistics.

There is something powerful about long-term social groupings and their influence on voting behavior. Even in the United States, electoral observers classify the electorate in social demographic terms such as the Catholic vote, African American vote, southern vote, union vote, women's vote, or other social groups. Election results tend to be broken down by such categories in newspapers and political science textbooks. According to the sociological model, class, ethnic, religious, and other group connections reinforce individuals' community socialization, which drive people to support the party associated with their group. The sociological model has held up better in other democracies, with strong ethnic and religious divides, but as Chapter 9 demonstrated, as social groups became cross-pressured by social changes, the power of this model has decreased.

Though the United States often reports voting by social group, American voting scholars find that the **social-psychological model** better explains American voting behavior. Accordingly, family socialization leads an individual to identify with a political party in ways similar to how they identify with their nationality (Irish-American, Italian-American, etc.) or religious denomination.[26] These are long-term identities that affect behavior even if the identification is not that strong. For instance, Christian churches tend to be packed on Christmas Eve and Easter because many people identify with their religious denomination but seldom act on that identity. Their faith may not be as strong as others, but it does not mean that their identity does not drive their behavior when they do behave religiously. These Christmas Eve and Easter church-goers are not jamming up the parking lot of any old convenient church; they go to their *own* church out of an important socialized identity. The same happens in elections; less politically engaged voters end up voting for a party based on identity rather than policy belief.

Psychological identifications are also important because they affect how people perceive the world.[27] If one identifies with a sports team, the fan tends to view the sport through biased lenses, emotionally rooting rather than rationally evaluating the game. Short-term objective reality is overwhelmed by long-term team identity. Such a fan is likely convinced that the referees or umpires are plotting against their team rather than objectively officiating, and the identity probably makes watching a rivalry game with a friend who identifies with the other team impossible. Similar identities drive voting behavior.

Most voting behavior scholarship recognizes party identification as a powerful long-term force that trumps short-term evaluations of policy or leadership in American elections. The strength of party identification comes from its direct effect on voting *plus* its indirect effects of coloring perceptions of the political world.[28] As Figure 11.1 demonstrates, the indirect effects of party identification on voting behavior are particularly powerful because it means that other explanations of voting—positions on issues and evaluations of parties/candidates—end up being driven by preexisting party identification more than short-term objective political evaluations.

Two dynamics have altered the complexion of how party identification operates in American elections in recent decades: (1) the relative number of independents and partisan identifiers and (2) the growth of negative partisanship or how party identification has increasingly led people to vote against the opposing party as much as vote for their own party.

While party identification is the largest influence on vote choice for Americans, there are increasing numbers of independent voters in the American electorate. Further, the number of independents who are politically sophisticated and engaged has quadrupled in the past fifty years to nearly 20 percent of the electorate.[29] This has led to a growing number of free agents who may vote based on issues and ideology. Yet, many of these voters lean toward one of the parties, and leaners tend to have strong fidelity to the party they lean toward. Moreover, the large number of strong party identifiers that really remain loyal to their party washes out any effect of these growing number of independents.

Further, party identification has increasingly led voters to be mobilized against an opposing party even more than for their own party. Beyond a positive identity with one's party, there is a "second layer" of party identification that drives partisans out of a distaste for the opposing party.[30] This so-called **negative partisanship** is the idea that voters are mobilized to vote against the opposing party more than they actually vote for their own party. Much like a sports rivalry, the dislike of the opponent fires people up as much as their love of their team. Rivalries lead to sold-out games and high television ratings. So like Red Sox fans who hate the Yankees and will root against the Yankees no matter if their own team is playing, Republican voters will vote *against* Democrats as much or more than vote *for* Republicans. Some have argued this helps to explain the lack of party defection in the 2016 presidential election, even though positive feelings for both Trump and Clinton were low. House Republican Jason Chaffetz exemplified this when he said he could not endorse his own party's nominee Donald Trump after the airing of an Access Hollywood tape where Trump bragged about grabbing women "by the p*&&y." Chaffetz tweeted on October 26, 2016, "I will not defend or endorse @realDonaldTrump, but I am voting for him. HRC (Hillary Clinton) is that bad. HRC is bad for the USA."[31] In fact, negative partisanship is considered a major reason why there has been unprecedented party loyalty in recent elections.[32] This helps to explain high levels of political incivility in party polarization and why negative advertising is so effective.[33]

For American voting behavior, the outcome of party identification for politics is important because Americans lack the ideological constraint of other democracies.[34] The fact that large majorities of Americans have identified with a political party has stabilized American political debate throughout history, even if the public did not fully engage in all issues. Some critics argue that party identification is less steady than the social-psychological model posits, though the psychological identification remains important to these critics even if issues and candidate evaluations can shift party identification.[35] There is general agreement that party identification as a long-term political force has an enormous influence on how voters come to their voting decisions, and that the voting decision is not entirely dependent on short-term political or campaign factors.

Many other democracies' citizens also hold a psychological identity to a particular party, though the identity itself is not as powerful of a force typically as it is in the U.S. case because many democracies' parties provide greater ideological clarity to voters. Further, voters switch party allegiance more than American

Figure 11.1 The Direct and Indirect Influence of Party Identification on an Individual's Vote Choice

Long-term Political Influencees   Short-term Campaign Influencees   Vote Decision

Socialization Agents
Family
Community
Ethnicityy/Culture

Party Identification
(Direct Effect on Voting)

Stance on Issues
(Indirect consequence
of party identification)

Evaluation/Image of
Candidates
(Indirect consequence
of party identification)

Vote Choice

Sources: Angus Campbell, Philip Converse, Warren Miller, and Donald Stokes, *The American Voter* (Chicago, IL: University of Chicago Press, 1960); Russell Dalton, *Citizen Politics,* 5th ed. (Washington, DC: CQ Press, 2008).

voters.[36] So short-term **instrumental political evaluations** affect voting more in these democracies. In fact, in many multiparty democracies, party identification does not exist in the same way as the United States. With numerous parties competing and many clustering in a similar ideological space, voters may identify positively with two or more parties. Instead of long-term single-party identification conditioning short-term voting behavior, short-term political factors lead voters to evaluate favored parties fluidly based on the conditions of particular elections.[37]

This is not to say that parties are not important to voting in these democracies; party government is the norm for most democracies as highlighted in Chapters 7 and 9. However, without that overwhelming indirect effect of coloring perceptions of short-term conditions, voters in these democracies consider public policy positions of parties, the state of the economy, or political crises much more instrumentally in their voting decision. As seen below, the nature of parties, clarity of responsibility for policy, and ideology of parties make it easier for voters in some democracies to evaluate governing performance and vote based on current political and economic conditions.[38] Table 11.2 summarizes the effect of electoral context on voting behavior.

NONVOTING BEHAVIOR

When discussing electoral participation, it is important to note that it is only one form of political participation, so it may be less influential than other forms of participation depending on the political context. The context of American campaigns lowers American *voting* participation, but Americans have participated more than other democracies' citizens in nonvoting electoral activities like political discussion, persuasion of others during campaigns, or volunteering for candidates.[39] This makes sense in the context laid out above. If one lives in a one-party area in the United States, it may make more sense to join an interest group, join a protest, write letters to newspaper editors, Resistbot, blog, or engage in many other modes of participation.[40] American participation patterns have changed. More Americans and citizens of other advanced industrial democracies say they are frustrated with political parties, do not feel that their government listens or responds to them, and have lower evaluations of governmental performance.[41] The disappointment with representative democratic institutions is juxtaposed with high levels of support for democratic principles—so democracies aren't democratic enough.[42] (Although, as discussed in Chapter 2, this is changing among younger populations.) This has led citizens to pursue other modes of participation in the United States besides voting and electioneering, such as voluntary work that addresses social problems outside of the political debate.[43] So flagging voter participation rates may simply mean political observers and commentators measure only *voting* participation but miss other important *civic* participation rates.[44] Similar patterns are occurring in other democracies as well, which makes empirical evaluations based on older behavior models difficult.

CONSEQUENCES OF ELECTORAL LAWS, CONTEXT, AND VOTING FOR DEMOCRACY

The results and meanings of elections differ greatly depending on countries' electoral systems, political contexts, and voter decision-making context. The results do not simply influence who represents the public in a particular office but also affect the **electoral mandates** of those officials—how closely policy follows election results; **electoral volatility**—how much governing control swings among parties, as well as citizens' overall satisfaction with democracy following election results. American political culture ends up leading to minimal electoral mandates, low electoral volatility, and broadly divergent levels of satisfaction with democracy. American exceptionalism also leads Americans to accept negative and unwelcome consequences from our electoral system that other democracies disallow because Americans prefer individualism and minimal government regulation in the political marketplace of ideas. Americans hate big money in campaigns, campaign negativity, incumbency, and never-ending campaigns but accept them when balanced against regulation of individual political liberty.

Table 11.2   American Electoral Context and Effect on Voting Participation and Voting Choice

Components of American Electoral Context	Common Elsewhere?	Effect on Voting
Election Laws and Rules		
Voting frequency and number of elected offices	Uncommon	Lowers voter knowledge/interest
Voter must register self to vote	Uncommon	Lower voter turnout
Tuesday voting	Unique	Lower voter turnout
Length of campaign	Unique	Lower voter interest
Campaign finance wide open to donors and money	Unique	Muddies clarity of electoral responsibility
Electoral College strategy	Unique	Lower/imbalanced voter turnout
Political Party Mobilization		
Weak party organization in the United States	Uncommon	Imbalanced voter turnout
Candidate-centered elections	Uncommon	Muddies clarity of electoral responsibility
Primary elections for candidate nomination	Uncommon	Lower voter turnout; weakens parties

(Continued)

Table 11.2   (Continued)

Campaign Information Flow		
Many actors with multiple messages	Uncommon	Muddies clarity of electoral responsibility
Horserace media culture	More common over time	Muddies clarity of policy-based responsibility
Clarity of Choice and Consequences of Voting Outcomes		
Liberalism and limited government	Uncommon	Lower turnout and muddies clarity of responsibility
Ideological similarity of parties	Uncommon	Lower turnout and muddies clarity of responsibility
One-party dominance	Also in other democracies	Lower turnout
Separate timing of elections— electoral mandate	Also in other democracies	Lower turnout and muddies clarity of responsibility

Electoral Mandate

There are many countries where responsibility for policy is much clearer given the electoral institutions listed above and the governing institutions highlighted in Chapters 6 and 7.[45] Voters in a single-party majoritarian parliament can reward or punish an incumbent party very easily because it is clear who is responsible for policies. On the other hand, voters in consociational democracies with numerous parties in coalition governments would struggle to hold a particular party responsible in proportional representation elections.

Even though American elections provide majority voting patterns that allow voters to hold parties responsible for policy, the separate legislative powers and sequence of congressional elections from presidential powers and elections reduces Americans' ability to hold parties responsible. Congressional elections occur every two years while presidential elections occur every four. As detailed in Chapter 7, often the surge of supporters in a president's successful election benefits his party in congressional elections. Two years later when the president does not run during the so-called congressional **midterm elections**, supporters motivated by the presidential campaign do not show up to vote as much as those motivated against the president.[46] In all but two midterm elections since 1934, the president's party has lost congressional seats. Aware of this trend, savvy and potentially strong candidates from the president's party sit out these midterms, minimizing further their party's ability to stop midterm loss.[47] Other democracies' voters tend to punish ruling parties or coalitions the longer they serve,[48] but in the United States, the surge and decline of voters brings patterns where Barack Obama wins the 2008 election rather comfortably, has his party lose an enormous number of seats in 2010 (sixty-three in House and six in Senate), but then he wins the 2012 election only to see the Democrats take additional losses in the 2014 midterm (thirteen in House, nine in Senate).

The result is that the American public appears to give the president's party a mandate to govern in one policy direction but two years later favors the party who wants to move in the opposite policy direction. This election policy zig-zag means that American elections do not create mandates nearly as clearly as elections do in other democracies, and the ability of the public to blame a single party or leader for not succeeding is not as clear in the United States. The president can point at Congress, and Congress can blame policy failures on the president. (This can be a bit harder to pull off when Congress and the presidency are controlled by the same party.) Ironically, the United States has the electoral laws to bring the responsibility of a single-party majoritarian democracy, but the political context and governing institutions end up more like consociational coalition governments in struggling to hold governments accountable.

Electoral Volatility

Despite Americans' historic distrust of parties and the relative weakness of parties in the United States, American parties are extremely stable. Electoral volatility is the overall change in party fortunes from one election to the next.[49] In other words, how much party turnover do elections produce on average? American voters do not swing between parties much from one election to another. Figure 11.2 illustrates the relative electoral volatility—the average turnover of parties in democratic elections—for numerous advanced industrial democracies. As the figure illustrates, the United States has the lowest volatility among democracies. This is partially because two parties dominate in the United States, so there are few parties to choose from if one were upset with his or her own party. This stability is the case historically, too, so it is unlikely that a dam of partisan frustration in America is about to break. As stated in Chapter 9, only four elections in American history could be considered realigning elections where one party dramatically outperformed the other party and changed the trajectory of party competition and governance. Meanwhile, other electorates shuffle their governing parties frequently.

Evaluations of Democracy

The results of elections affect how governments represent the public as well as how the public evaluates how well democracy works. Proportional representation elections tend to result in governments that better represent the ideological beliefs of the public.[50] This occurs despite the fact that the public's vote only triggers a bargaining of party leaders who build a governing coalition. So the results of

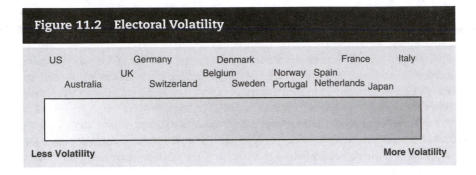

Figure 11.2   Electoral Volatility

US	Germany	Denmark		France	Italy
	UK	Belgium	Norway	Spain	
Australia	Switzerland	Sweden	Portugal	Netherlands	Japan

Less Volatility   More Volatility

voting in different democracies lead to different policies depending on the electoral system, electoral context, and political culture of democracies.

A very important component for democracy to succeed is the belief that people support democracy even when their favored party loses. But politics is about who gets what, when, and how, so those whose party lost an election might be sour on the process relative to the winners. The electoral institutions and electoral context shape this evaluation of democratic satisfaction beyond simply evaluating how well current elected officials are doing. Do the electoral institutions and context even affect how well democracy is evaluated? Yes. In a study of European democracies, supporters of winning parties in majoritarian systems were far more satisfied with democracy than were supporters of losing parties, where less than half of losers claimed that they were "satisfied with democracy."[51] Meanwhile, voters in PR electoral systems were less satisfied with democracy when their parties won compared to majoritarian winning partisans, but those who supported "losing" parties in PR systems were far more satisfied than losing partisans in majoritarian systems.[52] Thus, electoral institutions and context affect democratic beliefs beyond elections and into broader political evaluations.

CONCLUSION

The lack of ideological separation of U.S. political parties, coupled with the frequency of elections, Tuesday voting, and long and money-heavy campaigns has suppressed electoral turnout in the United States compared to other countries. That said, Americans' low overall relative participation compared to other democracies is offset by the amount of electing Americans do and participation in many nonelectoral civic activities. Such rates meet or exceed rates in other democracies.

American voters also tend to lean toward longer term predispositions of party identification when voting. Given long-standing social cleavages, sociological theories help explain the voting behavior of other democracies, particularly in Europe. Those democracies with clearer ideological cues may also allow more short-term instrumental evaluations to overshadow longer term predispositions.

Finally, volatility, common in other countries, particularly those with proportional electoral systems, is not nearly as pronounced in the United States.

In short, the American electoral system and electoral context fits the individualism component of American political culture just as other countries' systems fit with their ideas of communalism or consensus. As a result, the exceptional American electoral context, a key vehicle through which countries determine who gets what, when, and how, remains in place because the alternatives conflict with key American political cultural values.

POINTS TO REMEMBER

- Electoral system design is a trade-off between stability and representation.

- District magnitude, ballot structure, and electoral formula all impact stability and representation.

- District magnitude is the number of representatives elected from a constituency, or voting district. In the United States, district magnitude is one.

- Ballot structure refers to the way in which candidates are listed on a ballot and the number of ballots or elections a country has before a candidate is selected.

- The United States has a primary system to determine which candidates stand for general election. In other countries, parties generally select candidates.

- Americans go to the polls more often than people in any other democracy.

- Voting in many democracies is compulsory, and registration is automatic. In the United States, responsibility for registration and voting rests with the citizen.

- Several structural factors that are left over from previous points in U.S. history help to dampen voter turnout in the United States compared to other democracies, including Tuesday voting, registration rules, Electoral College, campaign finance, and long campaign seasons.

- There is strong support in the United States for the socio-psychological model to explain voter behavior, while in other countries, the sociological and instrumental models carry weight.

- While American voting is suppressed compared to other counties, Americans engage in a great deal of nonelectoral political behavior.

- Political volatility is not as strong in the United States as it is in other countries.

- The nature of U.S. institutions makes instrumental voting, or assigning reward or blame to parties, difficult. This, coupled with American cultural preference for liberty, limits much of American voting behavior.

KEY TERMS

Australian ballot 242
Electoral behavior 236
Electoral context 236
Electoral mandates 251
Electoral volatility 251

Gerrymandering 245
Instrumental political
　evaluations 250
Midterm elections 252
Negative partisanship 248

Political efficacy 237
Social-psychological
　model 247
Sociological model 247
Swing states 242

REVIEW QUESTIONS

1. Why is voter turnout in the United States lower than in other countries?

2. Explain how sociological, sociopsychological, and instrumental theories of electoral behavior explain vote choice. Which is most applicable to the United States?

3. What is electoral volatility? How does it play out in the United States compared to other countries?

4. In what other ways can people participate in politics other than voting?

5. What is political efficacy, and how does this impact participation?

6. How does nonvoting behavior look in the United States compared to other democracies?

7. In what ways do you participation in politics? How would you rank your level of efficacy?

8. How do electoral institutions and context influence voters' evaluations of democratic outcomes?

9. Do you think that Americans make bad democrats? What are the implications of lower voter turnout in the United States?

10. Look up Resistbot. What are the implications for participation with this sort of tool?

11. Does voting matter to you? What are the consequences of younger voters turning out at lower numbers than older citizens?

SUGGESTED READINGS

Anderson, Christopher, and Christine Guillory. "Political Institutions and Satisfaction with Democracy: A Cross-National Analysis of Consensus and Majoritarian Systems." *American Political Science Review* 91, no. 1 (1997): 66–81.

Campbell, David. *Why We Vote: How Schools and Communities Shape Our Civic Life*. Princeton, NJ: Princeton University Press, 2006.

Dalton, Russell, and Christopher Anderson. *Citizens, Context, and Choice*. Oxford, UK: Oxford University Press, 2011.

Grofman, Bernard, and Arend Lijphart (eds.). *Electoral Laws and Their Political Consequences*. New York, NY: Agathon Press, 1986.

Rae, Douglas. *The Political Consequences of Electoral Laws*. New Haven, CT: Yale University Press, 1967.

NOTES

1. For a more detailed explanation of the role of institutions, individual-level features, and electoral "context," see Russell Dalton and Christopher Anderson, *Citizens, Context, and Choice* (Oxford, UK: Oxford University Press, 2011). Crewe also provides numerous linkages between institutions and the consequences on a political environment and behavior as well; Ivor Crewe, "Electoral Participation," in *Democracy at the Polls: A Comparative Study of Competitive National Elections*, eds. David Butler, Howard Penniman, and Austin Ranney (Washington, DC: American Enterprise Institute, 1981).

2. Anthony Downs, *An Economic Theory of Democracy* (New York: Harper & Row, 1957).

3. Sidney Verba, Norman Nie, and Jae-on Kim, *Participation and Political Equality: A Seven-Nation Comparison* (Cambridge, UK: Cambridge University Press, 1978).

4. David Campbell, *Why We Vote: How Schools and Communities Shape Our Civic Life* (Princeton, NJ: Princeton University Press, 2006).

5. See a full explanation of direct, indirect, and contingent effects from electoral institutions and electoral context in Russell Dalton and Christopher Anderson, *Citizens, Context, and Choice* (Oxford: Oxford University Press, 2011), as well as Robert Jackman, "Political Institutions and Voter Turnout in the Industrial Democracies," *American Political Science Review* 81, no. 2 (1987): 405–424.

6. Crewe, "Electoral Participation," 232.

7. Jackman, "Political Institutions and Voter Turnout in the Industrial Democracies."

8. G. Bingham Powell, "American Voter Turnout in Comparative Perspective," *American Political Science Review* 80, no. 1 (1986).

9. George C. Edwards III, *Why the Electoral College Is Bad for America* (New Haven, CT: Yale University Press, 2005).

10. Catalina Camia, "Poll: Americans Bored with Presidential Campaign," *USA Today*, July 5, 2012, http://content.usatoday.com/communities/onpolitics/post/2012/07/presidential-election-boring-pew-research-poll-/1#.Uxy4Ts6GfFI.

11. Jeffrey Gottfried, "Most Americans Already Feel Election Coverage Fatigue," Pew Research Center. July 14, 2016, http://www.pewresearch.org/fact-tank/2016/07/14/most-americans-already-feel-election-coverage-fatigue.

12. For a fuller explanation of the origins of the Electoral College, see Edwards, *Why the Electoral College Is Bad for America*.

13. Calculated by authors, from Gerald Pomper, "The Presidential Election: Change Comes to America," in *The Elections of 2008*, ed. Michael Nelson (Washington, DC: CQ Press, 2010), Table 3.5, 65.

14. See https://www.nationalpopularvote.com/campaign-events-2016.

15. Daniel Elazar, *American Federalism: A View from the States* (New York, NY: Thomas Crowell Company, 1966).

16. Martin Wattenberg, *The Rise of Candidate-Centered Politics: Presidential Elections in the 1980s* (Cambridge, MA: Harvard University Press, 1992).

17. Michael Wolf, J. Cherie Strachan, and Daniel Shea, "Forget the Good of the Game: Incivility and Lack of Compromise as a Second Layer of Party Polarization," *American Behavioral Scientist* 56, no. 12 (2012): 1677–1695.

18. For clear discussions of political context and institutions, see G. Bingham Powell, Jr. and Guy Whitten, "A Cross-National Analysis of Economic Voting: Taking Account of the Political Context," *American Journal of Political Science* 37, no. 2 (1993): 391–414; Dalton and Anderson, *Citizens, Context, and Choice*.

19. See Powell, Jr. and Whitten, "A Cross-National Analysis of Economic Voting"; Dalton and Anderson, *Citizens, Context, and Choice*; Crewe, "Electoral Participation."

20. Warren Miller, "One-Party Politics and the Voter," *American Political Science Review* 50, no. 3 (1954): 707–725.

21. T. J. Pempel, *Uncommon Democracies: The One-Party Dominant Regimes* (Ithaca, NY: Cornell University Press, 1990).

22. See Alan Abramowitz, *The Disappearing Center* (New Haven, CT: Yale University Press, 2011), and Bill Bishop, *The Big Sort*, (Boston, MA: Houghton Mifflin, 2008), and Jowei Chen and David Cottrell, "Evaluating Partisan Gains from Congressional Gerrymandering: Using Computer Simulations to Estimate the Effect of Gerrymandering in the US House," *Electoral Studies*, Vol. 44, 2016, pp. 329–340.

23. Jeffrey Karp and Susan Banducci, "The Influence of Party and Electoral System on Campaign Engagement," in *Citizens, Context, and Choice*, eds. Russell Dalton and Christopher Anderson (Oxford, UK: Oxford University Press, 2011).

24. Powell, "American Voter Turnout in Comparative Perspective."

25. Quan Li, Michael J. Pomante II, and Scot Schraufnagel, *Election Law Journal: Rules, Politics, and Policy*, September 2018, http://doi.org/10.1089/elj.2017.0478.

26. See Angus Campbell, Philip Converse, Warren Miller, and Donald Stokes, *The American Voter* (New York, NY: John Wiley & Sons, 1960).

27. For a discussion of broader psychological identities, see Donald Green, Bradley Palmquist, and Eric Schickler, *Partisan Hearts and Minds* (New Haven, CT: Yale University Press, 2002).

28. Campbell et al., *The American Voter*.

29. Russell Dalton, *The Apartisan American: Dealignment and Changing Electoral Politics*, (Washington, DC: CQ Press), 2013, p. 43; and Michael Wolf, *An Attentive Public* (PhD Thesis, Bloomington: Indiana University, 2002).

30. Michael Wolf, J. Cherie Strachan, and Daniel Shea, "Forget the Good of the Game: Political Incivility and Lack of Compromise as a Second Layer of Party Polarization," *American Behavioral Scientist*, Vol. 56 (12), 2012, pp. 1677–1695.

31. Danielle Diaz, "Jason Chaffetz Appears to Flip-Flop on Trump," CNN, October 26, 2016, https://www.cnn.com/2016/10/26/politics/jason-chaffetz-utah -donald-trump-hillary-clinton/index.html.

32. See for example, Alan Abramowitz and Steven Webster, "Negative Partisanship Explains Everything," *Politico*, https://www.politico.com/magazine/story/2017/ 09/05/negative-partisanship-explains-everything-215534.

33. Michael Wolf, J. Cherie Strachan, and Daniel Shea, "Incivility and Standing Firm: a Second Layer of Partisan Division," *PS: Political Science & Politics*, Vol. 45 (3), 2012, pp. 428–434.

34. Philip Converse, "The Nature of Belief Systems in Mass Publics," in *Ideology and Discontent*, ed. David Apter (New York, NY: Free Press, 1964).

35. Morris Fiorina, *Retrospective Voting in American National Elections* (New Haven, CT: Yale University Press, 1981).

36. David Butler and Donald Stokes, *Political Change in Britain* (London, UK: MacMillan, 1969).

37. Jacques Thomassen, "Party Identification as a Cross-National Concept: Its Meaning in the Netherlands," in *Party Identification and Beyond: Representations of Voting and Party Competition*, eds. I. Budge, I. Crewe, and D. Farlie (London, UK: Wiley, 1976).

38. John Huber and G. Bingham Powell, Jr., "Congruence between Citizens and Policymakers in Two Visions of Liberal Democracy," *World Politics* 46, no. 3 (1994): 291–326.

39. Powell, "American Voter Turnout in Comparative Perspective."

40. Verba, Nie, and Kim, *Participation and Political Equality*.

41. Robert Putnam, Susan Pharr, and Russell Dalton, "What's Troubling the Trilateral Democracies?" in *Disaffected Democracies: What's Troubling the Trilateral Democracies?*, eds. Robert Putnam and Susan Pharr (Princeton, NJ: Princeton University Press, 2000).

42. Russell Dalton, *Citizen Politics: Public Opinion and Political Parties in Advanced Industrial Democracies* (Washington, DC: CQ Press, 2006).

43. Russell Dalton, *The Good Citizen: How a Younger Generation Is Reshaping American Politics* (Washington, DC: CQ Press, 2008).

44. Russell Dalton, *The Good Citizen*; Putnam, Pharr, and Dalton, "What's Troubling the Trilateral Democracies?"

45. Powell, Jr. and Whitten, "A Cross-National Analysis of Economic Voting."

46. James Campbell, *Congressional Elections: The Presidential Pulse* (Lexington: University of Kentucky Press, 1993).

47. Gary Jacobson, *The Politics of Congressional Elections*, 8th ed. (New York, NY: Pearson, 2012).

48. Powell, Jr. and Whitten, "A Cross-National Analysis of Economic Voting."

49. Scott Mainwaring and Mariano Torcal, "Party System Institutionalization and Party System Theory after the Third Wave of Democratization," in *Handbook of Party Politics*, eds. Richard Katz and William Crotty (London, UK: Sage, 2006), 204–227.

50. Arend Lijphart, *Patterns of Democracy in Thirty-Six Countries*, 2nd ed. (New Haven, CT: Yale University Press, 2012); Huber and Powell, Jr., "Congruence between Citizens and Policymakers in Two Visions of Liberal Democracy."

51. Christopher Anderson and Christine Guillory, "Political Institutions and Satisfaction with Democracy: A Cross-National Analysis of Consensus and Majoritarian Systems," *American Political Science Review* 91, no. 1 (1997): 66–81.

52. Anderson and Guillory, "Political Institutions and Satisfaction with Democracy."

CHAPTER TWELVE

CONCLUSION

Seymour Martin Lipset titled his definitive book on the topic *American Exceptionalism: A Double-Edged Sword.* In a powerful section of the book, Lipset juxtaposes reasons why he considered American exceptionalism a double-edged sword: "America continues to be qualitatively different. To reiterate, exceptionalism is a two-edged phenomenon: it does not mean better. This country is an outlier. It is the most religious, optimistic, patriotic, rights-oriented, and individualistic."[1] Lipset also noted other consequences of American political beliefs: its work ethic, high worker output and voluntarism, economic productivity, and highly educated and upwardly mobile society. Simultaneously, Lipset weaves in some of the other side of the sword of American exceptionalism—high rates of crime, litigiousness (frequency of Americans suing each other), low voter turnout, enormous income inequality, and high poverty.

Lipset's point is not to scold Americans for being terrible or to trumpet the United States as incomparably awesome. Instead he argues that the things Americans both do not like and that they admire about American society are deeply linked together by long-standing American political cultural values.[2] This insight is key to the theme of this book, which began by posing key questions that subsequent chapters tried to answer: What does it mean to study American politics from a comparative perspective? *How* and *why* is American democracy similar to and different from other advanced industrial democracies?

Using the comparative method provides the ability to explain why American institutions, political behavior, and policies differ from other democracies. The comparative method used does not just show a difference between the United States and others, it provides a method to analytically explain the contrasting democratic effects and features of long-term political cultural beliefs. Understanding American politics today requires comparison to evaluate how unique American policies, institutions, and citizen behaviors are from other democracies as well as understanding their similarities. Analysis that does not include comparison may do a fine job of describing American politics, but in isolation, it does not sufficiently or accurately explain the dynamics of American politics. It also leaves political observers to look at crime, voter turnout, work hours, poverty, economic productivity, litigiousness, voluntarism, income inequality, and other nuts-and-bolts aspects of American political life as isolated phenomena unconnected to our political values and just different than elsewhere; in reality, beliefs and values explain why those aspects of American political life both exist and exist differently than in other democracies.

As Lipset notes, these positive and negative aspects of American political life are not solely the way they are because of current economic and social conditions or the failings or personalities of political leaders. They also have not popped up due to sudden moral decay, slipping generational values, or because society has gone off the rails. Instead, these American political features are the trade-offs in contemporary American life of American political beliefs that are based on values long ago established about what legitimate government means. American political society stands where it is, not because of current conditions alone, but because American founding beliefs put it on a long path to this point. Americans have always believed, and continue to believe, that government should have an extremely limited role in deciding who gets what, when, and how in society. A legitimate government to Americans is one that first and foremost protects individual life, liberty, and property more than equality across society.

Other social democracies evaluate democracy through principles of equality of outcome and pursue policies that provide for the common good for society relative to individual liberty. This does not mean that Americans like high crime, low voter turnout, inequality, and poverty. Nor do Americans affirmatively choose policies to produce those harmful social characteristics. The alternatives to addressing these policies often conflict with principles of limited government. As a result, because Americans value individual liberty and limited government, their criminal justice system approaches suspected crime differently than civil law tradition democracies, which limits Americans' police and judicial powers. Americans may not like people suing each other, but their preference for limited governance means they would rather have private sector disputes resolved in court after problems pop up than have the government regulate the economy heavily at the front end as is the case in social democracies. Nobody likes poverty, but a society that values limited government delinks the role of the government from the role of civil society to address inequality and poverty in the United States, whereas societies in social democracies insist that government bring about more social equality and minimize poverty. These are the negative consequences of American exceptionalism.

In conclusion, American government is far better understood—its vices and virtues—when studied comparatively over time. That is the point of this book. Each chapter goes a long way to explain American politics through comparison with other advanced industrial democracies. Table 12.1 summarizes the major points of each chapter as well as highlights the broad similarities and differences of the chapter theme. The table is meant as a shortcut and summary and not as a stand-in for reading and wrestling with the content of each chapter.

Table 12.1 What Have We Learned?

Chapter	Summary	Comparisons
Chapter 2: Similarities Between the United States and Other Democracies	This chapter asked the question "What is a democracy?" and explored the broad foundations of democracy, areas where the United States is quite similar to other democracies. This is especially true when you compare democracies to other forms of government like authoritarianism, oligarchies, monarchies, and so on. The United States and other advanced industrial democracies have a representative form of democracy. This principle has been critiqued by some who advocate for more direct or radical forms of democracy.	**Similarities:** The United States stacks up similarly to other democracies on several broad measures: 1. Procedural democracy—Sometimes referred to as a Schumpterian definition of democracy; that is, all democracies share similar procedures. The main procedure we discussed was competitive elections, which has led some to refer to this criterion of democracy as electoralism. 2. Contestation and inclusion—Coined by Dahl, these terms refer to the fact that in all democracies, there is competition over policy positions and participation by large numbers of groups. While there is variation in contestation and inclusion among democracies, all advanced industrial democracies have high levels of both, deeming them polyarchies. 3. Freedoms—All democracies have relatively high levels of freedom or protection of civil rights and liberties. 4. Economic development—While not determinant of democracy, we discussed the idea that all advanced industrial democracies have high levels of socioeconomic development.

(Continued)

Table 12.1 (Continued)

		5. Dissatisfaction with democracy—Across all advanced industrial democracies, we are seeing younger generations report more often than older that it is not important to live in a democratic society. At the same time, Americans tend to be as happy in general as people in other democracies.

Differences: *This chapter did not explore differences.* |
| | | **Similarities:** *This chapter did not explore similarities.*

Differences: American democracy differs from other democracies in several broad ways.

1. Legitimacy—Legitimacy refers to what makes government popularly accepted. The United States has differing opinions of legitimacy and the social contract than other democracies. U.S. social contract theory and legitimacy is greatly influenced by the thinking of Locke, while other democracies, particularly in Europe, are shaped by the thinking of Rousseau.

2. Self-selection of the American immigrant—Many people who came to the United States by choice had a more entrepreneurial and individualistic spirit than their counterparts who stayed behind in Europe. |
| Chapter 3: American Exceptionalism | American exceptionalism has been used by some politicians and members of the media to discuss a superiority of the United States over other countries. This chapter explains that American exceptionalism in its analytical usage refers to how the United States is an exception, or different, on many measures from other advanced industrial democracies. This difference stems from different founding conditions in the United States as opposed to other democracies. Combined with differences in political culture, the different founding conditions put the United States on a different path than other democracies. | |

	3. Because of a lack of feudalism and a socialist movement, the United States did not develop the same sense of political communalism through the state as did other democracies. In the United States, settlers were always able to "go West" to seek their fortune rather than needing to rely on joining arms with fellow workers to press for claims.

4. Constitutional rigidity in the United States and constitutional longevity mean that the blueprint for U.S. democracy is based on a much older model than the blueprint of other democracies.

The above differences in founding moments led a more liberal democracy to develop in the United States, while other democracies developed a more social democracy. Today, Americans are less tolerant of taxes and redistributive social policies than citizens in other democracies. |
| Chapter 4: Political Beliefs: Political Culture and Ideology | This chapter asked how Americans' beliefs stacked up against their democratic cousins, examining both the political culture, or shared political norms and beliefs, and similarities among democracies as well as the unique aspects of American political culture. This chapter also explored ideology or the shared set of beliefs about the proper order of society and how it can be achieved and how it differs in the United States compared to other democracies. | **Similarities:** All democracies share a civic culture. This means people engage in politics, believe that citizens play an important role in government, and trust fellow citizens. Americans favor a limited role for government compared to other democracies. |

(Continued)

Table 12.1 (Continued)

Differences: American political culture is biased in a Lockean sense toward valuing protections of life, liberty, and property in decisions over who should get what, when, and how. Americans favor individualism over communitarian values. Though the sense of a commonwealth exists with Americans, Americans prefer the community to provide for each other outside of government policy or action. This leads Americans to favor individual, community-led, or market solutions to social problems rather than government solutions as found in other democracies. While Americans favor equality of opportunity, citizens in other democracies favor equality of outcome. This is most strongly seen in the economic marketplace and opinions toward inequality, competition, "hard work," and "fair" pay.

Additionally, due to the differences in historical trajectory laid out in Chapter 3, Americans have an ideological space that differs from the ideological space in other advanced industrial democracies. In short, the ideological space is truncated in the United States around liberalism—preferring limited government (not left-based policies)—and ends up being to the right ideologically of belief systems in other democracies.

| Chapter 5: Civil Liberties and Civil Rights | Chapter 5 discussed the civil liberties and civil rights of advanced industrial democracies. Some freedoms are referred to as negative rights that are protected because a government takes no action. These are called civil liberties. Other positive rights are freedoms that come from governments proactively taking action and are called civil rights. The chapter looked at the balance of governments' provision of these positive and negative rights. | **Similarities:** The United States provides core civil liberties like other democracies, including freedom of speech, press, assembly, religion, and rights of accused criminals. Civil rights are also something democracies have that protect citizens from discrimination based on race, gender, age, and other social divisions.

Differences: The American Constitution and Bill of Rights provides more negative rights—civil liberties—than other democracies based on American exceptionalism, individualistic rather than communal political culture, and the early adoption of the American Constitution. Fewer positive rights—civil rights—are protected in the American system relative to other democracies, whose political cultures look to provide equality of outcome more than just equality of opportunity. Most democracies have far more rights such as social welfare, healthcare, human dignity, and environmental rights explicitly written into their constitutions. Evaluation of civil rights in the United States comes from Supreme Court interpretation and executive branch activism, but both vary over time, which makes civil rights less protected in the American system, fitting the American values of limited government. |

(Continued)

Table 12.1 (Continued)

Chapter 6: Constitutional Arrangements	Chapter 6 examined constitutional arrangements among democracies, focusing on the longevity of constitutions, the vertical organization of government (unitary v federal) and the degree of majoritarian or consociational sensibilities in the constitution.	**Similarities:** The United States is a federal system of government, similar to what is found in some other democracies. Federalism is not the only way to organize, however. Many advanced industrial democracies are unitary in their vertical organization. The United States is majoritarian on Lijphart's executive-parties dimension, something it shares in common with many other democracies.
		Differences: The United States has a constitution that is much longer lived than the constitutions of other advanced industrial democracies. It is also more rigid, or harder to change. While there are many democracies that are majoritarian on Lijphart's executive-parties dimension, like the United States, others are consociational, a major difference between the United States and some of its advanced industrial democracy cousins. On Lijphart's federal-unitary dimension, most democracies are more majoritarian than the United States. The United States is highly consociational on this measure, something it shares only with Germany and Switzerland.

| Chapter 7: Governing Institutions | Chapter 7 discussed how both the vertical organization of government in the United States and the horizontal organization of government mark it as unique when compared to other democracies. Differences in civil versus common law traditions help to differentiate the American judicial system from judicial systems in some other democracies. | **Similarities:** Bicameralism, found in the United States' legislature is also found in many other countries' legislative makeup. The judicial system in the United States is based on common law tradition. It shares this in common with some democracies (like the United Kingdom). All democracies have well-developed bureaucracies that carry out the functions of government.

Differences: The most distinguishing difference of the United States is its horizontal structure, or presidential system. In this system, the executive and legislative branches of government are separate, and the roles of head of government and head of state are encompassed in one individual, the U.S. president. Most other advanced democracies have a parliamentary structure, where legislative and executive branches are fused. In other democracies, we are more likely to see party government in the legislature and unlikely to see primary elections, like we find in the United States. In most other democracies, the head of government and head of state roles are fulfilled by two different people, with many times the head of state being a monarch or a figurehead symbol of the country. This is why when we look at legislatures and executives comparatively it makes most sense to discuss them together. |

(Continued)

Table 12.1 (Continued)

	Following a common law tradition, the judicial branch in the United States differs greatly from judicial branches in other democracies, which follow a civil law tradition. The American judiciary is independent from other branches of government and exists to protect citizens' liberties in the criminal justice system. Judicial review is also uncommon among other advanced industrial democracies.
	Similarities: The United States is similar to other advanced democracies in that interest groups play an important role as intermediary institutions in preference articulation in the United States as in other advanced industrial democracies. Interest groups in all democracies go through similar life cycles, and we find similar types of groups, including violent groups, in all democracies. Additionally, groups in all countries tend to employ a mix of insider and outsider tactics.
Chapter 8: Interest Groups	The first of two intermediary institutions discussed in this book (the second is political parties), interest groups form the basis of this chapter. Explaining that interest groups bring together like-minded people, this chapter explored the life cycle of interest groups, the difference between social movements and interest groups, and different types of interest groups. Activities of interest groups, the expanding role of money in politics through interest groups, and the way in which institutions influence activities were also explored. Finally, pluralist interest groups versus corporatist interest group arrangements differ across democracies.
	Differences: The largest difference in the United States is its pluralist, some would say hyperpluralist, interest group arrangement. While other countries may have a degree of pluralism, the United States is the most pluralistic of all democracies. Many more democracies are corporatist in their interest group orientation. Additionally, interest groups have been viewed more negatively in the United States than in other countries. This is due to the growing influence of money in politics, much of which is funneled through interest groups to political campaigns.

| Chapter 9: Political Parties | Political parties are the major interest articulation vehicle in advanced industrial democracies and tend to operate differently in the United States than in other democracies. The focus of this chapter, then, was both the comparative development and operation of political parties in the United States and other democracies. | **Similarities:** All democracies revolve around political parties competing for political influence, organizing governmental institutions, and electoral competition. The strength of this influence and the centrality of parties to the operation of democracy are what differ among democracies. That said, confidence in political parties is declining, not just in the United States, but this is a sentiment shared in other democracies. American party unity, when it exists, is similar to what we see in other democracies. Over time, parties in other democracies have become more "American," by making broader "catch-all" appeals.

Differences: The American party system developed under different historical conditions than party systems in Europe. Thus, the cleavages in Europe that mapped to the political party system (à la Lipset and Rokkan) were not present in the United States as they were in Europe, and American parties do not reflect deep-seated societal cleavages like the parties of Europe.

Parties do not furnish the primary linkage between citizens and government in the United States that they do elsewhere. This is in part due to the fact that from the beginning of the United States, parties formed under an air of suspicion. |

(Continued)

Table 12.1 (Continued)

		Additionally, parties in the United States play a reduced role in governance compared to parties in other advanced industrial democracies. In part, this has to do with differing expectations among citizens as to the role of political parties in democracies.

Differences in founding as well as attitudes toward parties and politics in general help to explain why there are many fewer political parties in the United States than in other democracies, with U.S. politics dominated by two main parties. The party landscape (as well as ideology) is much more varied in other democracies.

Other democracies can be referred to as "party governments" because parties so heavily structure the political agenda and policies of those countries. Many countries even place parties in their constitution.

Similarities: The United States elects candidates in a single-member plurality system. This is similar to some countries, but it is not the norm among democracies. All countries' electoral systems are designed to address a balance between stability and representation. |
| Chapter 10: Elections and Electoral Institutions | This chapter examined electoral institutions. The chapter explored the different types of electoral systems and the consequences of these systems, noting that systems differ based on their preference for stability or representation. The United States has opted for a system (single-member plurality; SMP) that favors stability over representation. | |

	Differences: The United States has a primary system for candidate selection. This differs from other countries that tend to have candidate selection as part of an internal party process. Most democracies use some form of proportional representation system to elect candidates.
	The type of electoral system in a country has structural consequences. The plurality system in the United States, coupled with a presidential system, keeps the effective number of political parties in the United States much smaller than in other countries. Additionally, most other democracies operate using coalitions, which do not exist in the United States. In many democracies, quotas have been used as a way to increase the representation of underrepresented groups in politics, like women, a concept that tends to be foreign to most Americans
Chapter 11: Electoral Behavior	**Similarities:** Due to the frequency of elections and federated structure in the United States, instrumental voting, or assigning blame or support at the ballot box, is difficult in the United States. This is similar to proportional systems where parties operate in coalitions. Additionally, the United States, like many democracies, effectively operates in most locations with one party in dominance.
This chapter examined electoral behavior. Electoral institutions and rules, coupled with other institutions and culture, influence the way citizens behave in the political sphere. American political behavior, primarily lower levels of voting, is a function of several factors discussed in this chapter. Additionally, we found that the socio-psychological model rather than the instrumental or sociological models best explains voting behavior in the United States.	

(Continued)

Table 12.1   (Continued)

Differences: The structural differences mentioned in Chapter 10, in addition to Tuesday voting, frequency of elections, and nonmandatory registration, has kept American voting patterns depressed compared to other democracies. However, when we consider the number of opportunities Americans have to vote, and calculate participation differently, we actually find that Americans are quite participatory. Americans also participate a great deal in nonelectoral ways. Finally, volatility, something seen in many other democracies as voters shift between parties that operate a similar ideological space, is much lower in the United States than in other democracies.

NOTES

1. Seymour Martin Lipset, *American Exceptionalism: A Double-Edged Sword* (New York, NY: W. W. Norton, 1996), 26.

2. Lipset, *American Exceptionalism*, 26.

INDEX